FEEDING THE NATION

Yuriko Akiyama completed her Ph.D. at King's College, University of London.

FEEDING THE NATION:
Nutrition and Health in Britain before World War One

Yuriko Akiyama

Tauris Academic Studies
London • New York

Published in 2008 by Tauris Academic Studies, an imprint of
I.B.Tauris & Co Ltd
6 Salem Road, London W2 4BU
www.ibtauris.com

In the United States and in Canada distributed by Palgrave Macmillan, a
division of St Martin's Press, 175 Fifth Avenue, New York NY 10010

Copyright © 2008, Yuriko Akiyama

ISBN 978 1 84511 682 8

A full CIP record for this book is available from the British Library
A full CIP record is available from the Library of Congress

Library of Congress Catalog card: available

Printed and bound in India by Thomson Press (I) Ltd from camera-ready
copy copyedited and typeset by Oxford Publishing Services, Oxford

Contents

Acronyms and Abbreviations

A/NFC	Nightingale Fund Council at LMA
ADM	Admiralty Records
BL	British Library
CMO	chief medical officer
ED	series number for Ministry of Education records
HMI	His/Her Majesty's inspector
IML	Invalid Kitchens of London Records
JOD	journal housed at the National Maritime Museum
KCLA	King's College London Archives
KH/CM	King's College Hospital, Minutes of the Committee of Management
KH/N	King's College Hospital, Nursing Committee
LBK	letterbook
LCC	London County Council
LH/A	London Hospital, Administrative Records
LH/N	London Hospital, Nursing Records
LH/X	London Hospital, Records from unofficial sources
LMA	London Metropolitan Archives
MAB	Metropolitan Asylums Board Records
MH	Ministry of Health
MS	manuscript
NA	National Archives
NAM	National Army Museum
NMM	National Maritime Museum
NTSC	National Training School of Cookery
PP	Parliamentary Papers
PP/WILBY	Wilby Hart Diaries, typescript and manuscript at RLHA
PTR	Sir James Porter Papers

RAMC	Royal Army Medical Corps
RLHA	Royal London Hospital Archives and Museum
SA/QNI	Queen's Nursing Institute collection
ST/NTS	St Thomas' Hospital Records, Nightingale Training School at LMA
TEB	Technical Education Board

Preface

While exploring the importance of cooking and cookery instruction in health education in modern Britain it has been necessary to investigate a broad range of sources covering official records, private papers and contemporary publications. Archival materials belong to various repositories: the National Archives, local record offices, universities, museums, libraries and private organizations. The historical sources used have different natures, but all reveal cookery connections with either school education, medicine or the military services. Such diversity would be evidence that contemporaries in the late nineteenth and early twentieth centuries experienced cookery's educational influence widely.

Admiralty documents in the National Archives cover the variety of trials on cookery and health reform in the Royal Navy. Ministry of Education records include the broad range of instructional activities undertaken by the National Training School of Cookery. Ministry of Health records provide examples of social improvement through cookery education. Private papers provide further evidence. Florence Nightingale's correspondence in the British Library confirms links with nursing and health reform, especially when focusing on sickroom cookery. Records relating to nursing include further Nightingale correspondence and other papers in the Wellcome Library for the History and Understanding of Medicine. Furthermore, Margaret Pillow's letter books in the Norfolk Record Office and her additional papers in the Women's Library have received little attention, even though she was one of the leading educationists of domestic economy. Her papers led to investigation of the influential cookery schools in Gloucester and Liverpool, the archives of which, stored in the Gloucestershire Record Office and in Liverpool John Moores University, are not fully catalogued. They provided much useful original information on the various challenges in spreading cookery education.

Hospital administration and nursing records explain the progress of sickroom cookery instruction for nurses and chart the rise of dietitians – especially those of the London Hospital at the Royal London Hospital Archives and Museum. The records of St Thomas's and Guy's Hospitals in the London Metropolitan Archives, and those of King's College in the King's College London archives, also make it possible to compare such progress. Other records at the London Metropolitan archives, for example those of the Metropolitan Asylums Board, demonstrate the link with the Royal Navy regarding cooking's educational influence and the customs of healthcare among young boys on training ships.

Research on military service further reveals the health-related educational influence of cookery among men, which is unclear from studies of civilian history. For the British army, archival materials in the National Army Museum reveal soldiers' experiences of cookery and healthcare. The Wellcome Library houses the Royal Army Medical Corps records, while records in the National Institute for Defense Studies in Tokyo add an international comparison. For the Royal Navy, food and cookery reform was directly connected to the medical department – a class of Admiralty records. Private journals kept by naval medical officers describe the attention paid to food and health from early periods. Furthermore, the vast correspondence of Sir James Porter in the National Maritime Museum has not yet even been catalogued. As medical director-general, he was an influential figure. In addition, useful records were obtained from the London Metropolitan archives for technical education and charitable work, the Guildhall and Wellcome libraries for district nursing, the Royal Society of Arts archives on domestic economy congresses, the British Library of Political and Economic Science archives for Beatrice Webb's diaries and Charles Booth's London survey records, and from the Clendening History for Medicine Library, Kansas University Medical Center, which supplied a collection of Nightingale correspondence in digital format.

Contemporary publications on cookery and health education, printed public health lectures and accounts of domestic economy congresses, memoirs, books and articles found in general and medical periodicals (including military medicine) all showed an awareness that cookery instruction would become a vital educational solution to combat social problems. As for the secondary sources, early histories of domestic economy education by Yoxall and Sillitoe supplied useful background information for this research. They were written almost as contemporary studies.

I wish to record my sincere thanks to the staff and archivists who kindly offered professional help at archives, libraries and record offices. The research at Gloucester, Liverpool and Norwich was achieved by financial assistance of the Small Grants for Humanities Research from the School of Humanities, King's College, London, and by the Central Research Fund of the University of London. I am also grateful to my former research supervisor, Professor David McLean at King's College, London, and, above all, to my family in Japan who kept encouraging me for more than three years of study in London.

Introduction

Public health reform and scientific research on diseases were important in Britain throughout the nineteenth and into the twentieth century. In the early nineteenth century reforms focused on the infrastructure of drainage and water supply in order to control the spread of diseases, particularly among town dwellers. Legislation supported these developments; indeed, many argued that maintaining good health for what had become so large a population required an organized system run by the state. This, however, could never be the only solution to the problem; indeed, attention by the general public to the issue was essential. Reforms had to be seen not as something outside people's daily lives and dwellings but rather as being directly related to their individual health. While progress in medicine and sanitary engineering led to a gradual improvement in domestic sanitation, for most people cookery was to provide a vital part of the wider questions of nutrition and healthcare. Cookery could not, of course, act as an effective agent alone: however, combined with medicine, sanitation and educational work, it came to be important. To make it effective, it had to be both taught and practised by those with proper understanding and knowledge.

This is a historical study of developments in cookery in which cookery is considered as a vehicle for the widespread improvements in public health that began in the late nineteenth century. In this period, food and its preparation came to be recognized as a public issue and not just a private or domestic matter. It became an aspect of practical preventive medicine and a part of medical care, perhaps best represented by sickroom cookery. Nurses delivered sickroom cookery to patients in individual households as well as in hospitals, thereby extending the capacity to feed patients properly and providing an important alternative to medicine in curing food-related diseases such as diabetes. Sickroom cookery was designed to supply nourishment in suitable forms for individual patients with a view to aiding their recovery from an illness and getting them back to work. At the same time, through patients and their families the cookery instruction associated with it delivered valuable basic medical knowledge about healthcare to society generally.

Given that cookery is about how to prepare and eat food it requires a basic understanding of personal cleanliness and hygienic food handling. These are admittedly unspectacular activities, often requiring unremarkable changes in people's daily habits. Yet, if everyone could come to recognize their necessity, cookery would soon prove an effective agent for improving health and combating disease. Furthermore, better nutrition might protect people from infection, even during an epidemic. Culinary culture is not discussed here, for that is a branch of the history of food, but in this research I nevertheless shall show how scientific knowledge about nutrition and healthcare was delivered to the general public through cookery, especially when linked to educational activities. Such knowledge was delivered in schools by teachers, in hospitals through nursing and in the armed services by medical officers and hospital staff. Examining all these will reveal the growing interest in and the diverse connections between cookery and health across British society.

The establishment of the National Training School of Cookery in London in 1873 encouraged this movement; indeed, it opened a new era in cookery education by training cookery teachers to be instructors in elementary schools, hospitals and the armed services. Yet, apart from some coverage of such work among children in schools, this significant contribution was only briefly mentioned in the histories of domestic economy education written by Yoxall in 1913 and by Sillitoe in 1933. The 1966 history of the National Training School of Cookery referred to classes given at St Thomas', Guy's, the London and in military hospitals, and mentioned the school's support for improving general cookery in the armed services.[1] Even there, however, these facts are not examined further in the broader social context, despite them being both important turning points for those organizations and clear evidence of a growing understanding of nutrition and healthcare.

To date, the role of cookery in school education, as well as in nursing, the British Army and the Royal Navy has invariably been treated as an adjunct to their own mainstream histories. Its contribution is not highlighted, even though contemporary doctors, scientists and women educationists recognized its effectiveness and despite evidence from school inspections, Education Department and Board of Education committee reports, annual surveys of the health of the army and navy, and reports on overseas postings and reforms. Archival evidence illustrates the progress made via cookery instruction in all activities related to diet and healthcare, many of which were new to medicine, but also the many challenges and struggles those who undertook such work faced in the complex areas of sanitation, medicine, food supply and general habits.

In the following chapters I shall discuss the influence of cookery education on nutrition and health in different fields. In the first chapter I look at a growing public interest in cooking and health and at influential women reformers' views on cookery education in the late nineteenth century. Furthermore, the activities of cookery schools in Liverpool and Gloucester reveal extensive cookery education for local needs and its increased popularity among men as well as women. Chapter 2 is about cookery instruction for girls at workhouses and elementary schools. The Education Department commenced cookery education for elementary schoolgirls with grants from the 1880s, thereby encouraging the introduction of this subject. School education was theoretically the ideal way to instruct large numbers among the population, though it required systematic administration. Alterations in cookery instruction are further investigated in Chapter 3, with attention paid to mothercare and schoolchildren's health. By the early twentieth century cookery and domestic economy education were seen as means of tackling poor physique and they constituted an area of government reform before the onset of medical inspections and the school meals service.

Cookery education influenced several fields of health-related activity, which indicated its success, especially where groups of professionals could follow up on such understanding and could witness self improvement in the population, which was not generally possible on account of often only brief years of school attendance. In Chapters 4 and 5 I analyse the effectiveness of sickroom cookery in this context as an important part of hospital and district nursing.

As an aftermath to Florence Nightingale's work during the Crimean War and to the commencement of training for nurses after 1860, the matron of the London Hospital, Miss Eva Lückes, started training probational nurses in sickroom cookery as one of her reforms in 1893. Sickroom cookery instruction for medical students brought knowledge of dietetics into medical care and helped to improve the hospital catering system. Women even became significant in the British armed forces, whose medical services now requested specific cookery training for hospital orderlies. Cookery, alongside sanitary care, was considered a support to health both in peace and wartime as trained men became agents for maintaining hygienic conditions on campsites and in ships' accommodation.

At elementary schools, working-class girls were taught cooking and domestic economy, including hygiene and sanitation, and these subjects became more systematic after the 1880s. Boys, generally, had no corresponding classes. Some educationists, however, claimed their usefulness for boys in so far as knowledge of cleanliness was necessary for everybody, though in practice it was provided only for boys who lived near a port and expected to spend their future lives as seamen, soldiers or colonists.[2] If men worked as plumbers or cooks they might care about hygiene as part of their trade, but that still did not provide many men with opportunities to learn about sanitary matters. The large number of recruits for military service had little education and, though they might be taught about sanitation, it was initially only to maintain their health during service. But, increasingly, this gave men the opportunity to obtain skills and knowledge about personal cleanliness. In Chapter 6 I shall focus on the reform of army cookery after the disaster in the Crimea – not only in army hospitals and its medical services, but throughout the whole organization as the army struggled to improve sanitary conditions. The importance of such educational activities among soldiers was recognized even more after the Boer War. The navy had long tried to provide a healthy working environment for its men. Long-term experience of overseas service had encouraged more systematic medical care and victualling, all under a strict regime of daily cleansing of ships and men. In Chapters 7 and 8 I analyse cooking in the Royal Navy between the 1850s and 1890s and, more specifically, examine naval hospital and sick-berth cookery before 1914. The navy undertook a number of experiments designed to improve the quality of supplies, water storage and catering. Links with civil suppliers and professionals, such as nurses, widened the possibilities for what had become an advanced naval medical service.

Cookery and related areas of domestic economy education have usually been studied in the context of girls' and women's education or that of philanthropic work by middle-class women. The term 'domestic economy' covered the same areas as 'domestic subjects', 'domestic science' or 'home economics', and it is not easy to give clear definitions. They all consisted of cookery, needlework, laundry work, household management, sick cookery, housewifery, infant care, sick nursing and hygiene. Among historians, the term 'domestic subjects' has often been considered suitable if mentioning school curricula, for example when listing the subjects taught to schoolgirls or a teacher's title as a domestic subjects teacher.[3] Contemporary sources, however, used the term 'domestic economy' to refer to a type of education – one involving a practical curriculum for schoolgirls as well as the name of the subject itself. It thus described a combined and broad area of education, such as when domestic economy congresses in the 1870s and 1880s urged the expansion of practical teaching in schools or encouraged more middle-class women to undertake teacher training in these fields. Schools where girls might learn housework after their elementary education were called domestic economy schools: the girls would usually become domestic servants or housewives. Significantly, it was cookery schools that commenced systematic instruction. Other related areas of domestic economy education were then added. Cookery, therefore, had a founding role in this new education.

Cookery teaching provided middle-class women with a new career – albeit one that might be perceived as reinforcing a traditional woman's role – to add to those generally available to them, namely in the teaching profession, or as a nurse, shopkeeper, shop assistant, clerical worker, or civil service employee.[4] The development of the subject at university level can be charted through King's College for Women, which created a household and social science course in 1908. Compared with America, after the early 1900s Britain was slow to provide the graduates of its home science departments with new careers as teachers or hospital dietitians; in fact, hospital dietitians in Britain only really became another medically-related profession for women in the 1920s.[5] Yet, although promoted rather quietly and not highlighted as much as other activities, cookery and domestic science arguably formed an important part of the women's social movement in the late nineteenth century. Given that educated single women tended to work in the community in an attempt to improve the lives of the poor, being skilled specialists, cookery and domestic subjects teachers clearly undertook valuable social work.[6] Although largely neglected by scholars, this movement to improve health through educational activities, which several women national figures supported, is another significant element in the study that follows.

The history of modern British people's health has, for some years, been prominently represented by the works of Smith and Wohl whose approaches to public health questions span the whole range of activeties by the state, local government, medical professionals and voluntary work.[7] The living standard of the working classes has been much studied as it turned upwards around the 1870s when more households could afford to purchase meat and more food, though most writers accept that the story was not that simple. Differences have to be analysed not only for each occupational category and class but also between regions, depending on the types of labour. An analysis of wages and the nation's overall economic growth does not provide a sufficiently clear picture of the improvement in people's lives when compared with previous decades.[8]

The public health movement was one of the most important agents for change, even before the 1870s. It was connected to developments in science as well as to the local government and health administration systems that operated in the large towns. Edwin Chadwick's 1848 Public Health Act has been widely recognized as a milestone, while medical advances and trustworthy dispensaries aided many patients.[9] Cholera epidemics were prevented in Britain from the 1860s, which reflected progress in both sewerage systems and in the water supply.[10] Yet, although the infrastructure of modern urban life was being created at this time, it was not available for all and many public or private bath and washhouse facilities remained poor. Slum areas certainly remained in central London long after the Public Health Act of 1875 and it was still difficult to say that sanitary reforms had made British towns hygienic.[11] Controlling the water supply in towns frequently required great efforts and expenditure by the local authorities, although these now needed to be considered in the planning of housing and sewerage. The gas supply likewise grew from the late 1860s and its declining price allowed commercial gas cooking and heating. In the 1870s it was introduced into the kitchens of middle-class households and finally, by the 1890s, working-class families were starting to use gas for lighting and cooking, often as the slot-coin system that supplied gas for a limited period. From the last decades of the nineteenth century, therefore, the working classes had opportunities to cook warm dishes more easily and more frequently at home.[12] Nevertheless, the meat consumed was not always high quality: one textbook for elementary schoolgirls cited that as a fact. From the 1890s, however, when transportation of frozen meat from Australia was introduced, a large amount of meat was imported into Britain and this began to change the domestic market.[13] For the two decades from 1870 until refrigerated and other colonial produce became available, the working classes probably only ate cheap offcuts. While the lives of the poor were certainly getting better, it is, however, hard to say that they really comprehended much about cookery during this period. While their upper and middle-class contemporaries were interested in public health and sanitary programmes, it took a long time for the practice of domestic hygiene and an understanding of the importance of cookery and nutrition to spread to the wider public.

The British diet was analysed through household budgets to reveal the quantity and variety of food consumed, while nutritional changes over time were hailed as the effects of better living. Dietetic analysis of food value was also attempted in the nineteenth century, an early example being the report by Dr Edward Smith in the 1860s. Charles Booth and Benjamin Rowntree later analysed it as a part of their research into poverty and social conditions in London and York in 1889 and 1901 and explained the link between poor physique and the unequal quality of food intake between different social classes. From the 1960s new research areas combined social history and dietetics. These studies discussed trends in

consumption, focusing on specific food values such as carbohydrates or protein from a range of diets – school meals, workhouse
diets and the difference seen between the meals of the poor and the
rich. This research, using budget records, identified increased meat
consumption and the use of a wider variety of food after the
1870s.[14] This method, however, did not reveal much about the
reality of people's daily consumption, about how they cooked,
prepared and stored food after purchase. These remained important
questions to be examined. Scientists increasingly focused on protein
to discover the link between food consumption and bodily energy,
with research in the nineteenth century undertaken by the German
scientist Justus von Liebig and by British scientists such as Sir Lyon
Playfair and Edward Smith. Edmund Parkes also paid attention to it
through practical experiments for the British Army. Wilber
Atwater's dietary survey in the United States in the 1880–90s aimed
to show the range of protein sources available; this was followed by
Francis Benedict's 1906 analysis of labourers' diets in America and
Europe. More attention was paid to the link between health and
nutrition after the discovery of vitamins in the early twentieth
century: for example, vitamin B and beriberi. The development of
nutritional science thereby contributed to a gradual improvement in
health through an understanding of the amount of protein both
consumed and required.[15]

   In an attempt to understand nutritional values since the late
eighteenth century, changes of height were analysed demographic-
ally using statistics from military recruitment. Records of heights,
however, were not a conclusive measure of living standards and, like
mortality, morbidity, diet and housing conditions, only revealed one
aspect of the issue. Furthermore, the functional relationship between
income and welfare is unclear: for instance, investigations show that
urbanization was not always conducive to better nutrition. Even
though people could earn more, city life prevented the working
classes from growing taller and the standard of living was not always
connected to the health of the people. There is evidence to suggest
that increased nutritional intake after the 1870s effectively decreased
respiratory and waterborne diseases, though perhaps less directly
than the well-known thesis of Thomas McKeown might suggest.[16]

McKeown's work in the 1970s has produced one of the most influential historical studies of the British people's health. Through statistics, he ascertained that longevity and population increase in the nineteenth century were essentially caused by better nutrition; increased food production in the eighteenth and early nineteenth centuries simply led to the decline of many diseases. Environmental contributions, such as legislating to improve the water supply, work by philanthropists and advances in medicine were not the main factors when compared with a rising standard of living based on the benefits of a free-market economy. Szreter re-examined this thesis in the 1980s and concluded that better nutrition was not the only reason for a declining death rate; he cited improvements in public health as having a strong impact on society by raising the standard of sanitation. The point is that less nutrition among people is not always linked to lower fertility and higher mortality, as demonstrated in many countries in the late twentieth century.[17] In 1873 one Poor Law Union schoolmaster recalled his childhood and irregular mealtimes; though very hungry he could not eat a large amount, even when supplied to him on his first meal at the workhouse. It was widely understood in the early twentieth century that children in poor districts had 'slum stomach' and did not need a large amount of food; they were not starved, even though seldom full. Moreover, when those children had food they preferred only pickles or other highly seasoned food to nourishing rice pudding or soup.[18] Selecting what to eat and knowing how to eat it was essential. Just as Szreter referred to educating the public on sanitation, so such knowledge of food and how to prepare it was an important next step towards solving the problem of the nation's health.[19]

Knowledge about food would not only be useful in daily life but could also alter people's unhealthy habits, thereby supporting further public health reform. As seen in the demographical analysis of height, better nutrition was not the only answer and the contribution of the public health environment had to be considered. As a further example, in the late nineteenth century there were still complaints about sanitary conditions in the Royal Navy even though these were much better organized than in civil society. Strict naval regulations on sanitation had existed for a long time; however, it was not possible to alter habits across the whole organization. Regulations alone could not achieve better sanitation and one of the vital keys would be educational activities. Food safety in the nineteenth century has invariably been discussed from the perspectives of governmental administration and public health legislation. Recently, historical analysis has focused more on links between food and disease: for example, on typhoid caused by shellfish or tuberculosis in the milk supply. The Sale of Food and Drugs Acts in 1875 and 1899 became the foundation for food safety standards; selling poor quality meat, known as 'measly pork', with parasites, or such adulteration as seen in bread or tea was restricted thereafter.[20]

Therefore, to reveal the connection between cookery and healthcare in the late nineteenth century one still requires an analysis of how foods were eaten by the people. While public health reforms altered the living environment by improving the infrastructure, it was necessary also to change the general public's attitude to domestic hygiene. By obtaining an increased amount of food, people might well be able to live longer, but maintaining good health required knowledge of sanitation, for unless they understood that, even consuming more food could not free them from diseases. Cookery was effective as a vehicle through which to deliver this general understanding of domestic sanitation (water supply, drainage and care of cooking utensils), food selection, handling, storage and personal cleanliness (clean hands, nails, hair and clothes when preparing meals). Even if it involved only the one activity of cooking meals, it obviously had broader connections with public health and with medical progress via sickroom cookery. It was evidence of the translation of scientific knowledge and medical research into plain words and common sense.

By the early twentieth century smoking had also come to be regarded as a health problem among boys and youths, for until then it was not widely recognized as a habit that caused poor physique and illnesses. It was the Physical Deterioration Committee's report in 1904 and the 1908 Children's Act that recognized smoking as a public health problem. The habit was common among military men who had experienced it at a young age.[21] Admiral Sir Astley Cooper-Key, for instance, when young, had considered quitting smoking for the sake of better health.[22] Such self-consciousness helped to curb smoking, though it was not applicable to the whole of society. Particularly in towns, increasing opportunities for casual labourers to earn small sums of money allowed youths to purchase far more than just food to make them full, whatever its quality. It also introduced them to cigarettes and alcohol. Again, then, the rising standard of living was not always consistent with spending money for better health. No law prohibited people from purchasing foods and commodities; regulations only applied to those who sold them. Unless members of the general public became concerned about food safety they would always live with health risks, whether serious or not. Cookery instruction was vital to help spread that concern. Its place in the movement to improve the nation's health from the late nineteenth century will first be shown by tracing publications such as cookery books, public health lectures and domestic economy education congresses.

Chapter 1

Health Reformers and Cookery Schools in Nineteenth-century Britain

Publications about domestic management were not an innovation in the late nineteenth century: Mrs Isabella Beeton's *Household Management* and Alexis Soyer's *Charitable Cookery* were earlier examples.[1] These, however, were for wealthier readers who generally organized a household but did not have to cook for themselves except as a leisurely activity or occasionally to provide cooked meals for the poor as philanthropy. Thereafter, publications and lectures focusing on food and health increased in number, including those about cookery, elementary dietetics and sanitation. Even though the readers and audiences were limited to well-off men and women, the question was gradually receiving more public attention.

The books that teacher training courses in cookery schools recommended in the 1870s covered elementary physiology and nutrition. This shows the level of scientific knowledge required for students during training, even though that information would not be delivered directly to their future pupils. These books were popular publications on the subject at that time. Recommendations by the National Training School of Cookery and the Northern Union of Schools of Cookery comprised about five books each: one or two for cookery lessons, some on scientific analysis of food values and a book on health. Cookery schools recommended that their students read books on food, diet and dietetics published since the 1860s. Scientific analysis of food by Arthur Church was common because it was connected to the food collection at the Bethnal Green Museum (a branch of the Kensington Museum). Also, Henry Letheby's *On Food* shows the interest among both scientists and the public on food values. Dietetic studies by Frederick Pavy and Edward Smith were the basic texts for medical treatment of illnesses caused by diet and digestion.[2]

Cookery books in this period included many recipes that, from the range of ingredients, could be either middle class or working class. Textbooks for schoolgirls represented food in working-class homes by listing recipes for simple dishes,[3] but that did not mean that people ate them regularly. Nor did it mean that the meat the poor could afford was always suitable for the cooking methods proposed in the books, such as roasting or broiling. For example, to have a hot meal on Sunday, people in poor households in south London, with no oven or stove, would take their food to a neighbouring cookhouse where they could prepare it for a small fee.[4] The section on sickroom cookery in these books generally introduced beef tea or egg flip; however, they were not affordable for the very poor who had to ask charitable societies and philanthropists for the ingredients and for advice about basic sick care at home.

From the middle of the nineteenth century a number of sanitary associations sprang up in large towns for which medical doctors, scientists and philanthropists delivered lectures. The Ladies' National Association for the Diffusion of Sanitary Knowledge was organized early in 1857 and, as the name suggests, involved middle-class women. The medical men who delivered lectures for it suggested that women's influence on healthcare could solve many problems. The association even tried to start a college of hygiene and household science to make girls good housewives, mothers and experts in domestic economy. Unfortunately, this was unsuccessful, for the idea was perhaps ahead of its time by a generation. The association subsequently rose to the challenge of delivering wisdom about domestic hygiene through such educational work as cookery, needlework, nursing and the care of children.[5] In 1873 the National Health Society, which professionals like Chadwick and Nightingale supported, was organized in London. Other large cities, such as Edinburgh, also had health societies that arranged lectures on a broad range of issues, including cookery, sanitation of dwellings, sick care and the problems of daily life. The lectures were published and widely distributed: the Ladies' Sanitary Association published 70 tracts, while for each health lecture the Birmingham and Midland Institute would sell 20,000 copies of a penny pamphlet.[6] Food and cookery were dealt with from various perspectives. The nutritional value of food, more practically as energy value for labour, was covered, as well as living standards and care and food for the sick and young children. The lectures were frequently attempts to make scientific research understandable to non-specialists.

Lectures could also provide an introduction for those interested in public health, for example Edward Smith's research on dietetics, Captain Sir Douglas Galton's work on sanitary engineering and Sir Lyon Playfair's analysis of the diet and labour of working men.[7] The lecturers suggested that even educated people paid insufficient attention to the purity of the air and to personal cleanliness among the public, which were important with respect to housing and food. Workmen rarely washed their hands before eating, unless they were lead workers who knew of its necessity to avoid lead poisoning.[8] The lectures were effective in publicizing the importance of domestic and personal health education to help overcome problems caused by overcrowding and to suggest thrift in running the household. It was vital that people improve unhygienic conditions by themselves and not rely solely on sanitary regulations and medical officers' inspections. Without this, public health reform would be incomplete.[9]

With respect to cooking, such lectures suggested that cooking performed by 'guesswork' could not avoid unnecessary waste due to unsuitable methods and the lack of a clear understanding of basic principles. Cookery classes were expected to improve home cooked meals, to make them comforting and nourishing, and to prevent unnecessary visits to cookshops and public houses.[10] The females in the family, and not the males, generally prepared and selected the food; the cleansing and heating processes of cooking reduced risks for everybody from parasites.[11] Knowledge and skills were important to convert cheap ingredients into a variety of dishes. Of course, it was often poor women who most needed systematic instruction, although even among middle-class women some of them had less knowledge of cookery than in previous generations.[12] Meals had already been analysed experimentally at public institutions such as barracks and workhouses to identify what foods were essential for a healthy diet.[13] Now, attention to cookery and health via education could provide girls and women with more knowledge about the care of infants.[14] For girls, practical instruction in econ-omical cookery and housework was strongly recommended before they assumed this responsibility.[15]

For a decade after the late 1870s these lectures reflected progress in effectively conveying information on cookery and health to the public. The basic principles of healthcare, including diet, could indeed be learnt by attending a few lectures. Health lectures in most places were similar in that attendance was mainly by educated people, albeit often from more prosperous working-class back-grounds. At one lecture in Birmingham in the early 1880s it was pointed out that food was recognized as having 'the most direct practical bearing on the preservation of health'. 'Knowledge of good economical cookery' had educational value for the people and the nation; instruction for schoolchildren was recommended for both health and comfort. While the reasons for promoting cooking were to ensure better digestion and to encourage self-support among the working classes and the poor,[16] it was the middle classes who generally lived in the types of dwellings used as examples in the lectures, with a separate kitchen, bedroom and bathroom, water taps and a drainage system. Lectures were useful for those active in philanthropic work and for learning how to help others who lived in different circumstances. The obvious limitation of such lectures was that even when delivered by medical specialists using plain words, the people who really needed the information to improve their living conditions and eating habits did not attend them. Nightingale cautioned that lectures had to be combined with practical training suitable for individual circumstances. Philanthropic visits by middle-class women was one answer; they could deliver information and advice about sanitary conditions for homes and families, young children and the sick. But reformers believed that improvement had to be based on education for the general public and not depend on support, help and instructions from house visitors.

Just as these lectures were planned to publicize the importance of health education, so the Society of Arts, supported by Sir Henry

Cole, a civil servant and philanthropist who had organized the Great Exhibition in 1851, organized domestic economy congresses in 1877, 1878 and 1881 respectively.[17] These were further examples of growing attention to this question and calls for more cookery instruction in schools. Speakers, however, were not limited to the organizers of cookery schools; sanitarians, like Chadwick, educationists, scientists and, of course, women took a large part in them. All tried to focus on improving the nation's health through educational activities – for example by providing swimming baths, better ventilation, sanitary conditions in classrooms, and medical inspections for schoolchildren. Sanitation, nursing and wider views on health were also discussed, but the main focus was on domestic economy education, principally cookery and needlework. Representatives from cookery schools who attended offered their opinions both on cookery instruction and on teacher training and children's education.

Miss Christian Guthrie Wright, the honorary secretary of the Edinburgh School of Cookery, was among the congress speakers and she argued that cookery was of educational value for the whole of society. The increasing interest in cookery instruction could be seen from the attendance at public classes since the Edinburgh school's establishment in 1875; 37 towns and villages now arranged cookery classes. Wright claimed that all women must have the opportunity to learn not only home management but also the principles of political economy. Because the latter was necessary to understand the use of money, food, health and life, it would benefit the nation. If women of all classes understood more about food, unnecessary waste would not occur. Along with girls' education, the Edinburgh school had already undertaken specific instruction for men through camp cookery for soldiers and artisan cookery classes in the evening. The latter were attended mainly by ploughmen, suggesting that this demand for cookery instruction would justify the introduction of cookery classes for elementary schoolboys. Her school had become sufficiently specialized to deliver lessons to soldiers, sailors and intending colonists. Furthermore, sickroom cookery for medical students was provided. Naturally, to satisfy all these specific requirements, cookery teachers also had to understand the dietary arrangements and cooking appliances of hospitals and other public institutions.[18]

A suffragist leader, Miss Lydia Becker of Manchester, discussed education for boys and men from the viewpoint of equality and women's rights. She asserted too that knowledge of domestic economy was just as valuable for boys after they became adults and would equally benefit the nation. If boys had this knowledge they would become better husbands and fathers, especially 'when their wives were ill, or absent, or dead, to mind their children and attend to their houses, if necessary'.[19] No doubt, this vision reflected Becker's ideal society. At the same time, though, it acknowledged the vital roles of healthcare and domestic economy and their usefulness for all if promoted through school education. The general message from these congresses, then, was that knowledge of food and how to cook it should be available in elementary schools, for this was a precious opportunity for children, whether boys or girls, to learn 'how to live'. Lessons explaining the nutritive value of food were recommended so that people could eventually maintain health by themselves.[20]

The progress of cookery education has rightly been recognized as opening up new professions for many middle-class women whose work can be analysed from several perspectives, including feminism, the history of girls' and women's education, and the role of women in philanthropy and public administration. When cookery education was introduced into elementary schools it took more than two decades to become well-organized in many districts. Several hazards accompanied the preparation stages of practical instruction, most notably poor school facilities and a limited supply of trained teachers and training opportunities, but it was an important starting point for cookery and health reform in Britain. Educationists and women members of the Local Government Board in London supported it, as did School Boards, which acted both as organizers of local education and as part of a wider political movement.[21] Prominent among them was Mrs Catherine Buckton of the Leeds School Board, whose books on health and domestic economy instruction became standard texts and were introduced to School Boards across the country.[22]

Another of these figures was Margaret Pillow (née Scott) who, after 1891, commenced her career as the first woman to hold a diploma from the Sanitary Institute in London, the qualification that local government authorities required for their sanitary inspectors. Pillow believed that sanitation was equally important for men and women; she had even visited plumbers and dairies to acquire practical knowledge. At that time, however, no local authority wished to employ a woman as a sanitary inspector, so she worked as a lecturer on sanitation for the National Health Society and delivered lectures to pupil teachers and local sanitary associations. Her interest was not limited to domestic economy and hygiene. She claimed that women could contribute to social reform with respect to sanitation and she encouraged women in such work as well as engaging in the voting campaign. At the seventh International Congress of Demography in London in 1891 she commented that women could be effective agents to prevent diseases. Her professional knowledge on sanitation enabled her, jointly with Dr Arthur Newsholme, to write a textbook on domestic economy for teachers.[23] Even after her marriage to Edward Pillow, an engineer who organized technical education for Norfolk, Pillow continued her work in education both as an examiner and by standardizing cookery training for teachers of domestic subjects.[24]

Another two women, Miss Fanny Calder of Liverpool and Miss Ella Pycroft of London, played important parts in promoting domestic economy education. Calder worked as the honorary secretary of the Liverpool Training School of Cookery, which was established in 1875, and founded the independent group of cookery schools in northern England. Pycroft was a lady organizer of domestic economy at the Technical Education Board in London under Sidney Webb and she and Beatrice Webb had become friends while working as rent collectors for the East London Dwelling Company. Pycroft also helped Booth's famous London survey by providing the information used from School Board visitors.[25] She was the niece of a founder of the Liverpool school where she had studied for the teacher training course. Thereafter, until gaining an appointment with the Technical Education Board of London in 1893, Pycroft helped to establish the Gloucestershire School of Cookery under Mrs Mary Playne, Beatrice Webb's sister.[26] Calder was originally a social worker in Liverpool where she worked for the Liverpool School Board with Eleanor Rathbone (of the well-known philanthropic Rathbone family). In 1891 Calder published a textbook on laundry work for elementary schools. It was supposedly based on her real understanding of living conditions in Liverpool where there had been a movement for public washhouses in the early 1840s after the outbreak of cholera.[27] From their experience of social work, both Calder and Pycroft knew a lot about people's lives and the need for practical instruction on sanitation for every household.

Buckton, Pillow, Calder and Pycroft represented the views of the many who believed that women could make an important contribution to better health, who encouraged the education of working-class girls and women, and who implicitly confirmed the middle-class woman's position in teaching cookery and domestic economy. Because cookery and domestic economy education were not too scientific or professional, they could relate broadly to the debate on public health, offer many openings and attract women educationists. A cookery teacher's work was partly philanthropic, but it was also professional and entailed the study of science subjects. While cookery teachers were perhaps seen as amateurs in the medical world, they could conduct studies and could teach about health through cookery and domestic economy. The limited places for such teachers, usually only with a part-time status and salary, did not attract the increasing number of lower middle-class women choosing to study at the training colleges to become school-mistresses. As a result, it remained largely a profession for comfortably-off middle-class women, whether single or married. One of its attractions for these women was that it offered more flexibility than other professions available at the time.

The basic background for cookery teachers remained the same throughout the nineteenth century; indeed, Calder frequently stressed its suitability for middle-class women claiming that they were ideal people to deliver reliable knowledge on cookery and health. They could provide more intellectual and scientific instruction for cookery through a knowledge of chemistry, geography or botany; they were expected to be well-educated, being daughters of clergymen, doctors, lawyers or half-pay army or navy men who could afford to take modest salaries of between £80 and £100 a year.[28] This was commonly agreed among women educationists from the 1870s. For example, at the 1877 congress, Wright from Edinburgh and Mrs Fenwick of the Leeds School of Cookery both mentioned how district nursing for the poor undertaken by ladies showed great results.[29]

Between 1839 and 1846 almost twenty training colleges were founded for the education of both men and women, though mostly for men to be trained as schoolmasters. During the 1850s trained middle-class women worked as elementary schoolteachers. From the 1860s, however, lower middle-class parents tried to enrol their daughters in teacher training colleges with a view to raising their social status and earning a better livelihood. This tendency can be traced by looking at the social backgrounds of women candidates for the Whitelands Training College in London, which trained women as elementary schoolteachers from 1841. With the rapid growth of national education, more women participated in teaching and many from the lower middle class now entered the profession. Trained middle-class women teachers became more inclined to take part in secondary education for middle-class girls who were eager to progress to higher education at university.[30] The total number of middle-class elementary schoolteachers thus gradually decreased.

Salaries in the teaching profession both indicated its changing social status and enabled one to compare teaching with other occupations for women. Even in the 1890s women teachers' salaries were still higher than those of other professions, such as hospital nurses or clerks. Teachers, even from a lower social class, could often enjoy more independence than other women professionals. Salaries in London were higher than in any other town because of the high cost of living there, and the salary range for women teachers (of girls and infants) was between £50 and £125 for assistant teachers and between £120 and £300 for headteachers. Average salaries in 1890 were £88 for women assistant teachers and £195 for women headteachers. Middle-class women's salaries were not the same: in 1890 London staff nurses earned between £20 and £30, sisters between £35 and £60, and matrons between £100 and £350. Around 1892–93 there were 20,000 nurses in Britain: about 15,000 earned between £20 and £25 per annum and fewer than 200 of them could earn £100 or more in a year. Cookery teachers likewise could earn only between £60 and £100 a year. A woman organizer for domestic economy under the Technical Education Board of the London County Council, however, could earn £250 a year – albeit only a quarter of what the male organizers of the same board earned.[31] Middle-class women might be proud of their professions outside the home, the same as men, but they knew that their salaries would be lower than those of women teachers in elementary schools, as well as those of their male colleagues. Nevertheless, they greatly appreciated paid work for the respect it brought them while providing training for younger women who would become their future colleagues.

Pycroft and Miss Florence Baddeley – the daughter of an army officer and Pycroft's successor as organizer at the Gloucestershire School of Cookery and Domestic Economy – discussed the status of cookery teachers at the National Union of Women Workers' meeting in 1895. They stressed the importance of training teachers because of increasing demand after the commencement of technical education in domestic economy all over the country. Teachers required adaptability to fulfil the aims of cookery classes, given the different conditions within schools and the different requirements of country and town. To avoid the lessons being boring for pupils, teachers must have scope within general education to make their lessons effective both for better health and to raise children's spirits. Baddeley commented on the various responsibilities of teachers when they had to manage a diversity of students: they instructed very poor agricultural labourers' wives and daughters, factory hands, artisans and dwellers in both town and county. A sympathetic and educated woman who was a good cook and a lecturer could only handle cookery education properly by understanding her pupils' circumstances. The general difficulty of all technical instruction was that teachers had to talk and use their hands at the same time, which was not always easy for those who only had training as elementary schoolteachers.[32] Specific training was therefore desirable.

The qualifications of women lecturers and cookery teachers were also questioned because, employing them now for their professional skills, they had to be sufficiently well paid. The county councils only paid technical education lecturers £50 for six months, which entailed delivering ten lectures a week, two a day. If this continued, it was doubtful that properly qualified women would wish to work for them and the councils would eventually be accused of wasting money by employing unsuitable people. Cookery teachers who could teach several subjects earned between £80 and £200 a year, so their salaries were no lower than those mentioned in the 1870s. In Norfolk, for example, the school of cookery or the technical school for women paid its best cookery and technical teachers £80 a year, including board. They could claim an additional 5/6d for travelling expenses, if necessary, and 3/6d a day for lodging. Lecturers in health subjects earned £6 a week for eight to ten lectures. In London, the annual salaries of cookery and dressmaking teachers were £90, of health lecturers £100, and the heads of domestic economy schools £120. A lecturer in Gloucester could earn £120 a year.[33]

From the 1880s onwards, when cookery became a grant-aided subject at elementary schools, the profession received increased attention. In the early 1890s Pillow strengthened its connections with sanitary science when the examination for sanitary inspectors was reformed. In 1892, when the National Health Society began to emphasize the importance of training women as sanitary inspectors, a new course on sanitary science was started at King's College, London, which eventually made it possible for women to become sanitary officers. Further extensions in university education allowed women to study hygiene or physiology – and to make such knowledge the foundation for their occupations.[34] From the late 1890s, once factory inspectors and inspectors for needlework and cookery education had been appointed, women could enter administrative work as well as teaching. With the professionalism of cookery teachers now recognized in society, they were expected to become important both from an educational and a public health point of view. Even though some cookery training schools closed, with only 15 remaining in England and Wales in 1909–10, the number of candidates applying to become teachers of domestic subjects did not decrease.[35] It remained, however, a profession largely for middle-class women. As dietitians, they no doubt had the potential to act as administrators for school meals, but this step would have to wait more than thirty years until the commencement of the dietetics course at King's College for Women in 1933.

Although health instruction and hygiene were regarded as foundations for elementary school life, they were not actually included in the syllabus for children. Indeed, only in 1910 did hygiene even become a compulsory subject for prospective teachers – 30 years after cookery teachers had commenced their work to show that instruction on healthy habits at school was more important than just teaching knowledge.[36] At elementary schools, general instruction for later life would be obtainable for boys from citizenship lessons and for girls from lessons in domestic subjects. In 1914 it was thought that this type of education would transform a school into a social service centre.[37] For years cookery teachers had tried to fill the gaps in public health education, act as observers in matters of general health and promote widespread knowledge about the importance of cookery.

The cookery schools established in large cities across the country after 1874 led to a movement for cookery education in the 1880s. The first school, the National Training School of Cookery, opened as a result of the popular cookery demonstrations John Buckmaster organized at the International Exhibition in South Kensington in 1873, which, it was reported, even the royal family visited. Buckmaster also contributed to the foundation of the school, which the tuition fees from students who wished to obtain diplomas and certificates would finance. Its influential lady superintendent, Mrs Edith Clarke (née Nicholls), was a family friend of Henry Cole through her poet grandfather Thomas Peacock. The school, supported by Clarke's daughters, continued until 1962. It devised a system of teacher training and it was followed by the establishment of cookery schools in Liverpool, Edinburgh, Leeds and elsewhere in the 1870s; with the advent of financial support for technical education, the number of such schools rose to 27 in 1896–97.[38] This expansion depended on funds raised under the Local Taxation (Customs and Exercise) Act for technical and manual instruction and the Technical Education Act of 1889.

To uphold cookery teachers' qualifications and standards, early in 1876 the Liverpool Training School of Cookery organized the Northern Union of Schools of Cookery with other schools in the north of England. This was intended to standardize training at each school according to that at the National Training School in London. While the question of issuing a universal certificate from the National Training School was raised at the domestic economy congresses, it was not, however, put into practice. In 1897, under the influence of other women workers' organizations, the Northern Union was merged into the Association of Teachers of Domestic Subjects.[39]

The intention was for women both to organize the National Training School of Cookery and to tailor the instruction given by its graduates, both in and out of schools, to local and national needs. The executive committee did of course include some men, such as the chairman George Leveson-Gower, but women did have significant opportunities for administrative work.[40] There were three courses – for teacher training, high-class cookery and artisan cookery. Tuition fees varied according to the financial circumstances of those attending. The artisan course welcomed attendance for a single class. Teacher training and high-class cookery courses, on the other hand, took longer periods to complete. Prospective teachers were given two options for studying – a 20-week course for plain cookery practice and high-class practice (£20) or a ten-week course just for plain cookery (£8.8s). The 20-week course consisted of scullery work and demonstrations, with teaching experience in four-week rotations. The school recommended the longer course on the grounds that its students would be better placed to find employment.[41] The school encouraged its graduate teachers to arrange cookery lessons for schoolchildren if requested. Regulations pertaining to salary and employment allowed for a teacher appointed at a rural school to be paid £5.5s a week (for two hourly classes a week, demonstrations or practical lessons) as well as boarding and travel expenses if necessary. If it were only for a day, she could earn £1.1s for one lesson.[42] In 1907 new regulations were introduced for training teachers of domestic subjects. The Board of Education would now provide instruction at 18 training schools where cookery, laundry work, housewifery and combined domestic subjects were to be based on each individual school's administration and examination. For the full diploma in cookery, no fewer than 840 hours' training was necessary, with 80 to 100 hours spent learning about teaching methods for children by attending elementary schools. At least 40 hours were to be devoted to individual practice in teaching.[43]

In many respects, and as late as 1906, the training of teachers of domestic subjects was considered more suitable for middle-class women because of their 'womanly tastes and capabilities'. The tuition fee of £55 (for the full course of cookery, plain needlework, dressmaking and laundry work) had to be paid in advance, which was hardly affordable for the lower classes.[44] Yet, the work of training schools was in such national demand that, to extend their instruction, government support became essential, with Clarke pointing out that for cookery to make its important contribution to national education properly trained women teachers were needed all over the country.[45] Clarke wanted to hold more classes at girls' schools and also some for boys: indeed, from the beginning, the National Training School of Cookery did not close its door to men engaged in the cookery profession. Yet this health-related work by the school was not initially popular; it became so only following requests from some medical men who supported broadening the possibilities for cookery education. This was not limited to the National Training School of Cookery: the records of other cookery schools showed a similar experience.

An interesting aspect of the work of cookery schools was the classes they held for local needs, which reached beyond just following general schemes for educating schoolgirls and women. The activities of two influential schools outside London illustrate this well: the Liverpool Training School of Cookery (established in 1875 and later known as the F. L. Calder College of Domestic Science) and the Gloucestershire School of Cookery and Domestic Economy (established in 1891 and renamed the Gloucestershire School of Domestic Science in 1900 and then the Gloucestershire Training College of Domestic Science). Except for family and friendship connections between the founders and organizers of these schools, they were quite different in their administration. The Liverpool school tried to retain its independence as a private establishment from the beginning, but later agreed to provide technical education under the auspices of the county council. The Gloucestershire local county council, however, basically ran the

Gloucester school as one of its technical education institutes.[46] The instruction that both these schools provided for local nurses, for men in the shipping industry, for emigrants and for the army confirmed that cookery schools were recognized as making a valuable contribution to the health of the community.

Calder organized the Liverpool school and it undertook a variety of instruction. In 1879 a doctor at the Southern Hospital in Liverpool suggested and promoted lessons in sickroom cookery for hospital nurses and cooks and the first class was held at the Southern Hospital in 1882. Nurses from the children's hospital also appreciated these special classes and thereafter the lessons were held annually. The doctor and nurses arranged the specific instruction for the special diet, which was designed to spread reliable knowledge about sickroom cookery. From the 1890s onwards, doctors arranged for the Liverpool school to provide instruction at the Northern Hospital in Liverpool, at the Royal Albert Edward Infirmary in Wigan and at the Ancorts Hospital in Manchester; and certificates were awarded to those who attended. This continued into the 1900s for district nurses and for nurses at hospitals and infirmaries; in 1915 sickroom cookery was taught in Liverpool at the Royal Infirmary, at the Toxteth Infirmary, at the Royal Southern Hospital and at the Highfield Infirmary.[47]

The school also organized practical classes and demonstrations on plain household and high-class cookery, and provided lessons for local artisans and children. Through its classes it conveyed the message that cookery education was important for every girl. With its plain household cookery classes targeted to the general public the school based its instruction on the scientific principles of cookery and health, for it realized that high-class cookery was only suitable for households on an income of more than £500 a year. Classes for local people were therefore encouraged and, with philanthropic understanding, the school set different levels of tuition fees; the higher tuition fees for the high-class cookery lessons thus subsidized the plain household cookery ones. Cookery was useful, of course, for all classes, but the next generation of the wealthy could already manage their homes better while the poor might be taught to prepare nourishing meals at home and to reduce waste.[48]

Lectures on nutrition and health, in which breads made from wheaten meal were analysed for their economical and nutritive benefits, were another feature of the Liverpool school. Florence Nightingale provided the syllabus for lectures on cottage hygiene and sanitation for the teacher training courses.[49] The broader technical education that women now required meant delivering a large number of lecturers on hygiene, home nursing, cottage sanitation and health to various places. Furthermore, the school arranged health lectures in conjunction with the Liverpool Sanitary Association.[50] These lectures, which touched on the social and home life of the industrial classes, aimed to develop an understanding of domestic economy using a more sociological approach.[51] This tendency to link domestic economy to social science was evident at Bedford College in London, which planned to set up a department of social studies, including sociology and economics, after a course for a hygiene diploma, regarded as a training for social workers, was discontinued in 1919.[52] By the early twentieth century the domestic economy profession had arguably become much more geared to the needs of society. As an indication of her foresight, Wright had pointed out the importance of combining domestic economy with social science as early as 1877.

In addition to all these activities, the Liverpool school supported cookery instruction for boys and men, especially sea cookery, as part of the technical education arranged with the local education authority. From the 1880s the school also held cookery classes for emigrants and men setting off for the colonies. Troops and boy scouts had cookery instruction in the 1910s.[53] As these cases show, the school was flexible enough to meet all local requirements and would organize dietary and cookery education for everybody in need. After 1891 cookery classes for seamen attracted considerable attention all over the country, but the sailors' cookery class at Liverpool was the earliest attempt in the country to promote seamen's welfare. The seamen's working conditions, however, made it impossible for any of them to attend the classes full time, so the number of pupils would fluctuate wildly. Women educationists at the school were active in promoting these classes, which its head teacher, Miss Mann, had begun in February 1891. With its focus on social reform in the shipping industry, its economic influence was obviously stronger in port towns.[54]

With connections to the shipping industry and having a different character from other school-based instruction, these classes, in effect, formed part of the trade sanitation reform underway in Britain. Sea cookery demonstrations and exhibits at the Chelsea Naval Exhibition in 1891 publicized them, while the Shipowners' Association of Liverpool and other places like Glasgow, London, Hull and Edinburgh enquired about training details and requested instructors. When the Shipowners' Association asked for a male teacher, Alexander Quinlan, an experienced sea cook, was selected: he underwent training for three weeks in September 1892 to commence work as an instructor at £80 a year.[55] Two seamen attended initially, then boys from the training ship *Clio* joined the class. Three types of certificates were issued, depending on the size of the vessel for which the graduate would be working – sculling vessels, cargo steamers or passenger steamers.[56] Quinlan was sent to London to demonstrate his lessons to the London Shipping Federation Committee. His independence was controlled, however, and basically he was only working under a woman instructor's authorization. He therefore had no right to issue certificates according to his own judgement.[57]

Unfortunately, the numbers attending did not increase and even in late October 1894 only three men came, despite Quinlan's recent promotion of seamen's cookery at the health exhibition in Liverpool at which he used the daily rations of a sailor to increase attention. The lack of concern of individual shipowners was the reason for the low attendance. Even though their cooks had no instruction or certificate, they showed no interest in the matter so failed to encourage their men to join the classes. Quinlan then undertook more promotional work through the shipowners' meetings[58] and, in 1895, the seamen's exhibits were given a silver medal at the London food and cookery exhibition.[59] Over the years, with promotions and the increasing sales of the school's cookery books, which Quinlan and Mann published in 1894, seamen's cookery gradually became better known. Boys from the training ships *Indefatigable, Akbar* and *Clarence* joined and the certificate came to be valued as a guarantee of the holder's competence as a cook. In 1895, 120 certificates were issued, including to boys. A man who had heard about the class in San Francisco joined it in 1896, thereby proving the wide influence of the class in Liverpool.[60] A laundry class was likewise arranged to help men cope while they were at overseas ports. Meanwhile, captains were starting to recognize the value of cookery certificates and increasingly employed people with the qualification.[61] The importance of instruction for sea cooks was finally recognized under the 1906 Merchant Shipping Act, which made it compulsory for every vessel over 1000 gross tons to carry a trained cook. This naturally increased the value of school certificates and boosted attendance.[62] Evening classes in camp cookery were also made available for troops and scouts.[63] Cookery schools across the country regarded these activities as part of their war work after 1914, but, according to the records, such instruction for boys and men was not limited to the war period.

The main purpose of the Gloucestershire School of Cookery and Domestic Economy was to provide cookery, health education and teacher training for local people, including schoolgirls, the artisan classes and mothers. Hospital and district nurses also benefited, and there was an invalid kitchen to support the sick. In January 1885 the founder, Mrs Mary Playne, opened Longfords Eating House for the benefit of working men. Cookery lessons by a recent senior staff teacher from the National Training School of Cookery were arranged for two evenings that month and they dealt with sickroom cookery and cheap dinners. The eating house also served breakfast on every working day and dinner four times a week, but without a cookery lesson.[64] This local philanthropic work was the origin of the Gloucestershire School of Cookery. With county council financial support for technical education and with private gifts, by the end of 1891 some 1280 pupils were being taught at 25 centres, which increased to 40 in 1892. The first centre, built at Minchinhampton, employed a teacher from the Liverpool School of Cookery: because of Playne's friendship with Calder, the connection with the Liverpool school was strong.[65]

The Gloucester school required its students for the teacher training course to board during their period of study. In 1893, 17 students studied for the teacher's diploma, while a further 12 attended for the elementary schoolteacher's special certificate. With county council support, in 1894 the school buildings were relocated and the school was fully equipped to provide cookery education across the county. In 1903, having provided education for girls from all social classes on home management skills, the school marked its nineteenth anniversary of working in association with the county council.[66] Cookery education at Gloucester was divided into two parts – county classes and city classes. For the former, for example, in September 1914 a travelling cookery van was introduced, which was better fitted out than two similar vans used in Yorkshire. The van, which was for cookery, laundry and housewifery courses and could accommodate 12 girls, was one answer to the problem of accessibility, made necessary by teaching cookery in the forest district in 1906.[67]

From the early 1890s Playne worked with district nursing in Gloucester in an attempt to promote her views on the usefulness of instruction in cookery and domestic subjects. From 1895 onwards, during the course of a year the county would offer between 40 and 50 lessons a week at 42 different cottage kitchens. Classes in the city on sick nursing and ambulance work were held in the evenings. The training school's graduates were eligible for a range of posts after passing examinations in cookery, laundry, dressmaking, needlework and millinery. In 1898 a new subject, housewifery, was introduced and then examined by Pillow.[68] Cookery and sick nursing lectures were provided for young working-class women; indeed, the influence of sickroom cookery at the school became very noticeable. Special lessons for nurses were given in 1899 at the new Cheltenham branch alongside the lessons for ladies and cooks. Those who attended the teacher training course said that the lessons on cookery and housewifery there were very useful for a nursing career. The school noticed that the society, which was much in need of improvements in household management, appreciated its work: proper care of food for both the sick and the healthy was understood to be necessary to the maintenance of a healthy community.[69]

On this understanding, in 1901 the school sent Miss Beatrice Apperley to the London Hospital to work under Eva Lückes as a sickroom cookery instructor for nurses. Thereafter, Apperley worked at both the London Hospital and Gloucester school. She delivered lectures on hospital work, which she presented as a new career in professional cookery for students undergoing training, and addressed alumni at the meetings of the Gloucester old girls' guild.[70] Apperley was appointed because of Playne's contribution to district nursing and, possibly, because Lückes was from Gloucester and had been educated at Cheltenham Ladies' College before commencing her nursing training. Infirmary nurses attended a lecture on sick cookery from 1908. Similar cookery classes were also held for district nurses.[71] The invalid kitchen in Gloucester, designed to provide cheap meals for the city's poor, had links with both district nursing and the Charity Organization Society. In 1905–6, with tickets provided by district visitors, it supplied 329 dinners and 16 soups and jellies five days a week.[72] The school managed the tickets and the list of meal prices.

The Gloucester school continued its work even during the small-pox epidemic of 1896. During this period, with funding from the county council's sanitary committee, it prepared and sent dinners for the nurses at one hospital. The school's work was commended for improving domestic conditions and trying to bring 'good wholesome food within the reach of all, and make the homes of England more comfortable and prosperous and give to our women and girls that training, which is indispensable to the welfare, not only of the present, but of the future generation.'[73] In 1898 the school started to promote health-related lectures on hygiene and physiology, in the hope that these would be effective in improving the audience's home life. The school was still delivering hygiene lectures to nurses in the 1920s.[74]

More boys and men started to join when, in 1901, the school introduced classes on colonial living along the lines of those held in Liverpool. Classes for boys were revived and one centre at Westbury-on-Trym had a practice class for which boys could obtain grants. It was recommended that other centres should follow suit. Under the auspices of the Gloucestershire county council's technical instruction committee, boys were given a cookery class in 1903 and the Gloucestershire regiment requested an army cookery experiment for training individuals in cooking. The latter was for practical cookery – how best to turn raw rations into palatable meals outdoors. The ration provided for the experiment was bread and flour, a mess tin and a water bottle. A soldier who had returned from South Africa helped with the fire and the bread making and then ideal recipes were published for the benefit of the men.[75] Classes for recruits were increased after 1914 as part of the school's war work; the same was true for those in London and other areas. In 1915 two officers attended the Gloucester school for cookery classes with their mess rations.[76]

Providing instruction for well-educated girls at Cheltenham was another of the Gloucester school's novel activities. By 1892 it had already contemplated giving all girls who left school, including those from Cheltenham Ladies' College, the opportunity to learn household management.[77] Cookery and the whole subject of domestic economy was not generally taught in girls' high or secondary schools; they usually just conducted an examination to meet the technical instruction requirement, which had no practical effect.[78] Only a few high schools provided lessons by trained teachers; the usual hazards were that it was financially difficult to maintain the facilities and parents objected because it limited their child's intellectual studies.[79] Clearly, it was possible to prepare to enrol at King's College for Women from Cheltenham Ladies' College, even if most middle-class girls would regard such a choice as marginal.[80]

Cookery education therefore opened up various opportunities, though it also raised questions about the status of its teachers and how to gain widespread support among middle-class families. In the next chapter, focusing on such individuals as Calder, I shall describe its great expansion into elementary schools and show what pressures were generated by the increasing attention paid to poverty in the cities and throughout British society.

Chapter 2

Cookery for Poor Girls

Health and diet education for schoolgirls through cookery instruction was introduced in the 1860s. It made an important contribution to society, especially following the Physical Deterioration Committee in 1904 and the Committee on Medical Inspection and Feeding of Children attending Public Elementary School in 1906. Women who had both trained as cookery teachers and worked in philanthropic fields led the movement to achieve this. Domestic economy was one such field in education. Cookery and cleaning were already being taught to girls in workhouse schools in the early 1860s as training for domestic service and it provided a successful model for introducing these subjects into public elementary schools.

Cookery and related areas of domestic economy education for girls have been discussed historically in so far as they regulated girls' roles at home and in society and limited their chances of further education. Carol Dyhouse and Annmarie Turnbull, for example, emphasize the inferiority of domestic economy as an intellectual exercise, for it had lower status than other subjects and was often judged suitable for backward girls.[1] The women educationists in the late nineteenth century who promoted domestic subjects, however, were naturally focusing on girls' future lives as wives and mothers, with the latter of course being responsible for children. It was thus considered an ideal way of preparing young girls for adult life during their school years. Influenced by the 1904 and 1906 committees, schoolchildren's health inspections and school meal services commenced at the same time. Despite the link between school meals and cookery education, however, not even the 1906 committee gave the latter much encouragement.[2]

The formal introduction of cookery to elementary schools began in the 1870s with the establishment of training schools for cookery teachers; it then became necessary to install the educational facilities for such lessons. Physical education was also considered important; this was mostly for boys but it was claimed that girls should be given the opportunity to learn about hygiene and sanitation in cookery and related areas of domestic economy, but this subject was very difficult to understand unless taught practically. Practical instruction in cookery therefore helped to combine skills and knowledge – for example, they could learn to boil new potatoes with skins on to retain their nutritional value.[3] Naturally, there were always arguments about whether or not such basic instruction was really necessary for girls. Nevertheless, habitual instruction was expected to provide common sense about what people should eat to make them healthier.

The 1875 education code – a detailed directive of what should be taught in elementary schools – listed domestic economy as a specific subject. Even before then, however, in fact as far back as 1840, Sir James Kay-Shuttleworth had promoted practical instruction in household management as part of the industrial education component for girls.[4] Cookery became a separate subject with specific grants in 1882; until then domestic economy was taught mainly through reading textbooks. Setting up practical lessons in cookery was therefore an innovation. Domestic economy was for girls above Standard IV (the level for children of about 11 years of age) and the 1878 code stipulated a grant of four shillings per girl. Girls had to choose this as one of their two specific subjects, whereas boys were allowed two subjects without restriction. The 1879 code divided domestic economy into two branches, namely housewifery (with hygiene) and food, for each of which the grant was two shillings. The number of girls attending was thereby increased from 844 in 1874 to 59,812 in 1882.[5]

Initially, needlework was introduced in 1846, with domestic economy added as a new subject only after the 1870 Education Act placed more attention than before on girls' education. The syllabus for domestic economy covered the theoretical study of food, including which ones were best suited to the requirements of the human body, the composition and nutritive value of different kinds and their choice and preparation. Household management concentrated on warming and cleaning dwellings, ventilation, general rules of health and the management of a sickroom. Ideally, every girl would be taught these subjects at school, alongside the 3Rs, before assuming domestic responsibilities at home. A basic understanding of personal health and domestic hygiene was an important factor in the improvement of public health and sanitation throughout society. It was believed that if working-class wives created comfortable homes there would be a decrease in antisocial behaviour due to drinking; temperance education was thus viewed as a side effect of domestic economy. Cookery education for children would therefore promote home comfort, higher morality and improved health among the masses.[6] Cookery gave pupils an opportunity to learn about healthcare from an early age.

HMI William Jolly mentioned in 1876 that introducing girls to domestic economy was 'an excellent step' and he expected hygiene to follow as another specific subject supported by a grant.[7] Dr Mathias Roth referred to Jolly as the only person in the education establishment who supported physical education and school hygiene, which Roth had been advocating for 20 years. Roth was a founder of the Ladies' Sanitary Association, which was set up to improve children's care through the work of philanthropic women and which also provided instruction at colleges for older girls. He believed that the general public's lack of knowledge about health caused widespread misunderstanding of advertisements for drugs and medicine, and he claimed that schoolteachers must act as agents for children's health through instruction and inspection. School hygiene, along with medical inspections and instruction, should, as part of the children's scientific physical education, be combined with practical lessons. The recommended teaching method was to use suitable objects and diagrams to help scientific understanding and to make the subject interesting: a sanitary museum was an ideal facility.[8]

Among the leading proponents of such practical education it was certainly possible to find a keen interest in domestic economy teaching. The 1880s proved to be the breakthrough decade for domestic economy education when it became expected that every girl would learn the new method of instruction in cookery. If one compares the education codes for 1884 and 1894, it becomes evident that domestic economy extended its coverage of food, dwellings, clothing, sick care and rules on health in more detail – largely through starting to provide

practical instruction in cookery.[9] The establishment of the continu-
ation school system and technical education, which local government
authorities were increasingly providing from the 1890s, addressed the
problem of the early school leaving age. These industrial training type
schools taught domestic economy to enable girls to become good
domestic servants, while evening classes and polytechnics undertook
education and instruction more suitable for young working-class men
and women. Later additions included sick nursing, childcare and first
aid classes along with French or history. HMIs focused their attention
on the health of children and the progress of cookery and domestic
economy education across the country.

With a view to providing better living conditions for those
deprived of them at a young age, the workhouse schools under the
Poor Law Board's jurisdiction offered cookery and cleaning as part of
industrial education. The workhouse school was considered to be a
useful place in which to provide healthcare education through habitual
instruction.[10] Pauper children received a rudimentary intellectual and
industrial education, with the latter designed to provide foundation
skills for occupations.[11] The girls, who if fortunate would become
domestic servants, learnt cooking, needlework and cleaning, while
the boys were taught carpentry or tailoring and given training for sea
service. Children were told to maintain cleanliness and strength of
physique through school activities. The health of the children was a
high priority in every branch of the workhouse system.

The Poor Law Board had organized workhouse education even
before the Elementary Education Act of 1870 and, in 1902, the new
Board of Education started to play a role in its administration. In fact
there had been growing coordination since the 1880s when some
parish unions sent their pauper children to public elementary schools
to allow the workhouse schools to concentrate more fully on
industrial education. Support from voluntary associations like the
Metropolitan Association for Befriending Young Servants, which Mrs
Jane Senior established, and the Girls' Friendly Society, which looked
after girls in service, followed this move. Boys who had spent years on
training ships were also well looked after. Public elementary schools
had no such system and were less interested than workhouse schools
in checking their pupils' later progress and providing help to those

children who had not taken the initiative to join a supportive association. Though workhouse children were usually from unhealthy, immoral and uneducated backgrounds, education was expected to change them and make the nation healthier. Cookery and domestic training at workhouse schools were particularly successful at combining intellectual education with industrial training.

Inspectors' reports showed that industrial training for girls was extensive across wide areas and was not confined to the metropolitan district. Even in the early 1860s, in the eastern and midland district a schoolmistress supervising household management or laundry work was considered 'the nearest approach to the perfection of a workhouse school'; it was recommended that industrial training for children should be harmonized with other religious, moral and intellectual education. The workhouse in Monmouthshire provided a good model in that the children there were well instructed without any adult paupers around them. Boys were taught field work and tailoring while girls were instructed in washing, housework and cooking; four paid officers taught them also how to manage a dairy there in pleasant and healthy surroundings.[12] Throughout the 1860s HMI Edward Tufnell commented that girls' instruction had progressed and that they were taught washing, sewing, cooking and cleaning, being soon required as servants. He pointed out, though, that it was important for education not merely to support pauper children's employment or to be useful for emigration opportunities.[13] As these cases showed, inspectors widely recognized the usefulness of cookery training for girls, even though instruction methods sometimes had to be altered.

From 1870 onwards, more attention was paid to girls' industrial training. To make the instruction suitable for real life and to achieve the moral advantages likely to be derived from educating them in a homely atmosphere, girls were taught domestic work in cottage homes. And once this period had been completed, the Metropolitan Association for Befriending Young Servants or the Girls' Friendly Society would take responsibility for their aftercare.[14] Senior encouraged further domestic training to help ensure that the girls could control cleanliness in people's homes and specifically recommended cookery and needlework for their development, saying that these lessons should not be categorized as low intellectual teaching.

She also urged that the sanitary conditions in workhouse schools with respect to accommodation, food and exercise should be improved. On food, she pointed out the need for more fresh fruit and vegetables to maintain children's health.[15]

Industrial training in metropolitan workhouse schools was constantly improved, to such an extent, indeed, that HMI Wyndham Holgate cautioned against assuming that the children were there as hands to maintain the workhouse schools rather than for educational purposes. This was often truer of girls than boys, who were more like labourers in that they used machinery to handle the laundry, steam kitchens for cooking and metal vessels for preparing meals and as washing tubs. These were not useful experiences for them because the families that might employ them would not use such large machinery. One workhouse matron in the metropolitan union came up with a much better model when she formed classes of about twelve girls over 14 and provided them with practical opportunities to learn all branches of domestic service for themselves by practising cooking, washing, ironing and cleaning. A reduced rate of poor relief was clearly to be achieved by teaching children self respect, cleanliness and making them economically independent.[16]

There were some interesting educational trials after 1881. For example, 600 pauper children of the Kensington and Chelsea school district were sent to 20 village houses at Banstead where married couples would look after them. The fathers would teach the boys about industrial work while the mothers would supervise the cooking and household arrangements alongside the girls who received instruction in laundry work, cooking, household duties and infant care.[17] This experiment was reported to have been so successful that the cottages made similar arrangements for ordinary households. It also provided a good influence for the boys.[18] This was followed by another industrial training scheme, which comprised boarding the children out at foster parents' houses.[19] From the above trials, environmental factors were clearly found to have a beneficial influence on the children's instruction.

For the children of the metropolitan union, though, improvement in industrial training for both boys and girls was still desired, as was cleanliness in the schools. Even though the girls' needlework was considered to be of poor quality in 1882, they were still only employed for heavy scullery work and laundry, which Holgate complained of as being a waste of time.[20] By contrast, he cited a remarkably successful result for the girls of one residential domestic training class in which they were given four months' experience of working as cooks, house-maids, parlour maids and general servants in rotating two-week turns. Instruction contained some new and interesting points, such as sending the girl on duty as cook to the neighbouring shops to buy necessities, and teaching her the sort of bookkeeping that would be useful for a small household. These skills would obviously help them after they graduated and were very practical financially. Since aftercare by philanthropists alone was judged insufficient, school managers were encouraged to report on the girls' future progress.[21] In the late 1880s domestic training and manual work were considered necessary in poor law schools. Children were to be instructed step by step, with attention paid to their ability in both manual and intellectual work.[22]

Since the number of children per instructor was too large – typically about 60 – overcrowding was still a problem. In the country unions there were sometimes fewer to a class, but at schools in the metropolis the average was usually even higher. Training girls in cookery and cleaning was certainly in progress in the northern district in 1887; in fact, the aim of such instruction and its effectiveness were universally recognized. Of course there was still room for improvement in the system: for instance, cookery lessons needed more encouragement because generally only adult women worked in the kitchens in the workhouses, so unless they were taught it in the school there was no opportunity for girls to learn kitchen work. Establishing training homes was therefore seen to provide an ideal environment in which to teach girls domestic work.[23]

The Lancashire poor law schools showed particularly good results in girls' industrial training in housework, though it might have been even better had there been more opportunities. Cleaning was considered as useful as cookery, so often two or three girls would help clean the room of the matron or schoolmistress, which was sometimes the size of a small dwelling. Here too it was ideal to introduce the cottage house system for training.[24] In 1901 Pillow inspected the girls' cookery, housework and laundry work at the poor law schools in London. She said it was 'good, but the time does not suffice to enable girls to learn intelligently; for example, how to deal with hard water, why raw starch is used, how to remedy stains,' and added that girls should take notes by themselves, although their lack of intelligence sometimes prevented it.[25]

On the question of diet, in 1875 Tufnell had already observed that the older children were given a variety of meals, indeed rarely the same for two days, and were given green vegetables, which Senior complained had been scarce. He pointed out that such vegetables as cabbages, parsnips and spinach were raised in the school garden and cropped by boys, even at the London schools. Meals were served warm and, apart from the newcomers who had no experience of eating anything except bread and potatoes and were unfamiliar with nourishing foods, the children left nothing on their plates. In some pauper schools the children's diet would in fact be altered following the medical officer's advice.[26]

To promote children's health it was desirable for public elementary schools to take part in transforming domestic training into a more educative activity. The good results seen in the workhouse schools on training for life often stemmed from their residential environment and hence the opportunity to control every aspect of health whether in education, diet or treating disease. This was why Senior recommended cottage home instruction, which was continued in the late nineteenth century as a boarding-out system, as the most effective for girls. Such control was not possible at public elementary schools, for these children returned to their own homes after lessons where the educational authorities had no influence over the health and sanitary conditions. However, it was possible to believe that, as a member of the family, every child attending school could deliver healthcare information to every door. Educationists interested in cookery and domestic economy saw this as a new possibility and a challenging environment into which to expand knowledge about diet and health at the edges of society. In 1887, at the Royal Commission appointed to enquire into the working of the elementary education acts in England and Wales (Cross Commission), Calder commented that workhouse schools had a record of successful teaching to make children intelligent through cookery and domestic training, while Holgate claimed

that the workhouse school was the perfect system of education, combining elementary, industrial, moral, religious and physical training.[27]

Cookery at elementary schools, involving practical training by a
girl's own hands, was made a grant subject in 1882 and by 1896 the
number of pupils had increased almost twentyfold. At the same
time, while discussions continued about women's work and
housework, infant mortality came to be recognized as a social
problem. Girls had to learn about infant care, especially from 1904
onwards. Teachers who knew the principles of sanitation and had
the ability to convey such knowledge to children should be put in
charge of managing and instructing unhealthy children about
malnutrition. The central authority's slow pace of administration,
insufficient financial grants for practical lessons and a shortage of
women inspectors, however, delayed the introduction of better
nutrition and healthcare for schoolchildren. In this context, it is well
worth analysing cookery and domestic economy education from the
1880s to c.1910 as a subject for which there was a government grant.

Looking through the development of cookery and domestic
economy education requires some focus on the people who actively
promoted it. All the leading figures, namely Calder, Pycroft and
Pillow, had connections with prominent individuals like Nightingale
and the HMIs. The latter of course were able to explain in detail what
progress was being made across the country and it was they who
recognized that the proper teaching of the subject could make an
important impact on altering people's way of living. After a series of
influential congresses on domestic economy education, which the
Society of Arts arranged, the 1880s marked the starting point for
cookery and domestic economy education as part of officially organized health education for elementary schools. HMIs had commented
on the vagueness of domestic economy teaching in the 1870s,
although the supportive opinions they voiced increased year by year.
The need for women inspectors was stressed because they would have
a deeper understanding of the subject than their male counterparts
who had little opportunity to learn it. Even so, male inspectors tried to
report what they saw, analysing its influence among children.

The provision of grants, particularly for cookery, made the subject
popular, though there remained a problem over instruction, which

varied from place to place depending on what facilities were available. Many teachers suggested introducing domestic economy, with instruction on sanitary principles, but HMI Revd W. Campbell, in the division of Chelsea, criticized the vagueness of the scheme the Education Department had put forward and requested practical revision. For girls who were learning this subject in the Lancashire area it would 'be useful in the state of life': they could reduce crime and immorality in society by producing comfortable homes.[28] These were typical images and opinions about promoting domestic economy education. HMI John Hall of Scotland strongly recommended domestic economy and housewifery as practical education for girls by suggesting it would alter working men's lives through 'cheerful homes, clean and neatly mended clothes, and palatable food'.[29] As the above reports from different places show, attention to domestic economy was increasing even before cookery became a grant subject.

Of course, there was not always approval for teaching domestic economy when based only on a hope of transforming habits through the application of common sense. The general downside of domestic economy education was that there was no scheme to confirm whether instruction followed the syllabus or whether girls enjoyed the lessons. Revd J. Lomax of the Stockport district said it had been successfully taught there for two years, though more progress had been expected. At mixed schools male teachers undertook lessons with only knowledge acquired from books and it was often the same for women teachers on food and its preparation, washing or managing a sickroom.[30] During this experimental period with its increasing classes, the Revd D. Stewart, in the metropolitan district of Greenwich, reported in 1879 that from his examination of domestic economy there was no doubt it would prove useful if well taught, but, as girls' answers often revealed, they showed no real understanding, as 'infection' and 'contagion' were commonly mixed up. Instruction on food produced similar confusion: even when questions were set about the girls' daily food (as was common among poor families) they were not understood and answers were not combined with any practical training or knowledge.[31] Cookery and health education in schools suffered from a lack of properly trained staff and methodology of instruction. Domestic economy textbooks also tended to be too scientific and more suitable for girls who already had basic education and were interested in medicine or science.[32]

When introducing nutrition and sanitary science to elementary schoolchildren, more effort should be made to transform professional and technical terms into plain words while still retaining an accurate understanding of sanitary engineering or dietetics. This would make the whole subject digestible, especially when combined with sufficient practical lessons. This was the principle Calder, Pycroft and Pillow proposed for promoting cookery and domestic economy education in schools. From the 1880s Calder's strategy influenced the Education Department's decision to use the grant system for cookery following her experimental instruction at Liverpool. In her capacity as a member of the London School Board, Rosamond Davenport-Hill was another important figure at this time to organize cookery education. They tried to establish cookery education at elementary schools in a systematic form and as a practical education for a better life.

Calder also explained that after schools of cookery were established in several large towns like Edinburgh, Glasgow, Leeds, Leamington and Liverpool, various hospitals, teacher training colleges, industrial schools, night ragged schools for boys and girls, and mothers' meetings also then started to offer opportunities for cookery lessons. Although artisan classes attracted adult women, these were not a long-term remedy for improving poor people's homes and lifestyles because, despite the instruction given, the women generally still considered that decent cookery would cost more than their uneconomical methods. Since wives and mothers found it difficult to adopt new methods and knowledge after classes, teaching house-keeping and health to young schoolgirls, the future mothers and wives, was therefore considered a better investment. Practical cookery instruction would become an excellent intellectual training in that it would turn girls' everyday lives into experiments and confirm the lessons 'more firmly in their minds'. Ideally, girls at any standard should have an opportunity to study domestic economy in case they had to leave school early due to a family need to earn money. Calder believed that cookery instruction for elementary schoolgirls would help poor families: for example, a young girl who learnt cookery at school could be a support for her widowed father. Calder argued for more public support for cookery instruction to encourage a wide range of learners to attend what she referred to as 'social progress', namely liberal and efficient activities delivered by cookery schools.[33]

In 1884 Calder attended the Conference of Education at the International Health Exhibition in London at which she drew attention to the problem of underfed children. Often this was caused by poverty combined with a lack of knowledge about household management such as thrift, sanitary principles and wholesome food. She opposed supplying food to poor children on the grounds that philanthropic help would only turn them into paupers; she was convinced that education with health instruction for girls was the best way to change their circumstances.[34] Practical activities throughout the lessons could also alleviate stress. At the 1877 congress Edwin Chadwick had made the same point by claiming that physical movements during domestic economy classes would improve girls' health and do no harm. More qualified teachers were required to instruct their pupils on how to prepare nourishing, but economical dishes for those on low wages; moreover, sickroom cookery was necessary since it was 'almost unknown amongst people'. The latter required a clear understanding of physiology, hygiene and chemistry. Only specifically trained teachers could cover all those requirements.[35]

The reports of HMIs in the 1880s showed hopes of benefit from better facilities and the professional education of teachers. Based on the idea of education for a better life, a systematic method was encouraged. Literary instruction was a potential hazard for girls whose knowledge would never enable them to distinguish nitrogenous from carbonaceous elements in food. Girls just had to learn by habit how to cook potatoes without wasting the most nourishing part as well as understanding theoretically their nutritional value as starch. When delivering scientific research results on nutrition and sanitation, as with ventilation and drainage, there had to be a good balance between the intellectual and the practical, with demonstration. These were the opinions of HMI Heneage Harrison, for the Liverpool district, after examining nearly 2000 girls on domestic economy. HMI Henry Oakeley in Manchester agreed that if literally-inclined instruction continued in domestic economy classes, the subject would lose its real educational value.[36]

HMI reports showed that these arrangements were making cookery classes more effective and that schools were becoming health instruction centres for children. In the Blackburn district of Lancashire, where well-prepared food was necessary to retain the factory workers' healthy physique, some ladies instructed girls even though they were not specially trained. As this case showed, there was both demand and recognition that knowledge of cookery was expected to counter the 'deteriorating influences' on people's health. Examinations showed that while an understanding of clothing, health and ventilation might be learnt from experience, answers on food remained unsatisfactory. To understand the art of cookery it was essential to have an elementary knowledge of chemistry and physiology. A typical problem was reported from Maidstone in Kent in 1883 where domestic economy was taught only from books containing a bulk of useless detail on food. Cookery knowledge was not recognized for its 'high sanitary and social value'.[37]

Gradually, progress was seen in the reports from 1883–84 onwards. The proper home management women derived from attending cookery classes would also encourage temperance and an improvement in poor people's dwellings.[38] Adding a reference about the temperance movement was understandable in that ideas about cookery and domestic economy education easily tied in with the wider moral reform of the working class. In the minds of educationists who were aware of the real conditions of the working classes, reforming the living environment of the people was associated with cookery and domestic economy education. Temperance, cleanliness of homes and knowledge on health were all necessary for them and elementary education provided learning opportunities for the largest number of people. Based on Calder's opinions and activities, Oakeley's report on Liverpool showed in detail how in a large industrial city regular schooling could control the cleanliness of children. At Liverpool, practical cookery was introduced where a course of 20 lessons conveyed knowledge about the values and usages of various foods like meat, fish, vegetables, soups and puddings, and where the pupils were also taught how to make economical dishes for invalids.[39]

In London, Davenport-Hill promoted cookery education so that even the poor in the worst slum areas might gain some skills for a better life. Systematic training by the London School Board had been started on a small scale in 1875–76, though a lack of trained teachers caused delay in making the scheme popular. For convenience, about 30 cookery centres were prepared: by 1884 these centres were all over London and approximately 21,000 girls were attending them every year. Davenport-Hill even criticized the National Training School of Cookery for inclining too much towards culinary arts rather than cookery teaching. She therefore proposed that the London School Board train mainly ex-pupil teachers to give 20 lessons in six months beyond the diploma of the National Training School of Cookery. That diploma was not enough for teaching purposes, though she did consider it was good to have one recognized body issuing teachers' certificates and eventually, by 1887, a large number of teachers were being trained at recognized training schools. The importance of instructing girls on cleanliness was stressed, especially washing their hands and cleaning their nails before cooking, and cleaning utensils after the lessons. There were initial objections from parents to such lessons, though in time they became more supportive. In London the number of cookery centres kept increasing in every area, averaging one centre for every five to eight schools. In the 1890s additional centres started to open up to teach such subjects as laundry work and housewifery.[40]

These promotions across the country increased the number of girls who received a grant: indeed, the number doubled in 1884–85. In 1884, 7579 girls were awarded four shillings each at 457 of the 541 schools and departments that taught cookery. The next year it increased to 17,754 girls in 643 of the 715 schools and departments. Cookery was by this time defined as the most important subject after the 3Rs and sewing for girls in public elementary schools. The benefits were not limited to practical skills, but the process of proper instruction was also expected to enhance the girls' interest and intelligence. They would learn cooking for themselves and not just end up on a course with lectures and demonstrations.[41]

If non-certificated teachers had enough practical experience in cooking both to mount demonstrations and give practical instruction, they were still accepted in the 1880s. One case was reported in Gloucester of a mistress of a girls' school holding a weekly lesson on cottage and invalid cookery in which she tried to instruct girls systematically and not waste their time by just copying recipes. They spent as much time as possible cooking by themselves and showing recipes on the blackboard that afterwards the girls copied into notebooks.[42] This was the method Calder proposed – theory, principles, knowledge of foodstuffs, demonstration and recipes then acted on during practical lessons. Calder's many visits to different places strengthened her influence on cookery education.[43]

At the 1887–88 Cross Commission, which since the 1870 Act and following the several minor changes in the codes had tried to identify progress across the country, cookery education was supported in elementary schools. Among the witnesses called were Calder and Davenport-Hill, who presented specific evidence on the current progress of cookery education, and some educationists who provided supportive opinion on the subject either from their inspections or their experience of teaching it at schools. The commission wished to promote cookery education, even though there were difficulties over finance and arrangements for teachers, since it could be a unique opportunity for girls. Witnesses made plain that the development of cookery classes was not limited to School Board schools and that voluntary schools were likewise quite keen to introduce it; for example, in Liverpool 1503 pupils studied cookery, though only 500 were in board schools.[44] To promote cookery education in more schools, Calder asked for more financial support to be given to voluntary schools. A system based on cottage cookery was valuable for real life, with four points mentioned as beneficial effects: such lessons let girls know about domestic servants' work, the skills learnt were simply useful for their families at home, they relieved classroom overpressure, and they taught girls to become thrifty and careful housewives.[45]

Davenport-Hill stressed the point that some children prepared dinner at home and thereby carried out their lessons in practice.[46] One of the witnesses, a job printer called Henry Williams, said that his eldest daughter, aged 11, could cook meals at home and would always tell her father about her interesting cookery lessons.[47] Calder found from following up girls who had received lessons at schools that parents were glad about their daughter's knowledge of cooking.

She added that doctors highly valued the subject for it was 'one of the greatest boons that education has ever given in making girls understand a little sickroom cooking, which is often more wanted than medicine'. Employers were also happy with those girls who already knew about their work before starting in service. Furthermore, Calder claimed, cookery education reduced mortality and helped maintain healthy homes among the working classes.[48]

The numbers of grant-receiving classes kept increasing throughout the 1890s, 1900s and after 1910, which meant that more opportunity was provided for girls to learn the subject as an aspect of broader technical education. Analysis by HMIs showed that the quality of instruction improved little by little. As at the Cross Commission, the value of cookery education was widely recognized. Not every school had facilities though and, in rural districts, the difficulty of finding qualified teachers continued. In the London area, the sale of the food cooked in lessons was considered important income to allow the instruction to continue.[49] After his inspection in Marylebone, HMI William Martin wrote that he would support cookery education for every girl – though they might learn more effectively if recipe books were given. He also proposed more systematic instruction and complained that girls were spending too much time copying recipes at cookery centres rather than actually cooking dishes. Oakeley had already mentioned to the Royal Commission on Technical Instruction in 1884 that the syllabus was not effective for learning practical subjects – learning recipes by heart about unfamiliar food with unknown prices was unsuitable.[50] The more cookery was promoted practically, the more specific inspection of practical lessons was needed, which in turn encouraged the introduction of women inspectors.

Cookery instruction showed steady improvement after the Cross Commission, with HMIs paying more detailed attention to its quality; for instance, in Norwich there was a trial during which, to claim for a grant, the schools recorded what dishes had been taught to the girls. To standardize the value of practical lessons, these records were taken as evidence of instruction.[51] In 1889 three schools in Gloucester claimed for a grant, though only two were successful. Due to the Bishop of Salford's wish to improve the working classes, girls in Roman Catholic schools brought the food they had cooked at home after cooking classes to school: they made the parents purchase the ingredients and then they brought what they had cooked to school the next day as proof. At school, girls prepared fried fish, pease soup, cottage pie and apple tart. Sometimes these dishes were sold. In Liverpool Calder's influence ensured that up to 1600 girls at School Board and voluntary schools had cookery lessons. HMIs certainly found that cooking facilities for lessons were improving, were widely used and that teaching food values was expected to reduce dyspepsia among working men in a generation or two.[52]

Calder summarized her work on domestic economy education during the 1880s in the context of an analysis of the national economy. For the wealth of the nation it was necessary to consider a thrifty use of food to support the rising population because 'waste of food would not contribute to maintain the health and strength of the people'. She quoted Lord Brabazon's opinion that in England 60 per cent of the wages working men earned were spent on food, which should be for their comfort and nutrition as well as for the national benefit. As for educating young girls, their strength, habits, tastes and ambitions were developed during their school years and cookery, as both an intellectual and practical subject, would work as a bridge to connect school and real life. Cookery was the more essential, said Calder, because even a very poor family would buy clothes rather than sew them for themselves, '*but no amount of money can buy* a well ordered home and the thrifty management of its resources'. They could not, therefore, obtain knowledge for a better life except through education and it was this that would surely raise the people's standard of living. The immediate effect of cookery lessons was seen even during school life in that practical work provided a relief for the brain; meanwhile, practical instruction in choosing and preparing nourishing food would provide girls with wisdom for the rest of their lives.[53]

Chapter 3

Cookery Education, Mothercare and Schoolchildren

Calder remained an inspiration for promoting cookery, both as education and to improve girls' lives. Her work with elementary schools was highly influential in that it paid much attention to extending educational opportunities for girls that combined useful knowledge and skills with scientific understanding. Pillow and Pycroft took this further, especially after the commencement of technical education made it possible to extend the health education element in cookery without losing the benefit of practical lessons. This in turn extended understanding. The appointment of women inspectors for needlework in 1888, and for cookery and laundry work in 1890, made the analysis of progress more detailed and improvements in health through cookery instruction were increasingly highlighted. More cookery centres were set up in this period; the 1890s developed into an advanced period for cookery education at schools, based now on a firm ideology constructed during the 1880s. Technical education was innovatory, stemming from the Technical Education Act of 1889 and the Customs and Exercise Act of 1890. It was also the first step in a decentralization of education policy whereby county councils became the chief authorities and provided the finance for secondary education.[1]

In London children who took cookery classes could clearly improve their lives. According to Booth, 10 per cent of the 40,000 children attending Board schools and 11,000 more children at voluntary schools were in want of food. It was proved that a large number of children were not fed properly at home and that the meals of almost all suffered due to poverty. Generally, these children helped parents at home in nursing or domestic work. Teachers recognized the usefulness of cookery classes for pupils although there was no time to spare for instruction outside the code. After their commencement in all Board schools and many voluntary schools in the 1880s, girls liked these lessons and proudly talked about their cooking experiences at home when they prepared the dishes learnt at school: for example, shepherds' pie, rock cakes and Irish stew were common dishes and usually had been eaten by their fathers. Booth expected this to be an agent for raising the standard of living.[2] Cookery education in London was thus recognized as useful to support environmental reforms, for, as Booth mentioned, one asset of cookery and domestic economy was the cleanliness and other health related matters learnt alongside it. Influence from sanitary inspectors came via Pillow. She devised a standard of sanitary knowledge appropriate for cookery and related subjects of domestic economy teachers. Arthur Newsholme was associated with much of Pillow's work.

Newsholme was already known for his work as a medical officer of health and as an author of books on health and hygiene, such as *School Hygiene* and *Lessons on Health*. In the section about state medicine at the seventh International Congress of Hygiene and Demography in 1891, he observed that 20 per cent of the total population consisted of elementary schoolchildren, which meant that if all of them were taught the principles of health the knowledge would spread in a few years and be beneficial for the nation's future by preventing diseases. He referred to the Education Department's 1890 returns on special subject pupils, which showed that 23,094 of a total of 88,354 girls had been examined on domestic economy, whereas only 1554 had been given specific cookery instruction. Newsholme supported cookery as 'an important branch of hygiene' and he supported instruction on hygiene in schools because of its impact on people's lives.[3] Houses were as overcrowded as they had been 50 years earlier; also, architects and builders were ignorant and misunderstood sanitary science. Hence, school education would be the best way to educate the larger population, ideally by teaching hygiene to make 'every man his own doctor'.[4]

Newsholme's early works on school hygiene were for financial gain rather than research interest. Nevertheless, his work with Pillow came to be regarded as essential to cookery and domestic economy teacher training and 40,000 copies were printed.[5] An innovative point was that it made a clear link between public health and domestic hygiene. The latter, in particular, required a better understanding of sanitary principles, which, it was expected, could be spread to every household by education. Because it was necessary to make cookery at elementary schools useful for real life, the recommended method was first to introduce children to the principles of cookery through an understanding of digestion. Then, practical lessons in cookery had to use recipes based on the variety of foods available from parents' wages. Time, labour and fuel also had to be considered, which meant instruction on recooking cold meat. Children's cleanliness was, of course, stressed in the instruction on preparing food, such as care of nails and hands. Knowledge of cookery could turn all food into 'palatable and nourishing dishes' even if the available ingredients were only scraps. Understanding elementary sanitary engineering regarding water and sewerage was basic for comfortable and healthy households; this too had to be introduced properly by teachers.[6]

Nightingale was another prominent figure to support cookery education and healthcare for schoolchildren. From 1886 she corresponded with the schoolmaster of Lea Board School in Derby, W. J. P. Burton. Lea was the ancestral home of the Nightingale family, which was the major landowner and which supported schools financially and educationally.[7] Burton was a keen gardener as well as a schoolmaster and his instruction for boys was thus suitable for the local area. Around 1888 Mrs Shore Nightingale gave a quarter acre of land to the school for horticultural purposes.[8] Florence Nightingale encouraged Burton's attempts to teach science through lectures and collecting geological specimens, which would encourage the boys to teach themselves. The boys were all working class and expected to become miners, quarrymen or factory workers. Nightingale said that educating children by this method would turn them into good citizens, and good fathers and mothers. She drafted a letter, at Burton's request, outlining the need to teach hygiene and sanitation to boys and girls leaving elementary schools, which stressed the need for schoolmasters to pay attention to sanitary questions. This was based on her theory of nursing education in which practical training was essential to support knowledge from books. Her detailed memorandum consisting of

instruction for girls was also impressive. Here, Nightingale emphasized that they had to think for themselves on hygiene and sanitation.
She wished children to consider the nutritional value of common
food, such as brown and wholemeal bread and fruit. Preventing food-
related ailments such as diarrhoea and constipation was mentioned.
Care of babies was added because, from ignorance, infants were often
given fat bacon instead of milk.[9] Among all these suggestions for
better health, care of food was considered the most important.

It was thus easy to understand why Nightingale supported work on
rural health with the health missioners in Buckinghamshire. She
worked for this scheme from the 1870s and by 1892 it was flourishing.
She nevertheless remarked that although its instruction would benefit
mothers, there was still no opportunity for women to acquire sanitary
training to become instructors. While nursing training schools could
teach sick care, they did not teach healthcare, and the latter was insufficiently understood by schoolteachers. They, therefore, had to be
properly trained professionally to deliver sanitary ideas.[10] In January
1892 Nightingale and George De'ath, the medical officer of health for
Buckingham, discussed the provision of 'Health at Home' lectures.
These were for missioners who delivered knowledge about health to
uneducated rural women in their homes. Such missioner women had
to pass examinations to prove their ability; the examinations put
more weight on teaching health – as for district nurses.[11]

During this work, Nightingale met Calder and learnt of the latter's
support for education in rural home sanitation and of her wish to send
women to train under the health missioners' scheme. She welcomed
another professional woman's interest in the subject.[12] Nightingale
wanted to make girls and mothers in the countryside understand how
sanitation affected their health and, to achieve this, she believed the
rural health missioners' approach was best.[13] Nevertheless, she
mentioned to Calder that the 'health at home' approach was not the
best way to succeed in all sanitary matters; it only aimed to maintain
the health of a cottage (even though this had admittedly not been
considered good enough until then) and Nightingale felt that the
work needed more emphasis on sanitation. Nightingale prepared a
syllabus for Calder to use at Liverpool to instruct teachers, while
tactfully thanking Calder for her practical hints.[14]

In 1892 Nightingale told Calder that the health at home missioners' scheme had commenced in north Buckinghamshire and that
she had sent pamphlets to Liverpool. She also praised Calder as 'Saint
of the Laundry, Cooking & Health'.[15] Not surprisingly, Calder wrote a
paper on domestic science for the 1893 Chicago exhibition where a
women's congress was held on the subject of philanthropic work and
where a paper by Nightingale was also read. Calder spoke on her
speciality, namely that cookery had now become a branch of national
education within the grant system and was taught by trained teachers.
She pointed out that scientific instruction in domestic skills would
reduce all sorts of waste due to ignorance; food was wasted from poor
cooking and garments from unsuitable washing. A penny manual
would ensure instruction by making facts easy to learn by heart.
Elementary schools and technical education classes were two
widespread systems of education that had a huge potential to improve
the way people lived, and instruction for home life should now be
accessible to every woman and girl. This was expected to become 'an
essential factor in the development of national welfare'.[16] Nightingale
and Calder were both keen to improve the health of individuals but
equally believed that if efforts were not focused on domestic matters
then better sanitation throughout society would never be achieved.

HMIs began to confirm general cleanliness among girls and
attributed it to the good effect of cookery education in that it taught
girls to be habitual, to tie up their hair and, in combined lessons, to
make aprons in needlework classes and wash them during laundry.
Systematic teaching schemes helped: writing up could be done after
and not during lessons, giving maximum use of the time allowed.[17]
The Education Department's first woman inspector of cookery, Miss
Mary Harrison, argued that lessons would obtain their maximum
effect if suitable utensils were installed and it was ensured that
instruction was suitable for working-class households.[18] By the 1890s
cookery was taught at both board and voluntary schools in London,
though not all the lessons were satisfactory enough to qualify for
grants.[19] Inspectors checked five points about cookery lessons –
systematic instruction, attention to cleanliness, suitable dishes for the
neighbourhood, using the cooking appliances found in working-class
homes and delivering knowledge on the value of foods for children.[20]

The value of domestic economy was succinctly defined: it was based on those scientific principles for 'the necessary condition of a healthy dwelling, the value and proper treatment of food, and due care of clothing'. It was necessary, inspectors concluded, to increase centres for cookery, laundry and housewifery for every girl over ten.[21]

Manual training at school was also considered necessary in order to catch up with other countries. Miss Hyacinthe Deane, Harrison's successor after 1896, acknowledged that large towns where the authorities were keen on the subject naturally showed good results, although the standard of instruction still varied due to the lack of utensils. More attention should be paid to obtaining grants. Children should be given written instructions and important points put up on the blackboard to help understand the principle of any demonstration before the children prepared a small dish.[22] More systematic instruction was required to help teachers reduce time wasted and to increase the educational effect. The sale of dishes, however, was approved. Having only 40 hours of lessons a year was not, of course, the remedy for providing a healthier lifestyle for the working classes, though parents were happy that their daughters could learn these skills. Furthermore, attendance was often irregular.[23] It was not easy to convert administrative plans into pupils' attendance.

In London, Pycroft's approach was different from Calder's in that she was more active on the administrative side of cookery education. Her work covered vast areas, including elementary and secondary schools, evening schools, voluntary societies and schools of nautical cookery. Under the Technical Education Board of London, Pycroft organized evening classes and polytechnics, and scholarships for girls who wanted advanced training opportunities at the National Training School of Cookery or at polytechnics. Classes were in domestic economy related subjects, sick nursing, hygiene, first aid and infant care – all designed to extend knowledge in areas useful for life. She arranged them in her role as organizer of the Technical Education Board's domestic economy subcommittee and frequently reported on activities, while involved in the appointment of teachers and in examinations. She investigated the current instruction in London and advised on cookery, laundry, dress cutting, needlework, sick nursing and hygiene classes for such external associations as the Girls' Friendly

Society and the Young Woman's Christian Association. She also pressed
the Board for the financial support necessary to organize her work.[24]

At the same time Pycroft began to organize one of her more
interesting projects: cookery lessons for merchant seamen. It was
started at the Sailors' Home in the London dock area and arose from
the increasing attention shipowners were paying to sailors' welfare and
the new scale of provisions the Board of Trade issued in the 1860s to
bring about long-term improvements in sailors' conditions. Following
the Liverpool Training School of Cookery's successful trial of seamen's cookery classes at Liverpool, the Technical Education Board
offered annual financial support. Pycroft visited the Sailors' Home and
examined the kitchen used for instruction, communicated with the
organizer regularly, and checked the students' achievements when sent
out to the merchant service. Certificates and examination became
important for the Board of Trade's compulsory system whereby all
men had to spend at least four years at sea as cooks as part of their
course. Practical experience was thereby necessary. The Nautical
Cookery School soon became well known by taking part in displays
at universal cookery and food exhibitions.[25]

In 1894 Pycroft also outlined the Technical Education Board in
London's plans to supply free of charge teachers of cookery,
laundry, needlework and dressmaking to women's and girls' organizations. Domestic economy schools for girls at polytechnics such as
Battersea, Borough and Regent Street were to be two-thirds filled
with free scholars under the board's proposals, and girls between 13
and 15 years of age were to be recommended by their school-
mistresses.[26] For the proposed extension of instruction on sick
nursing, hygiene and first aid, Mrs Bedford Fenwick, matron of St
Bartholomew's Hospital and of the Royal British Nurses' Association, advised that the Technical Education Board must employ
qualified nurses who had experience in teaching. This project
commenced for six months as an experiment from February 1894.[27]

The contribution such technical education made to cookery and
domestic economy was that it extended opportunities for girls, and
not just by occasionally attending individual lectures and lessons. The
high-standard classes held at voluntary associations for girls and
women were conducted by qualified teachers from the board either

free or for small charges, with even the latter acceptable because of the quality of the lessons. Instruction for men was also one of the characteristics of technical education, since boys were not included in cookery lessons at elementary schools unless in port towns. Technical education was thus intended as a follow-up for all those who had already left elementary school but wished to extend their professional or personal opportunities. Like elementary education, it was based on the idea that people might learn something to improve their lives.

With Beatrice Webb, Pycroft and Baddeley attended the National Union of Women Workers' conference in Nottingham in 1895 to read papers on technical education. While Pycroft represented the LCC, Baddeley spoke about her work in a predominantly rural area. The conference was intended to create a federation of all women's societies in the industrial, philanthropic and educational fields; the audience consisted of about 600 middle-class, mostly middle-aged, women who were largely professional philanthropists and guardians of the poor.[28] Pycroft analysed her work in London as an example of technical education, based, of course, on the LCC's experiments from 1890. She stressed it would allow people in all social classes to learn about cookery. The results that would follow were clear – increased opportunities for women and girls to learn useful skills and knowledge, and extending employment for domestic economy teachers.[29] Obviously, Pycroft viewed technical education as having benefits for both the poor who took lessons and for the teaching staff drawn from middle-class women.

Pycroft's main point, however, was economic conditions in heavily residential areas, where, especially in London, there was great local diversity. The Technical Education Board worked to maximize girls' attendance and the domestic economy centres increased from 96 in 1893–94 to 113 in 1894–95. Basically, evening classes presented a good opportunity to revise cookery classes attended at elementary schools. The demand for properly trained teachers kept increasing, with Pycroft claiming that their work was a remedy for the poor's ill health.[30] Baddeley then introduced the case of Gloucestershire, claiming that it was the only county to finance women's classes separately, which stressed the importance of such instruction. An affordable tuition fee was proposed: 1s or 1s 6d for ten lessons. In some cases 6d was returned to encourage regular attendance, the intention being to support self-help among women, not to pauperize them. Gloucester had high levels of local interest and systematic instruction. Baddeley even quoted interest from a working man who clearly understood that more nutritious food was needed. This, she said, showed an increasing demand from the working classes to improve their living standard.[31] Nevertheless, educational instruction for women required some fresh ideas because even if details were circulated in newspapers, advertisements would never reach those for whom they were intended. In Liverpool, now a large city, relying only on word of mouth was obviously ineffective when announcing new classes. Alternative methods included putting notices in shops and informing communities through employers or clergymen in their parishes. These problems notwithstanding, the introduction of technical education appeared to allow more flexibility regarding the needs of each district when broadening useful knowledge about healthcare.[32]

Pillow compiled progress up to 1896 in her milestone report 'Domestic economy teaching in England', which analysed developments since the 1870s. Pillow traced several alterations in the codes and in the grant system for elementary school subjects, technical education, examinations at high schools and secondary schools. She argued that upper grade schools also should introduce domestic science to assist their pupils' development and for the national benefit. Meanwhile, practical lessons in good home management, for both economy and health, would surely have a permanent benefit, even though rural areas still suffered from a lack of facilities and teachers. Pillow observed how teachers let girls bring leftover food from home to use when preparing dishes themselves and how marketing entered lessons as practical instruction for girls to understand economical as well as good food, though this was not always easy to manage.[33] Under Pillow's growing influence, more encouragement was given to technical education and other programmes to produce better wives and mothers, with cookery and domestic economy becoming confirmed as fundamental for mothercraft education.

In addition to its greater flexibility, technical education's other asset from the 1890s was that it provided instruction on demand, as opposed to teaching children of varying enthusiasm in elementary schools. Acquiring useful skills when needed was clearly an advantage; however, without a compulsory system of attendance or examination, it was not easy to investigate effectiveness regarding, for instance, knowledge of hygiene. Hygiene instruction was originally included in cookery and domestic economy for elementary schoolgirls, but had since been translated into the more common notion of cleanliness, while cookery and domestic economy education became more closely linked to national welfare. The 1904 Physical Deterioration Committee, however, which concluded that health knowledge must be spread more widely in society, laid much stress on the need for hygiene. It supported domestic economy educationists' long-held goal to teach children from an early age to change their way of living. Medical professionals likewise generally approved of feeding children at school as a remedy for malnutrition and to reduce disease rates.[34]

From 1900 onwards, HMIs' attention to schoolchildren's health and instruction was increased for both boys and girls, and not only through cookery and domestic economy education. To maintain hygienic conditions in the buildings, and to control disease among the children, more medical officers for schools were urged.[35] Support from nurses also developed from the early 1900s, for they could cover for infrequent visits by medical officers, check children's sanitary conditions and provide advice to parents. The School Board also advised teachers on how to undertake basic examinations on behalf of medical officers, particularly during epidemics.[36]

Even though systematic cookery instruction increased, some districts still suffered from a lack of facilities. As late as 1902, instruction in cookery was still complained about and even misunderstood as designed to turn children into professional cooks (practically impossible on only 40 hours a year) rather than for raising the standard of home cooking and health. Instructing younger girls was confirmed as potentially the most rewarding since they could learn cleanliness through their cookery education, which would later affect their habits as adult women.[37] This theory, of course, dated from the earliest days of cookery instruction for elementary schoolgirls, as represented by Calder. To improve the nation's health, the 1904 committee broadened the range of social problems requiring remedy: these now included urbanization and the people (overcrowded accommodation, pollution of the living environment, occupational health), alcoholism, food (cleanliness, processed food), the juvenile population (infant mortality, mothers' employment and pregnancy, breast-feeding and milk, parental ignorance and neglect) and finally the school system (feeding and medical inspection, special subjects). To reduce infant mortality and to produce a better way of life among working-class families, cookery instruction and infant care were elevated. House-wifery and hygiene for both schoolgirls and mothers placed more responsibility on women for the health of their families – currently perceived as a problem in an unhygienic and unhealthy nation where the deaths of so many young children and large numbers of rejections among army recruits made the matter immediately relevant and required prompt action to improve the people's physique. The lack of cooking facilities at home still called into question the value of cookery lessons for elementary schoolgirls in that they had little opportunity to repeat the lessons at home; at the same time this was also the reason for many poor mothers choosing ready-made food as the family staple. Using simple words to explain food values and to convey practical understanding about the chemistry of food was also recommended. The report concluded depressingly that these conditions 'may take generations of educative influence to correct'.[38] Until such time, instructing girls about hygiene required no less than a reconsideration of the education system.[39]

Healthcare education for boys was likewise sometimes linked to their future occupations, often in military service, and it was therefore important to reduce the number of recruits rejected on medical grounds. This meant more attention to tooth care, and an opportunity to learn cookery at elementary school, as was already common in the training of naval boys where it was combined with instruction about personal health.[40] Although the aim of instructing boys was simply to improve their general health, and was not connected to parenting or childcare as it was for girls, medical officers nevertheless commented on the effectiveness of introducing more education on hygiene. Dr James Kerr, medical officer for the London School Board from 1902, recommended hygiene education for all schoolchildren. James Niven, medical officer for Manchester, claimed that cookery was so important that it should not be left as voluntary but made compulsory. Domestic economy for girls had also to include cleaning, selecting food, dietetic knowledge and the care of clothes. Boys too should be given an opportunity to learn about food and health.[41]

Robert Hutchison of the London Hospital, an expert on dietetics in medicine, said that from his experience instructing working-class mothers on diet through practical lectures was effective. He did not, however, show similar support for instructing schoolgirls. Regarding instruction on infant care, this, he felt, would be more influential if delivered through health visitors' advice to mothers.[42] Alfred Eichholz, an inspector of schools, explained why adult men should also be given health instruction. He further explained that advice given by lady health visitors to mothers about childcare and food values would be more effective than just letting girls learn housewifery generally at school, only vaguely referring to their future lives.[43] Hutchison and Eichholz considered effectiveness from a medical perspective. For them, instructing schoolgirls and mothers was best arranged separately so that each could obtain benefit from instruction suitable for their ages and social circumstances. In contrast with such medical professional opinion, focusing principally on health education, most educationists tried to improve childcare and mothercraft education with an emphasis on social welfare. For maximum effect, domestic economy for girls might even be concentrated in the last year of school rather than started at a younger age.[44]

Supplying food at school was another subject the 1904 committee discussed, although this was separate from just conducting cookery lessons and such activity could only be appropriate for older boys and girls.[45] Charles Loch, secretary of the Charity Organization Society, was critical of the idea, saying that providing meals after lessons could only be a temporary solution.[46] Nevertheless, selling food after cookery lessons was already a popular practice; it was considered beneficial for schools financially as well as educational for children. Within a school meal system they could understand healthy diets as well as learn cleanliness through their lessons. Inevitably, disposing of cooked food after classes depended on the facilities available for cookery lessons, but much, of course, could be turned into meals. The first suggestion was to sell food, at the cost price of the ingredients, to be consumed at home; indeed, it was often mentioned that parents and children purchased dishes after lessons. The second was to cook, as meals, food for some schoolchildren at 1d or 1½d each, as discussed later in 1906 on introducing the school meal service. The third was to sell food as teachers' meals, referred to as a good opportunity to show the results of such lessons. The fourth was to supply cheap soup to poor neighbourhoods in cold weather, philanthropic work. This was more likely to be adopted when teaching domestic economy to middle-class girls and recipes for them frequently had this philanthropic purpose in mind. Finally, girls could take orders before cookery lessons, which would perhaps be the most economical way of solving the cooked food problem afterwards.

Davenport-Hill commented on one case where girls cooked many orders for meat patties and fruit pies from boys' and girls' schools and soup for teachers.[47] Naturally, this was not always educational because the girls had to cook dishes solely for sales. Selling food meant finding customers soon after it had been cooked, although that was the responsibility of managers, along with preparing suitable appliances and all the ingredients for lessons. Trials involving cheap school meals for very poor children were conducted in Manchester in 1885. A penny was charged for midday meals because under-feeding was considered a priority. Its educational value, however, was vague because there was no organized plan, while just giving food to children would be ineffective in making them self-supporting.[48]

Nonetheless, voluntary associations like, for example, the Destitute Children's Dinner Society, had been supplying cheap meals for poor children since the 1860s. In 1881 Lord Brabazon, commenting on the need for better health in Britain and expecting to benefit parents, schools and children alike, recommended supplying meals for children and selling them cheaply (or for a little more to the children of well-to-do parents). Preferably, though, for educational reasons, the children should cook the meals.[49] Brabazon was not the only one to show such support for children's cookery. Loch conceded that providing meals, at least for some poor schoolchildren, was essential because of their family circumstances. He introduced a trial in one district in London where girls cooked penny dinners by themselves, under instruction, using familiar utensils. Loch claimed that this would be educationally worthwhile and would influence their parents because the girls could show how to do it at home.[50] In 1890 the London School Board also recognized the necessity to feed children when so many of them came to school in want of food. Financial support was accordingly asked from the Education Department.[51] One scheme was reported in the Exeter district of southwest England in 1891 where girls prepared the school dinners every day: the lessons were much appreciated by their mothers. Against that, it was argued that even if cheap school dinners were provided as a result of cookery lessons, parents still had to take seriously the responsibility of feeding their own children.[52] Harrison, inspector of cookery, proposed a solution to the cooked food problem. She mentioned that if the price of the cooked food were kept low there would be no difficulty selling it, but that the establishment of cookery centres would otherwise satisfy the needs of local residents for cooked meals.[53]

Starting school meal services from 1906 onwards did not enhance the roles of domestic economy teachers, even though Pillow proposed this possibility. As Calder mentioned, feeding children on its own was not a remedy for social ills unless accompanied by education, and the school medical inspection system and school meal service ultimately had little direct connection with cookery and domestic economy lessons. State-organized school meals started to feed malnourished children whose parents were on low wages or in ill health, or those attending schools too far away from home to go back for lunch. Meals were therefore for selected children chosen by teachers and medical officers.[54] Yet, because feeding them properly was another element in producing healthier children, it was linked to their education. More positive sentiments towards cookery education and the management of cookery centres were thus to be expected from the 1906 medical inspection and feeding committee, the membership of which comprised school inspectors, examiners and local government medical officers. One member, Maude Lawrence, the chief woman inspector of the Board of Education, undertook a specific analysis of both cookery education and school meals.

In trials using cookery centres as school meal outlets, benefits were found for both the instruction of cooking and feeding the children. Pillow, in Norwich, and Robert Blair, executive officer of the LCC, both supported these arrangements. The problem in both places, however, was that they could only cater for small numbers of children and that the location of the centres was not always close to schools. Unfortunately, it clearly did not work perfectly because, due to the limited scale possible, it was only implementable as a side effect of cookery lessons. Nevertheless, the 1906 committee was demonstrably sympathetic to ideas about making cookery lessons more effective for improving children's home life.[55] In that context it is worth referring to Pillow's evidence because she was the only witness who had undertaken domestic economy education practically.

In Norwich, Pillow organized voluntary school meals for needy children during the winter of 1905 and the local education authority allowed her to use cookery centres. Teachers and attendance officers selected what children would be eligible for free meals. They were planned for three times a week: however, because of lack of funds the children were given only one meal a week. Apart from that, the feeding scheme at three cookery centres, each for 60 to 80 children, seemed well organized. Cookery teachers had entire responsibility for supervising, preparing and serving the meals to children and were supported by head teachers. Children who attended cookery lessons spent almost all morning preparing the meals. Meals were always for at least ten people, so they were not just preparing toy-sized dishes using ¼ lb of flour and 2 oz of meat. Pillow claimed that they could learn the principles of homely dishes for the family, though one inconvenience of the scheme was that it was impossible to teach good methods of using up cold meat, for they were unsuitable for so large a quantity of catering. She nonetheless insisted that feeding proper food would be most beneficial when accompanied with an opportunity to practise its preparation.[56]

Norwich was undertaking an extended scheme of cookery education based on an effective plan for the disposal of cooked food. Pillow explained that there was no complaint from parents about cooking meals for other children because it was recognized as an educational activity and that they were not being used as free labourers. This was a point Lawrence raised over a similar experiment in London in July 1905. The latter was conducted at five cookery centres attached to LCC schools and it aimed to supply cheap dinners for the children of those schools. According to Blair, domestic economy experts for the council, head teachers and school managers checked it and it was very successful.[57] In 1906 Lawrence reported on inspections of 550 centres and schools all over the country, referring to the increased interest by parents, how instruction was well-adapted to the pupils' homes and how dishes used commonly available staples. She warned, however, that classes must be educational and only if so could selling food be allowed.[58] Feeding at cookery centres had also caused another problem: it became necessary for teachers to learn how to organize and instruct a syllabus, and even Pillow was a little anxious that this might lead to a lot of extra work.[59] Even so, witnesses at the 1906 committee who were keen to provide nutritious meals for children at school, especially for those in poor areas, anticipated the usefulness of domestic economy. At the same time, the importance of parents feeding their children properly was not to be neglected.[60]

In 1910 a report investigating the school meal service confirmed that preparing meals at cookery centres had been initially regarded as a good opportunity for girls to learn cookery principles, but because of worries about its educational value it had since been suspended.[61] To offset this limited success of the school meals scheme, however, there was progress with the start of the school medical service in 1907, which likewise aimed to improve children's diet and health. Medical officers recognized the effectiveness of diet, especially, as preventive medicine, but did not encourage the children to alter their eating habits or give them any instruction. Instead, they tried to educate parents to look after their children's diet and health. Their idea of mothercraft emphasized parental responsibility for infant feeding. Medical officers, generally, were less interested in cookery and domestic economy for girls as the way of achieving this long-term goal.

The increasing attention school medical officers paid to children's health after 1907 eventually led to their more direct involvement, though they had to work closely with teachers in areas such as a child's difficulties with lessons, fatigue, overpressure or personal health.[62] The second International Congress on School Hygiene in London in 1907 encouraged instruction about hygiene and one of the speakers, Dr Janet Campbell, mentioned the need to have hygiene in the curriculum, ideally from the youngest age. She emphasized the

nutritive value of food, which, she said, the poor scarcely understood.[63] To improve children's health in the wider context, instruction
on hygiene in elementary schools and for prospective teachers at
training colleges commenced at the same time as the school medical
service began under the Board of Education's chief medical officer,
George Newman. While it seemed that an identifiable administration
for health inspection was now finally underway, its educative effect
was vague.[64] Compared with the medical officers' role in combating
disease, the domestic economy teachers' contribution to health education now came to be seen as less important, even though they
supplied the obvious and tangible educational benefits. There was
some collaboration between domestic economy teachers and school
medical officers, but this never seemed sufficient because teachers
were increasingly regarded as amateurs in the medical field, despite
their knowledge and ability to instruct about health. Henceforth, more
weight came to be put on medical officers' opinions following their
investigations of various aspects of schoolchildren's health.

Newman saw that if teachers played an educational part in
school meals then children could learn from their experience. He
strongly recommended this again in his 1914 report when, because
of the war, national health and strength were given high priority. He
cited data collected since 1908, which showed that introducing
school meals did reduce malnutrition, especially if combined with
the 'follow-up' by school nurses scheduled to check on improvements. This administrative idea was based on established principles
in public health work using a system of preventive medicine at
environmental as well as individual levels. To improve hygiene by
focusing on living conditions as they affected schoolchildren would
obviously benefit society greatly.[65] Hygiene education in elementary
schools was therefore designed to improve the habits of all children
through practical instruction from a young age in such matters as
cleaning teeth, brushing hair and cleaning boots.[66]

The issue that constrained the promotion of hygiene education via
cookery and related domestic economy subjects, compared with such
work via medical inspection, remained that of parental responsibility.
Annual medical inspection reports clearly showed that, although the
prevention of tuberculosis was connected with feeding children and

that where malnutrition was linked to the disease proper feeding would be the key to combating it, this would only be effective if accompanied by further care and attention to personal health.[67] This being so, the medical officers' approach to preventing the disease was to instruct parents rather than children on how to maintain a high standard of sanitation within their dwellings. This, of course, conflicted with the general idea of instructing the young on cookery for its long-term benefits. Even though the numbers of pupils, teachers and cookery centres were increased and cookery remained an important point of discussion as a key factor for health, responsibility within this whole area was still felt to rest ultimately with parents.

With medical officers' reports from 1910 onwards constantly stressing the importance of home care in combating tuberculosis among schoolchildren, the question of how to feed future children better by teaching schoolgirls how to become able mothers was bound to receive more attention. Better parenting and mothercraft were linked via the Children's Act of 1908 to the whole question of parental responsibility. In schools, hygiene education tended to focus on personal cleanliness rather than a logical understanding of health and nutrition; the latter remained part of cookery and domestic economy education for girls, despite its usefulness for boys being added to the code in 1901. As stated already, the scientific approach to what it was hoped would become common sense about life originally expected from domestic economy had instead become narrowed into mothercraft and addressed less and less the wider aim of making people generally healthier. Nonetheless, discussion published in the *British Medical Journal* in 1907 explained how far the wider community had a responsibility in this matter beyond the work of medical professionals. It concluded that controlling general sanitary conditions should be done through systematic hygiene teaching at every state-funded school and that women in particular must be taught how to feed infants. The activities of sanitary inspectors, health visitors and nurses were also, of course, essential; ideally, district nursing and health visiting should be part of sanitary and preventive medical organization.[68]

In the 1910 circular, instruction about infant care was stated to be of benefit to all girls, even those who were a bit backward, just as hygiene was useful for everyone. It was conceived in two parts, according to ages. Girls between the ages of 7 and 12 would learn basic sanitation for the home, including knowledge of eating and drinking. Then, girls still at school between the ages of 12 and 14 would be provided with more advanced skills, such as infant care, along with housekeeping (management of income or marketing), lessons about temperance, or home nursing.[69] Teaching mothercraft required women of all ages to be involved, from girls to mothers. An example of this was the instruction at the school for mothers in St Pancras where, through home visiting, mothers could receive cookery lessons at home, even though this could not lead to studying at home afterwards because taking notes, as in schools, did not occur.[70] Infant welfare was emphasized in a 1913 report in which Newman pointed out that by 1913 infant mortality had been reduced to 108 per 1000 births from 145 in 1904, probably due to improved feeding, sturdier maternal physiques and appropriate infant management.

The questions of malnutrition, preventing childhood diseases and infant care finally came together in 1914 as being pertinent to the war effort and the responsibility of mothers was increasingly stressed. School meals, besides being expected to 'improve home feeding', undoubtedly helped malnourished children. Inviting parents to help serve them at schools would speed up their educational effect by spreading an understanding of health via wholesome eating to both parents and the next generation. This was especially valuable in war time when it was necessary to make instruction as economical as possible. Mothers were encouraged to prepare cheap, nutritious meals at home to support children's growth. The local education authorities, assisted by the Board of Education and its pamphlet *Some Suggestions for Simple and Nourishing Meals for Home*, tried to provide instruction for them. The question of food education for children thereby became in part replaced by education for mothers. Using the extra time now devoted to cookery lessons to prepare school meals, in 1914 the idea was revived in London of utilizing cookery centres as feeding outlets from which girls could serve cooked food for infants.[71]

In reality, of course, in non-residential elementary schools it was impossible to control children's lives throughout the day. At least in schoolrooms, however, they should be able to study in a hygienic atmosphere. The objectives of health instruction at elementary schools, which in turn were expected to influence children's families, were to improve physical strength and instil hygienic habits through regular training. The 1904 Physical Deterioration Committee emphasized the need to encourage better cookery and healthcare by creating a school meal service, a school medical service and active instruction in mothercraft. With questions of nutrition and health becoming ever more urgent during the war and with even more attention being paid to households in the 1930s, dietitians began to be employed in schools. The foundation in 1936 of the British Dietitian Association, which supplied the dietitians, had made a more professional consideration possible almost half a century after the issue had first emerged. The British Medical Association had also formed a nutrition committee in 1933, which promoted cookery education for better health.[72] Due to the widespread malnutrition identified between 1929 and 1935, school feeding became widely recognized as an agent through which to change family diets, and the value of food knowledge as a preparation for adult life was generally understood.[73] Nutrition was finally being delivered to the general public as common sense and was widely associated with a healthy lifestyle. Choosing and preparing food with a view to its health value was taken seriously across society.

Overall, cookery teachers did not commonly direct school meals, but children cooking school meals was often welcomed, even in medical terms. There were at times thoughts of introducing it further because if girls had a cookery class every morning they at least had one nutritious meal a day. Learning about cooking and handling food helped prevent diseases, while costs could be recovered by selling the dishes they prepared. The notion of encouraging boys as well as girls to cook, expressed in the *British Medical Journal* in 1904, showed that cookery education was also recognized as an aid to independence. Knowledge of cookery would be invaluable to young men setting off to the colonies. Even at home it would prevent them marrying too young because they depended on their wives preparing their meals. Needless to say, it would also help those men interested in the cookery profession.[74]

In the medical field, 1900 was a landmark in the study of dietetics and medical science because this was when Hutchison, in *Food and the*

Principles of Dietetics, defined the role of dietetics in curing diseases. Pycroft verified how influential his book had been when she devised her lessons on the nutritive value of food and digestion. His was the first book she had come across that stressed that eating even nutritious food could be useless unless it was prepared in a suitable way. Although chemical analysis of food values had been taught for years, Hutchison was now suggesting that only when food was taken in a suitable form could human digestive organs obtain its nutritional benefit. Pycroft wanted this information included in the City and Guild of London Institute examinations[75] – evidence of the serious attention educationists gave to the question of nutrition and to the challenge of providing correct information based on scientific research. Admittedly, some dietetic study for medical students had existed for years, which cookery teachers had supported with respect to sickroom cookery for patients and cookery being introduced into nurses' general training. Yet, in the early 1900s dietetics remained undeveloped as a field and was still not commonly taught to medical students, despite its value in healthcare as an alternative treatment to medicines and indeed being often more suitable as a cure for particular diseases related to diet. Above all, it had huge potential as preventive medicine.[76]

In the late nineteenth and early twentieth centuries cookery teachers worked alongside other professionals in various areas of health and nutrition. Their pioneering and often high-profile work among children and the extension of cookery and domestic science teaching in schools was and has since been the focus of much attention. Yet, arguably, cookery education played just as vital, though less public, a role elsewhere – in hospitals and in military service. In fact, within these organizations, the professional skills of cookery teachers helped provide breakthroughs and reforms in selecting food supplies to fit their specific needs. In the following chapters I shall reveal significant developments in cookery in hospitals, the nursing profession, the British Army and the Royal Navy. In all these institutions cookery proved to be a key element in raising levels of nutrition and the overall standard of health.

Chapter 4

Nightingale, Lückes and Feeding the Sick

When the Nightingale Training School opened at St Thomas' Hospital in 1860, with support from the Nightingale Fund Council, which had been set up following Nightingale's impressive work during the Crimean War, nursing became available as an educational opportunity for women. The training was mainly for middle-class women in their mid-twenties to early thirties when they started. Apart from Nightingale's reforms, through lectures and practical classes medical men instructed the nurses in subjects like anatomy, digestion and ambulance work. Matrons and sisters also gave their probationers lectures on nursing .

Sickroom cookery classes for probationers, which Eva Lückes started in 1893 in her role as matron of the London Hospital and which either a sister or professional instructor taught, developed as a special area of training. Although its basic theories were explained in medical lectures, medical men did not cook the sickroom food. In the middle of the nineteenth century large hospitals acquired their own kitchens in which meals were prepared for patients and staff, so nurses no longer had to prepare their patients' meals, though they were required to cook light meals for some patients and for themselves during night duty when the main kitchen was out of service. After the 1870s many hospitals reorganized their central kitchens into catering departments for staff and patients, after which nurses became free from cooking in sometimes unhygienic conditions and shopping for their own meals using the rations provided for them.[1]

By the late nineteenth century, however, it was considered impossible for nurses to care for their patients properly if they lacked knowledge of cooking and had not attended sickroom cookery instruction. By then sickroom cookery had come to be regarded as a healing part of nursing care, though knowledge of it would also be reflected as a cultural influence on patients. Obviously, unlike medical doctors, nurses could not perform surgery, but their support in the care of patients was just as necessary and included providing medicine and meals at the correct times for each patient and washing his or her body. They had more direct contact with patients at every stage of their treatment than medical men, so had more opportunities and more of a responsibility to deliver professional knowledge about diet, ranging from the basic principles of health to information on specific illnesses like diabetes, in which the patient's diet was a particularly important part of the medical treatment.

Sickroom cookery came to be included as an integral part of the dietitian's role and of the hospital's catering and food services. After various innovations in kitchen equipment in the 1860s, hospital catering came to be recognized as a necessary hospital reform. A survey of infirmaries at workhouses in 1866 showed very few skilled cooks employed in hospital kitchens and, although the large hospitals in London in the early nineteenth century had provided their patients such food as gruel, porridge, meat, bread and beer, they had not given them any vegetables. Later, in the early twentieth century, hospital life was discussed more from the patient's point of view, in particular following the National Insurance Act in 1911. In 1922, following yet more complaints about hospital food, the journal *The Hospital* proposed establishing a hospital school of cookery with a view to obtaining better cooks.[2] The topic was still being mentioned as late as 1951 at the launch of the King's Fund School of Hospital Catering at the St Pancras Hospital (part of University College Hospital) by the fund's catering and diet committee. This was a training school for hospital kitchen staff and it functioned quite separately from the nursing and medical staff.[3] The object of the training was to acquire skilled professional caterers who could manage hospitals more economically and who could therefore make the cost per bed lower for the hospital management. Aside from this, sickroom cookery for probationary nurses was acknowledged to be for the benefit of patients, even though curricula and training methods varied until nursing professionals fully recognized its effectiveness. It is worth focusing on the training of sickroom cookery because it formed the necessary practical application following lectures for a nurse's study of digestion, chemistry of food and hygiene.

Considering the importance of feeding patients, training in sickroom cookery is given insufficient weight in the history of nursing. In fact, discussions centred on nurses and diet arose mainly from considerations about nurses' welfare or hospital management rather than from the medical aspect of the profession.[4] Practical sickroom cookery was taught in the wards to probationers, even though in the late nineteenth century the duty of nurses to cook for patients was limited. Their responsibilities had shifted from simply feeding patients to monitoring food as part of the medical treatment: nurses had to manage and organize a patient's intake and provide information about it. This training had great importance for private and district nursing because sometimes it taught the sick poor and their families how to alter their way of living. The training provided for nurses was thus important not only for the development of modern sickroom cookery but also as a starting point for health and food education among the common people.

By focusing on nurses' training in sickroom cookery, in this chapter I shall show how sickroom cookery came to be recognized as a part of medical education. First, I compare the curricula of training schools for nurses in the large voluntary hospitals in London and trace the history of cookery training from Nightingale's experiences in the Crimean War. I then analyse the detailed work of the preliminary training school for nurses at the London Hospital, which had a great influence on this training. In the following chapter I shall then discuss the impact outside hospitals of the cookery training delivered by private and district nurses. I shall also consider the alterations in hospital diet for patients brought about by both the practices of hospital management and amendments in the nurses' training.

In the 1870s, when cookery lessons for elementary schoolgirls had started, teaching cookery became a specific profession for middle-class women. At the same time training colleges for cookery teachers started to spread all over the country and, needless to say, this movement had an influence on nurses' training. At girls' high and secondary schools, however, practical education in cookery was given little attention; in fact, it was usually ignored altogether through lack of equipment and insufficient time available within the more advanced curriculum that usually formed the nurses' educational background.[5]

Information about common sickroom cookery was accessible to educated girls from books, though it would be impossible for them to learn more about medical sickroom cookery without attending training at the hospital. Around this period cookery was starting to be considered from a scientific rather than merely an artistic viewpoint – a development some medical professionals eagerly encouraged. An article appeared in a medical journal that ascribed the high levels of malnutrition among people to ordinary cooks learning simple cookery through practical lessons without any scientific lectures on food and nutrition. Such ignorance, the author held, unnecessarily lowered the nutritional value of food and led to discomfort, disease and even death.[6] Education at elementary schools at least introduced this idea to girls who would become mothers in the future, although there was no guarantee that it would be useful for them. On the other hand, cookery training for nurses in hospitals had a clear vision of its aim: first, the patient's hospital diet must form part of his or her medical treatment and, second, knowledge of hygiene and sickroom cookery skills would be put into full use as soon a nurse started to work as a member of the hospital staff.

In 1903 *The British Journal of Nursing* reported on the progress of training schools for nurses in the large London hospitals, namely St Thomas', Guy's, London and King's College. These were regarded as preliminary schools for young women wishing to start their careers as nurses. The preliminary schools provided the young women with a basic training and knowledge of nursing before they became probationers and commenced their more practical training on the hospital wards. The article concluded that preliminary schools that taught sickroom cookery during the course became more desirable and that it was possible that those hospitals raised the standard of nursing.[7] The movement for the registration of nurses that started in the late nineteenth century looked at the quality of the training school as well as the qualifications of an individual nurse. Advances in nurses' education owed much to the efforts of nurses themselves and to their leaders Nightingale and Lückes. Lückes had started her career by training at the Middlesex and Westminster hospitals.[8] She formed a friendship with Nightingale when she encountered difficulties with hospital management and training (after some former probationers and nurses had sent letters to *The Times* in 1890). This was also the time between 1890 and 1892 when a House of Lords Select Committee was set up to investigate the efficiency of metropolitan hospitals. The two women understood each other very well, both having entered the profession from middle-class backgrounds and they frequently discussed the quality of nurses and the standard of training with a view to improving nursing as a whole.[9]

The purpose of sickroom cookery training was explained in the prospectuses and regulations of the nurses' training schools at St Thomas', Guy's and King's College hospitals. In 1860, when Nightingale started training nurses, the idea of teaching invalid cookery had already been raised, although no systematic method existed as a model until Lückes claimed its importance as a compulsory subject for probationers and introduced it at the London Hospital in 1893. In the Nightingale Training School prospectus, sickroom cookery was described as a skill that both lady probationers and ordinary probationers must learn, as too must those educated to become matrons of relevant institutions and those trained to be hospital nurses. The duties of probationers under the Nightingale Fund were made plain to candidates. They were required to be sufficiently skilful to prepare gruel, arrowroot, egg flip, pudding and drinks for the patients.[10]

The actual method of sickroom cookery training was not clearly explained, for it was included in practical ward work rather than taught separately in classes. This guidance was used until 1910 when the preliminary training school started at St Thomas' Hospital set up sickroom cookery in its training curriculum. Sickroom cookery was taught at Guy's Hospital's preliminary training school in 1902 and the aim of its cookery training was clearly shown in the Nurses' League of Guy's handbook, which set out detailed instructions while extolling nursing as a women's profession. Sickroom cookery training was recommended to nurses in such a way that their own housekeeping experiences might help them understand it, for such experiences

increased their worth as candidates to become matrons.[11] Since a
matron was in charge of the whole nursing department, she needed to
manage hospital catering and housekeeping in addition to the nursing
and management of the hospital. At King's College Hospital, a series
of examination papers and examiners' annual reports on sickroom
cookery from the 1890s demonstrates that the training aim there was
the same as that of the Nightingale Training School.[12] Although their
systems of sickroom cookery training differed, all the hospitals recognized the usefulness of that training to nurses' careers.

In 1878 a teacher from the Edinburgh School of Cookery started
sickroom cookery lectures for medical students at Edinburgh because
making decisions about and ordering a suitable diet for patients were
recognized as an important part of a medical doctor's work. The
classes, which were held at the Royal Infirmary in Edinburgh and
related institutes, consisted of demonstrations on how to prepare such
sickroom diets as beef tea, whey, milk jelly and gruel; the students
were 'invited to examine for themselves practically the various diets
ordered for patients', and they showed much interest. Annual courses
were expected to provide students with more knowledge. This trend
in education at the medical schools, however, did not include
practical lessons on diet; indeed, the new instruction on cookery at
the medical faculty of Minnesota State University was reported as a
special case. By 1890 sick cookery instruction at the Royal Infirmary
in Edinburgh had been opened to all medical students as an adjunct
to the medical curriculum.[13] This type of instruction was always
separated from the medical school and attached to the nurses'
training school. To understand the background to the modern-
ization of hospital catering and the nurses' role in it, it is necessary
to analyse the hospital diet problems Nightingale faced in the
Crimea and the related work done by her subsequently.

Nightingale's correspondence during the war shows a specific
difficulty with hospital catering even amid such general troubles as
inadequate supplies. This became a matter of public interest and a
professional French chef, Alexis Soyer, who worked at the Reform
Club in London, came out to the battlefield at his own expense to
cater and help Nightingale. Even so, Nightingale still needed to solve
the problem of catering because some patients disliked both Soyer's

and her diets.[14] This experience in the Crimea generally brought home to her the need to systematize the training for nursing staff. Apart from Cooper, who discussed her work as the British Army dietitian, the important issues of feeding patients, hygiene and hospital kitchens have scarcely been mentioned in recent studies.[15] As soon as she arrived at the Barrack Hospital in Scutari, Nightingale prepared the kitchen for extra diets and cooked for wounded soldiers herself. She discovered that the cooks did nothing properly and was obliged to act as both cook and housekeeper during her nursing work.[16] The lack of supplies, the hospital system and the inadequate training of the nursing staff exacerbated these problems.

In the Crimea, Nightingale worked to create the nursing department staffed by gentlewomen as a distinct section. This is clear from her correspondence with and reports to the army hospital inspector during the war, Sir John Hall, under whose direction Nightingale worked in her capacity as the superintendent of the women's department for nurses. Until that time, Hall had trouble improving health and dietary conditions, but as soon as possible and thereafter he worked with Nightingale, controlling her ladies in the nursing department.[17] According to Nightingale's report from the Balaclava general hospital, in May 1856 there were only 23 women in four hospitals in the Crimea performing the work of superintendents, cooks, nurses, nuns and washerwomen.[18] Nightingale complained to Hall about a problem with the medical officers in charge there. She felt that since nurses undertook all the sick cookery at the hospital, the medical officers should at least take responsibility for the supplies.[19] Furthermore, between Nightingale and the medical surgeon, David Fitzgerald, there was another argument over the nurses' diet being compromised to cut the cost of running the hospital.[20] There was also a shortage of nursing staff. When Nightingale decided to send some skilful nurses to support one of her senior assistants, Miss Wear, she selected ones with experience as cooks and tried to encourage Miss Wear by sending two of the best ones to help her out in the difficult conditions under which she was working. Wear herself had had to handle sick cookery. One of the nurses Nightingale sent had 16 years' experience as a cook and the other was also reliable as a cook.[21]

Over and above their busy ward work, skilled nurses acted as hospital cooks because they understood what sickroom cookery required. No doubt Nightingale could have solved her catering difficulties more easily had all her nurses been trained in sickroom cookery. The inferior knowledge and experience of army hospital cooks, a shortage of supplies and unhygienic conditions in the hospitals were significant problems for the British Army and Nightingale reported all these to the War Office. Her reports and work in the Crimea provided a spur to reform hygiene in the British Army and the army's medical department started to prepare its medical school accordingly. At the same time proper practical training for nurses urgently needed to include sickroom cookery. However, that was separate from military service, so was not reflected in their training during Nightingale's time.

After her return to Britain and having set up the Nightingale Training School for nurses at St Thomas' in 1860, Nightingale embarked on trying to improve the hospital as well. In her memorandum after an inspection of the new St Thomas' Hospital in July 1878, she remarked on the poor hygienic condition of the wards. The construction of a new building by chance solved the specific problem of the hospital's kitchens and cookery. She observed, however, that the meals delivered for patients looked distressingly unappetizing with poor quality meat. She further commented that sickroom cookery in ward kitchens was limited to such items as beef tea, barley water and custard pudding.[22]

These defects at the hospital were thought to be avoidable by attending to familiar concerns – the nurses' role and the hygienic condition of the wards. Even though the training of nurses had already started at St Thomas' Hospital, sickroom cookery was not carried out for patients. By this time it was, Nightingale argued, necessary for hospitals and nurses; furthermore, its rationale had already been explained in the nurses' training prospectus as something to be learnt during the course. She then wrote a draft memorandum on training probationers in hospital wards, which she discussed with her cousin, Henry Bonham-Carter, who was secretary of the Nightingale Fund Council. Mrs S. E. Wardroper, matron of St Thomas' Hospital, who worked under Nightingale as acting principal of the training school, finally got it printed as a guide for ward sisters in 1879. It indicated that at St Thomas' Hospital, at least, sisters taught sickroom cookery to probationers on the wards. In the first section, Nightingale sets out three basic points that the sister specifically should teach every new probationer about how to do their work to the ward sister's satisfaction in such areas as watching patients and cleaning wards. Then, as training in district nursing, they should be taught sick cookery beyond merely making beef tea; for this they should be provided with proper cooking utensils and taught the way of 'Observation of the Sick', including 'the reason why' on medicines or dressings.[23] In the draft of the published version of the memorandum that Bonham-Carter and Nightingale had revised, according to Bonham-Carter's notation Wardroper had said that sick cookery could not be done more extensively because the ward sisters had reported that nothing was being cooked in the ward kitchen. Nightingale added a further note: 'everything is cooked in Ward Kitchen for some patients and probationers provide utensils at own expense' for that purpose.[24] Finally, sick cookery teaching intended for probationers was described in detail. Each probationer had to be taught sick cookery with the use of cooking utensils and methods and the amount of ingredients for beef tea, egg flip, gruel and drinks.[25] Nurses and sisters organized ward kitchens, so it is clear that from the early years of the training school for nurses instruction in and the understanding of sickroom cookery was necessary for future work in the hospital ward.

At Nightingale's request, in 1883 Mrs Edith Clarke, the lady superintendent of the National Training School of Cookery, sent a teacher to the training school at St Thomas' to give classes in sickroom cookery. Clarke was pleased to work with hospital matrons to organize cookery lessons for their nurses and offered to provide the classes at the lowest possible cost, just to cover expenses. She offered a detailed plan to Nightingale of three hours a week of practical lessons for six weeks. The fee for a course of six lessons was £1.1 for each nurse.[26] Matron Wardroper wrote to tell Nightingale that Bonham-Carter had asked John Buckmaster at the National Training School of Cookery about lessons in August and September, and that she hoped the lessons would be useful. Furthermore, she was interested in the effect of them on the nurses.[27]

Afterwards she submitted an annual report to the committee of the Nightingale Fund Council along with the syllabus and a list of nurses who had attended the course Mrs Berry gave during August and September in the kitchen attached to the nurses' dining room. The annual report said that all the probationers had attended, though the number in the matron's report shows that there was no precise definition of the course and examination: special probationers and pupils in the three different years of study were all mixed together.[28] These lessons were more akin to the special lectures an instructor from an outside body might occasionally give. This record therefore shows that even in the 1880s the nurses' training school had difficulty adding cookery classes and that the facilities were not good enough to allow them to continue it on a regular basis. The instruction and methods of the National Training School of Cookery, nevertheless, were in progress for sickroom cookery training at that time.

At St Thomas' Hospital basic sickroom cookery was taught to probationers as practical training in the wards and the sister of each ward marked the results.[29] Cookery classes were not, however, organized until after the foundation of the preliminary training school in 1910, along with other subjects such as elementary hygiene, anatomy, physiology, bandaging and bed making. The matron pointed out that cookery classes especially were of great benefit to the nurses when they worked in the wards.[30] Nightingale's educational policy was to emphasize the practical side of learning rather than relying on classes or lessons, though clearly it would be difficult for probationers to learn everything about nursing from practical training in the wards.

Lückes, the matron at the London Hospital, considered it would be more useful if probationers had time set aside to acquire basic knowledge of nursing. She thus altered the educational programme to comply with her own experience, which was one of the reasons why the London Hospital was the first to start systematized sickroom cookery training for nurses. In 1892, just a year before this training began at the London Hospital, an article in the nursing journal urged the introduction of sickroom cookery training in England as soon as possible. Even though diet generally was important, the nursing authorities and doctors recognized a sick diet as 'a powerful factor' in treatment. It had to be taught practically to nurses, for being able to prepare a special diet would also be beneficial in the private nursing service.[31] This type of instruction was eagerly advocated within the nursing profession because, it was argued, it would be a great help if nurses commenced their work with this skill. The writer explained that sickroom cookery was already included in nurses' training in America and with good results. Being wanted by nursing professionals and of interest to them, systematic training of sickroom cookery began at the London Hospital in 1893.

In contrast to St Thomas', Lückes made regular sickroom cookery a compulsory subject for probationers at the London Hospital. From their correspondence it is clear that Lückes respected Nightingale and considered her methods for nursing and training to be basic. She asked Nightingale for advice on training at the London Hospital and then tried hard to improve on it by introducing new methods. While the records of the Nightingale Training School reveal its character to have been ward-based training, Lückes's reforms at the London Hospital were considered to be more modern and set a new standard for nurses' education.

It is important to understand something about the character of the management at the London Hospital and how this systematic training for nurses operated. After Lückes was appointed matron in 1880 the nursing department of the hospital became more centralized and had a stronger position. At the house committee, Lückes argued to improve nurses' welfare and training.[32] This meant a change of cook for the nursing home (nurses' accommodation), a private nursing institution and a preliminary training school, which would require financial support from the hospital. After 1898 the committee was regularly informed about the appointments of cookery teachers. In 1905, following inspections of some infirmaries, her assistant and other hospital staff submitted a report that advocated alterations and improvements in hospital management. Specifically, to maintain their funding and quality, this meant managing each bed at the hospital more economically and providing detailed reports on hospital catering and housekeeping expenses. There were also a number of reports about diet tables that related directly to the hospital management. The hospital's house committee and medical council discussed these diet issues from a management perspective and in terms of nutritional values, and the outcomes were immediately conveyed to the nursing department.[33] In this hospital the nursing department was clearly recognized as an independent section.

Lückes had worked at the London Hospital before as a staff nurse and knew of the nurses' terrible working conditions. She first tried to improve their position in the hospital and then started to educate young women to become nurses. In 1881 she began giving 12 nursing lectures herself while the hospital physician and surgeon each gave 16 lectures a year.[34] She considered that the training school for nurses attached to the hospital should have the same practical value as medical schools and that if the medical school and nursing school of the same hospital cooperated it ought to be possible to obtain mutual benefits.[35] At the London Hospital the preliminary training school, Tredegar House, was established in 1895 where probationers were given basic instruction in nursing for six weeks, followed by examinations after lectures and practical training in such areas as bandaging and sickroom cookery. Tuition was arranged in sets of 12 lectures and 12 classes: physiological and anatomy, theoretical and practical cookery/nursing/bandaging, hygiene, with a further six lectures on the theory of food and six classes on ambulance work.[36] In 1892 Lückes sent Nightingale a copy of the report on the hospital nursing department she had drawn up for the house committee. In this report Lückes stressed the importance of sickroom cookery and pointed it out as the only alteration she could suggest to the committee. For satisfactory results, attendance should be at small sickroom cookery classes and they should not take place in large and busy wards.[37]

Since it would be difficult for a sister in charge of a probationers' residence (termed a home sister) to instruct probationers in sickroom cookery during regular duty, Lückes suggested employing a professional teacher from an outside body for that purpose. She was confident that nurses would welcome the introduction of these lessons and emphasized that these practical skills would define them as highly qualified nurses. She reported to the house committee in late May 1893 that the provision of sickroom cookery was for the benefit of the nurses of the London Hospital. When the London Hospital finally started 'systematic instruction' in sickroom cookery training in June she expressed her pleasure to Nightingale. This instruction became permanent, as did the other lectures introduced since 1881.[38]

Because Lückes considered systematic training for sickroom cookery essential, she arranged for professional instructors from the National Training School of Cookery both to instruct and to examine nurses during the course. She planned demonstrations and practical lessons for her probationers, although first she selected pupils from among sickroom sisters (who looked after nurses when they were ill). Lückes hoped that staff nurses could manage instruction for other nurses and probationers after six months, for it would cost too much if they continued with classes held by outside teachers.[39] The sickroom cookery scheme was approved by Nightingale who strongly argued that the method used should be practical and that 'the pupil must do everything with their own hands'. Classes run only as demonstrations by instructors 'are almost useless', she continued; however, she admitted that this type of cookery teaching was common in hospitals.[40] As with general training for nursing, she considered that sick cookery could not be learnt without practical lessons as an aid to remembering thoroughly.

For Lückes, diet for the sick and invalids was as significant as the treatment medical men prescribed. She was insistent that care of patients was the main object of nursing. In her books on nursing she described how to serve food to patients as part of their medical treatment: it was necessary for nurses to check the patient's appetite and the appropriate amount, quality and quantity of food for every condition – such as after or before operations. In addition, it was the matron's general responsibility to order the patients' diets as directed by doctors from the stewards along with the diet table, so it was impossible to ignore the training on diet. Lückes reiterated that basic knowledge about food and diet was essential for nurses because without this knowledge they could not help doctors feed patients properly, thereby restoring them to health.[41] The correct diet provided nourishment through digestible food, adding that 'while people are ill, food is even more essential' than for those in good health. Selecting the right diet was therefore necessary for nurses because if the preparation and administration were unsuitable, patients would not take it.[42]

In a later edition published after the preliminary training school had started, she devoted a separate chapter to the topic of feeding patients. She again described why cookery training was invaluable and stated her objective to be that nurses not only learn the common sickroom diets but also need to practise making more nutritious dishes that would be effective in giving patients the power to recover from diseases and for their convalescence.[43] Beyond this, it was the sister's duty to watch whether patients had extra food that was not provided by the hospital. Sometimes patients' friends visited the hospital with gifts like stimulants, cakes, puddings and pies. Sisters needed to consider whether or not they were harmless and give advice on them pending the doctors' decision before consumption. A sister needs to protect her patients from accidents caused by these extras.[44] These were the reasons why Lückes strongly urged paying attention to patients' diets, for a poor understanding could give rise to difficulties in an age before the dietitian became an established profession within hospital catering.

It is possible to trace Lückes's technique of teaching sickroom cookery to the training of instructors and their methods. Miss Hannath, a sickroom sister, was, along with other staff nurses, taught how to become a sickroom cookery instructor by a professional teacher from the National Training School of Cookery. For a few years after 1893, three evenings a week Hannath would hold practical classes containing ten pupils each to which a number of hospital staff came. From 1895, when the house committee accepted sickroom cookery as part of the curriculum for probationers, certificates of proficiency in this subject were required before they started their careers as nurses. After that time the sickroom cookery teacher was specially appointed and asked to live in the nursing home with the status of a sister, even though she was not a trained nurse. Her salary was £40 a year. The instructor was Miss Maude Earle of the National Training School of Cookery who gave demonstration lessons for 30 pupils every Monday evening in conjunction with Hannath's practical classes. Preparations in advance of the theoretical examinations held at the end of each course were also charged for: each examination cost 10/6d for the whole class while practical examinations cost 2/6d a head. This training required a larger payment than just doing it in the hospital wards. Miss Margaret Thompson-Hill and Miss Cathelin du Sautoy were appointed after 1896 as cookery teachers, and then from 1902 Miss Beatrice Apperley worked for the London Hospital as a professional instructor for 15 years teaching elementary hygiene, physiology and anatomy as well as cookery to probationers.[45] Although the appointment of instructors and examiners from outside undoubtedly increased costs, it did mean that the skills of nurses from the London Hospital were judged formally and independently and their abilities thereby guaranteed.

One characteristic of the instruction at the London Hospital was that it was not only for probationers but also open to hospital sisters and private nursing staff who had already finished their training. The hospital nursing reports show the number of pupils in cookery classes: 158 pupils (57 hospital staff and 101 probationers) in 1896, 153 (64 staff and 89 probationers) in 1897, rising to 181 (25 staff and 156 probationers) in 1904, and 169 (21 staff and 148 probationers) in 1906.[46] These numbers show that the classes were mainly for probationers, though staff nurses attended them freely if they had opportunities. The matron's annual letter of 1904 reveals that a new kitchen was built solely for sickroom cookery training. Lückes started to encourage established nurses working at the London Hospital's Private Nursing Institution occasionally to join the cookery classes in the morning if they were in the hospital and had time off duty to refresh their memories and to expand their knowledge of sickroom cookery. She claimed that the number of nurses who recognized 'the advantage which this expensive course of instruction proves to them in their work' was increased and added that private nurses frequently reported to her 'how they have rejoiced to be able to prove of service to their patients in this respect'.[47] At the London Hospital the period of training was two years with a further two years work in the hospital; therefore after 1900 many nurses trained there commenced their work either in the hospital or outside as private nurses or staff nurses at another hospital. Lückes was proud of her sickroom cookery course, which, she exclaimed, was just as necessary for private nurses. All the private nursing staff of the London Hospital found the sickroom cookery training useful.[48]

Like Nightingale, Lückes always tried to put herself in the position of her patients and to consider how best to care for them and to make their condition comfortable. In this context it is worth examining how nurses experienced and regarded their training in sickroom cookery. Even though an instructor was invited to St Thomas' earlier than to the London, the National School of Cookery did not then have proper experience of teaching sickroom cookery specifically: its curriculum was too complicated and less practical than the one introduced at the London Hospital about a decade later. The textbooks written on sickroom and invalid cookery seem to confirm this in so far as the London Hospital's training was of greater interest to publishers.[49] At St Thomas' the syllabus comprised 12 cookery lessons held in August and September 1883. The dishes selected were not taught in any order that would make them easy to remember. There was no examination record or explanations on practical classes: the 12 classes were given as six demonstrations and six practical classes. Each lesson taught two meat and fish dishes, two soups and light meals, such as poached eggs, and puddings and drinks such as lemonade.[50] The lessons were intended to be completed as a course menu each time and only the instructions on apple water, lemonade, soufflée and poached eggs were repeated during the whole course.

By way of contrast, the timetable at the London Hospital in 1907 shows that quite practical lessons were given to the nurses: 12 demonstrations followed by 12 practical classes. Two main (meat and fish) with two light meals (puddings and jellies) were taught at one class and these were planned to be repeated: there were six sets of classes twice, 12 practical classes in total. According to the schedule of Miss Grace Easton, who started her training at the London Hospital in 1907, these practical classes were marked to the value of 20 points in full: her record shows that almost all work acquired 20 points at the second running of the class.[51] This reflects the systematic training on sickroom cookery that Lückes devised. Understanding was checked at the end by examination on the methods of cooking each dish, effective use of such food as eggs, rules to select suitable fish for patients and so on. Examination questions show that this knowledge of sickroom cookery could be easily learnt by heart if nurses confirmed what they had seen in demonstrations by cooking with their own hands. Similarly, information about the chemistry of food, which was included in medical lectures, would be also remembered most effectively with the aid of practical training.

Hospital doctors gave lectures at the King's College Hospital's Nurses' Training School on medical knowledge and treatment. Sickroom cookery was included in the syllabus for examination from 1904. Sister Matron (the matron of this hospital) decided to arrange free cooking lessons for nurses once a week by a teacher from the London County Council's Technical Education Board, for which the nursing committee was required to pay up to £15 of the cost. In June 1910 the theoretical examination paper the LCC set on sick cookery for hospital nurses makes it clear that they provided more general lectures than those that formed the training at the London Hospital. Nurses were required to understand general rules about cooking for invalids, recognize the value of milk for patients, and know how to prepare peptone beef tea, milk puddings, gruel and beef tea custard. In 1914 the LCC charged the class £1 per nurse in order to continue and the instruction it provided lasted until the 1930s.[52] From the examples of dishes, however, the training by instructors from the LCC was clearly more limited than that delivered at the London Hospital.

The sickroom cookery training Lückes advocated as essential for nurses had a great influence on other hospitals and nursing institutes. In 1897 *The Nursing Record* highlighted the progress made at the London Hospital, of which, it asserted, the systematic instruction in sickroom cookery was characteristic.[53] The LCC's Technical Education Board now extended the range of its lessons, providing technical instruction for schoolchildren and adults at schools, which included cookery classes in independent schools or institutes given by the board's staff teachers. In November 1899 the board received applications from the matrons of the Poplar and Stepney Sick Asylum and the Kensington Workhouse Infirmary. The managers stated the objective of the class to be that nurses who trained there should be taught cookery suitable for the sick and invalids. The matron of the Westminster Hospital also requested teachers to train its probationers. Although there were differences in management between workhouses, infirmaries and voluntary hospitals, the new method of training for nurses at the London Hospital was widely recognized and many medical institutes decided to follow its trial and to update their

training schemes for nurses, enquiring whether the Technical
Education Board could provide the instructors necessary.[54] As these
examples show, the London Hospital's innovation in commencing
sickroom training for its nurses in 1893 was soon highly valued.
Although this aspect of training became common for nurses at the
London Hospital, its maintenance and effectiveness depended on the
extra expense incurred by the teacher's salary and Lückes recognized
that, given the hospital's voluntary character, this would become a
financial problem for the management. When she started sickroom
cookery training Lückes asked the house committee to allow it even
though the instruction would be costly. After a few years it was again
referred to the committee as a request for support by the hospital
chairman, Sydney Holland, Viscount Knutsford. In 1892 Lückes had
explained to the committee that it would cost between about £60 and
£80 a year: in 1897 Holland said that its cost was about £200 a year,
though he was glad to continue and encourage this training, which he
believed would become the strong point of nurses from the London
Hospital. He commented on this training, both in lectures for nurses
and elsewhere, as a distinctive feature of the London Hospital and
explained that it should be made standard for all nurses' training.
Holland added that it was useful for private nursing as well as in
private life.[55] It is widely known that hospitals had internal struggles
over the independence of their nursing departments and the London
Hospital was no exception. At the London Lückes afforded Holland
the respect due to his position in the management of the whole hospital, while his appreciation of the importance of nursing supported
her scheme for training.

Nurses trained at the London Hospital who became hospital
nurses and educationists at training schools or who engaged in
private nursing, had great respect for the training they had received.
One nurse directly instructed by Lückes was Miss Edith Cavell, who
later became well known when she was put to death in Belgium for
rescuing British soldiers during the First World War. She worked as
matron at the training school for nurses, l'Ecole belge d'infirmières
diplômées in Brussels. The probationers there were not as well
educated as those in London and she introduced the English
method – the training of the London Hospital she so admired.[56]

Cavell mentioned the beneficial influence of her training in her correspondence with Lückes. She spoke about it to her brother-in-law, Dr Wainwright, and the surgeon, Mr Wallace, and they praised the nurses Lückes had educated to so high a standard. Cavell was glad to have the opportunity to introduce the characteristics of her training to other people in the medical profession. These men thought highly of the general condition of the hospital wards, were impressed that the patients' rooms were kept in such good condition, and appreciated the unstinting efforts the nurses made to keep everything in the rooms running smoothly. More specifically, Cavell was proud of the London Hospital's sickroom cookery instruction. For her, the various lectures at the London Hospital were unforgettable; indeed, she kept using her notes for reference.[57] In the lecture notebooks on feeding patients she took during her training, Cavell had written about the amount of food necessary for a patient compared with that for a healthy working man, especially when on a diabetic diet, which required gluten for meals instead of starch.[58] Until insulin became available for diabetics, the only medical treatment for them was a strictly controlled diet with no products that turned to sugar after digestion. For this reason, the diabetic diet was one of the most common instructions recorded in nurses' lecture notebooks, for it was understood that this lecture could avoid the problem of serving unsuitable food. If nurses had practical training in sickroom cookery beyond the medical lectures attended by them, their knowledge would be reinforced, which was Lückes and her supporters' objective.

Some nurses from the London and St Thomas' hospitals also mentioned sickroom cookery classes in their later years. One, Miss Margaret E. Broadley, who started her career in 1923 at the London Hospital, said that during her training as a probationer, 'for some unknown reason great stress was laid on' invalid cookery; however, she remembered that it was well taught.[59] A probationer at St Thomas' in the 1920s had a similar memory of sickroom cookery instruction. This was after the preliminary training school had been established there, which included sickroom cookery in the curriculum. She remembered that her cookery training was given first as a preparation class by a sister in which the important points to be remembered were pointed out. Then, on the next day, four probationers, including her, were told to take the dishes they had cooked over to the wards and they visited the hospital kitchen with a nurse to see the kitchen equipment of the hospital catering. She mentioned that, for practice, she cooked beef tea in three different ways and baked custard.[60] These memories at least reveal that after the 1900s sickroom cookery training for probationers was standard, although it was not always easy for them because of its practical character.

Sickroom cookery took a long time to become accepted as an integral part of the training and as a standard part of nurses' skills. Since the problem of diet had first occupied Nightingale and the nursing department during the Crimean War it required almost a half century for its importance to be reflected in the training provided for nurses. Lückes's response was recognized as a model for nurses' training. In 1907 *The British Journal of Nursing* claimed in its editorial that knowledge of sickroom cookery was 'a most valuable asset to a nurse'. It was essential for nurses to be well enough trained to supply suitable nourishment for patients during convalescence. Therefore, understanding the nutritive value of the food and developing the skills to prepare palatable and well-presented dishes were high priorities,[61] and became standard practice when the Royal British Association for Nurses included examination in sickroom cookery for its certificate.[62]

Sickroom cookery required medical knowledge, and, even when they did not feed them directly, nurses needed to give advice to patients on food either while they were sick in the hospital ward or at home while nurses tended them as private or district nurses. Interest in cookery training had risen from the 1870s; however, medical men did not pay much attention to it even though they chose the patient's diet. Their experience of sickroom cookery was poor and essentially they all depended on nurses who had more opportunity to look after patients directly. The need for this training became obvious and it eventually provided progress not only in medical sick cookery and the science of dietetics but in turn more commonly to the whole of society through nursing care. The spread of such knowledge about food, hygiene and cooking in society via district and private nursing is the focus of the next chapter.

Chapter 5

Nursing Instruction and Hospital Cookery

Nursing was a way of conveying information to the poor about principles of health and nutrition. From the early 1900s in particular, when imperial ideas were popular and strategies were being devised to build up model citizens for Britain, improving the nation's health was of increasing and widespread interest. Because of this changing attitude in society, girls at elementary school now had compulsory classes in domestic subjects, which provided them with more opportunities to learn how to manage their homes and the health of their families in the future. However, it was always difficult to check on achievements. Mothers' schools tried to provide information about childcare to young and poor mothers in their area, though this did not directly include tips on how to improve the health of the whole household.[1] With their professional medical education, nurses who worked in the district or for private patients could, however, make more effective checks. By the end of the nineteenth century, nurses had practical training in sickroom cookery and had attended lectures on hygiene and dietetics delivered by medical doctors – indeed, such training was recognized as standard after 1895 following Lückes's efforts at the London Hospital.

To study the movement for health and diet education by nurses and hospitals in this chapter, an analysis of nurses' educational work with patients outside hospital, as district and private nurses, is first required. If they were to turn their visits into opportunities to convey health education they required great skill and knowledge about nursing. Before maternity health visitors for women and infants became common, a number of charitable women's associations would visit poor neighbourhoods to provide help, but this was very different from nursing care by properly trained professionals who were not simply almoners.[2] In Nightingale's opinion, these nurses were the most effective agents for the provision of health advice to people.

Second, it is also important to understand what opportunities doctors had to give advice to inpatients and outpatients at hospitals. The administration of outpatients and their diet was frequently discussed as a charitable issue, associated, for instance, with the activities of invalid kitchens to feed the sick poor. The medical lectures doctors delivered to nurses on dietetics were probably based in part on research conducted with their inpatients, though the common approach to patients' diets by hospital doctors was different from that of the nurses: basically, doctors did not feed patients but just issued orders about feeding them to the nurses. But, as Hutchison of the London Hospital's milestone work on dietetics in 1900 demonstrated, some doctors did take diet seriously as a part of therapy and undertook examinations of food and its nutritional value in the hospitals. This was because treatments for diabetes, rickets and scurvy among young children, for instance, depended mainly on diet rather than medicine. Hospital diet was now regarded as more than preventing starvation and was increasingly being acknowledged as an important part of a patient's treatment. Doctors' research on diet-related diseases was as much tied up with hospital catering and management as it was with the reform of diet tables. However, knowledge of their work on diet seemed to be imparted only to nurses and very little directly to the patients. This was probably due to a lack of opportunity for wider dissemination and the appalling living conditions and poverty of so many patients. There was little general understanding about health, the value of food or nutrition and hygiene at that time – against that background doctors were largely confined to making suggestions to aid recovery from specific diseases. Yet, even this essential instruction from medical professionals could not be spread by doctors alone; the strong support of nurses was also necessary.

The issue of hospital diet and the nurses' educational role in it rarely appeared in medical journals as a main subject. As late as 1945, however, an article in *The Lancet* drew attention to the common and long-term inadequacy of hospital diets, which remained a problem in Britain even after the many reforms of the late nineteenth century. The article was written during a period of wartime food shortages and after 1943, which was when the King's Fund established a committee on hospital diet to support catering systems. The issue was still presented primarily as a social problem that hospitals were expected to solve through their educational work. The hospital was considered the best place to learn what to eat, in conjunction with district nursing. Nurses were thus recommended to keep a 'critical eye on food' through their training, which would allow them to provide a high standard of diet both in the districts and in the wards.[3]

District nursing began in England through the work of charitable or religious bodies to help the sick poor who needed home care. Home nursing had several benefits for families; if a sick mother could stay at home she could take care of her children when she felt better, and if the husband were sick at home then the wife could nurse him immediately after her own work outside, for hospitals did not always accept the sick poor. This type of work had started with independent nursing associations drawing upon the services of lady nurses or ordinary nurses. William Rathbone planned and started organized district nursing in Liverpool, and its theory and methods were based on the ideas of Nightingale who believed in the importance of nursing in a patient's home as the most comfortable way for the sick poor to recover from illness. Nursing at home fitted into the curing part of nursing work, while at the same time it provided an invaluable opportunity to supply basic knowledge about how to stay healthy and to keep residences hygienic for patients and their families. Early district nursing has been mostly studied from its social perspective and its connection with health visitors' work for mothers and babies and not mainly from an educational motivation to improve domestic hygiene and eating, which at the time it was supposed should receive more attention.[4] The training of district nurses adopted the same changes in the late nineteenth century as that of hospital nurses, with the growing influence of health and food education.

From the mid-nineteenth century charitable bodies organized lectures and produced printed material on health education. One such body was the National Health Society, which delivered practical lectures on people's health in many places from the early 1870s. For a few pennies it also sold health calendars to members of the audience with advice on how to live a hygienic and healthy life over the years.[5] The society's activities were well known through its many lectures, famous members and publications related to them, and its influence spread through its ideals and educational work. Even Nightingale had worked with the society, though she had reservations about its village nurses scheme; she entirely agreed that a scheme was necessary for rural areas but was critical that the training for nursing care under technical education was not the same as a practical training at a hospital. Systematic training was necessary.[6] Her opinion was that insufficient educational effect would be supplied to village people if the nurses' training method were limited to lectures.

Nightingale frequently mentioned the benefits of district nurses teaching health in poor people's homes; she regarded it as an ideal arrangement and expected they would work as health missionaries as well as sick nurses. This was clear from examples cited in her book. In India, she wrote, lectures and school teaching through textbooks on health and sanitation had no practical effect at all, 'as that kind of teaching is not instruction, and can never be education'. The essential point about health education was that it should provide opportunities to inspect progress regularly through direct contact with people's living circumstances. A plan to have health missioners, a group of women trained in healthcare with professional lady superintendents, in Buckinghamshire to improve health conditions in the area, started in 1892. It was considered a good alternative to district nursing and it would be a great help to medical officers of health in combating disease among the ignorant poor.[7] To promote health education in society, direct instruction by district nurses was recognized as the most effective way in many subjects, including care of the sick, sanitation, domestic hygiene, infant healthcare and, last but not least, nutrition and diet through cookery lessons.

As health promotion work expanded after the 1890s so too did district nursing. It was, of course, influenced by the nurses' training at individual hospitals, which had commenced by that period, and also by the way in which the merger of organizations affected district nursing training. Nightingale's idea of district nursing had stressed the very practical way of nursing, especially in London, which had a wide diversity of poor people. There were two large voluntary district nursing societies in London – the East London Nursing Society, established in 1868 with non-lady nurses for the very poor, and the Metropolitan and National Association of Providing Trained Nurses, formed in 1874. Medical doctors thought especially highly of the latter's work and called them Bloomsbury nurses or nurses of the Metropolitan and National Association. It was a professional organization for gentlewomen whose members were given salaries ranging between £35 and £50. They were normally sent to cases by doctors who had applied to the association.[8]

Its influence was strengthened by the foundation of the Queen Victoria's Jubilee Institute for Nurses in 1887, which adopted the training method of the Metropolitan and National Association in London organized by Miss Florence Lees, later Mrs Dacre Craven. Training for these nurses required one year spent at a recognized training school for nurses attached to one of the general hospitals, with six months' district training and three months' maternity training. Craven's educational plan for nurses was to keep the very high standard of nursing established at the central home in Bloomsbury, with its hospital training and further training specified for district work. Rathbone believed that district nursing by the Bloomsbury ladies in London would become the principal centre and provide great opportunities for educated women to commence special training for district nursing with a view to becoming future superintendents who would extend such work to the provinces.[9]

Since sick nursing and instruction were the main objectives of district nursing, it followed that the visits of nurses from better educated families would be more productive because, after checking drainage systems and the use of back yards, which affected the cleanliness of the dwellings, they could report any sanitary defects in their districts to superintendents and health officers. Nightingale saw this as a district nurse's duty.

The quality of trained nurses became a still more pressing question after the Queen Victoria's Jubilee Institute for Nurses merged with the Metropolitan Association, at which point the latter turned its attention to training both sets of nurses. It was accepted that a district nurse's training had to be more systematic and of a higher standard, so one reform proposed was a collaboration between Nightingale and Miss Amy Hughes, who was later appointed as superintendent of the Queen Victoria's Jubilee Institute for Nurses. The Bloomsbury nurses followed the same curriculum as hospital nurses from the start, including practical instruction. Practical instruction, however, had not been much emphasized in hospitals in the 1880s.[10] It thus becomes possible to analyse alterations in hospital training as district nurses experienced them as a result of Hughes's work.

Hughes started her career as a lady probationer at St Thomas' Hospital in 1884. The following year she met Nightingale who suggested she become a district nurse because that offered 'the opportunities and openings for the national welfare in such an inspiring way' and, from that autumn, Hughes trained at the district nurses' home in Bloomsbury. Later she wrote articles on district nursing in the journal, *The Hospital*, which she eventually compiled into a book, or manual, along with additional advice from Nightingale and Bonham-Carter; Nightingale hoped the book would raise both the standards and the ideals that attached to district nursing. The overall thrust of the book was that a district nurse's work should be primarily to care for the sick with only limited or elementary training in midwifery.[11] In their opinion, district nursing had already proved its worth with the scheme in Liverpool, with the Bloomsbury nurses in London and with the Queen Victoria's Jubilee Institute for Nurses, which the Metropolitan Association trained from the 1890s; it was therefore time to set up a standard for training district nurses. This would require more practical knowledge and skills to manage hygienic conditions in people's homes; Hughes clarified these in her book, *Practical Hints on District Nursing*.

By 1890, Craven's *A Guide to District Nurses and Home Nursing*, which explained the basic method of nursing and the theory of district nursing, was already in wide circulation. Beyond this, Hughes now tried to illustrate the more practical application of district work. She pointed out that free nursing of the poor at home had to be more focused than free nursing in hospital and was expected to make more impact on the patient's neighbourhood. Teaching children was one way of bringing the laws of health into the home, and the information health visitors delivered about children and home care should be categorized as pioneering work.

In meeting these challenges, district nurses worked in 'a quiet, unobtrusive manner'. Because they understood the home they visited, they could choose appropriate instruction for that home regarding cleaning and hygiene. It was, for instance, no use talking about the importance of a sunny room and avoiding dampness if it were not affordable in those lodgings. She suggested nurses spend about half an hour giving a practical demonstration during their work instructing a family how to prepare a savoury meal with 'the most economical materials'. Furthermore, nurses had to encourage girls at home if the latter had learnt cookery at school, because 'it benefits the household and trains the girl[s] to apply their knowledge practically'.[12] This last suggestion of cookery training for girls could, in fact, be quite effective if district nurses had the chance to try. They used to teach the eldest girl in the patient's family to help her mother alongside the nurse, so understandably nurses sometimes gave revision lessons for girls on any knowledge of hygiene or cookery they might have learnt at school. The benefits arising from this were potentially extensive since, according to Education Department records, 134,930 girls from 2729 schools received classes in cookery in 1895–96; in the London area the London School Board further encouraged this subject, so the girls had even more possibilities.[13] District nurses therefore came to play a useful role in elementary education regarding certain aspects of domestic hygiene.

District nursing was also mentioned in Booth's *Life and Labour of the People in London* as a better way, compared with other charitable work, of altering and improving living conditions among the poor. The work was educational and it enlightened 'the common ideas of the people', not only by delivering care in sickrooms and cleanliness of infants but also by 'the preparation of food not for invalids alone' combined with many other aspects of domestic economy that nurses could deliver naturally to patients' homes. The section on district nursing was based on a number of interviews that a surveyor, George Duckworth, conducted with nurses and matrons engaged in such work, including Lückes and the superintendent of the Queen Victoria's Jubilee Institute for Nurses. Booth concluded that 'district

nursing was the most successful to alter people's way of life directly. It
is almost true that wherever a nurse enters the standard of life is
raised.'[14] Since the survey incorporated widespread research on
poverty in London, district nursing came to be seen as a key element
in analysing social needs and medical welfare services in each district.

As honorary secretary of the Scottish branch of the Queen
Victoria's Jubilee Institute for Nurses, Christian Guthrie Wright
further developed the role of district nurses as hygiene instructors. She
also acted as secretary of the Edinburgh School of Cookery, which
from 1878 frequently delivered sickroom cookery classes to medical
students.[15] The training of nurses in the Scottish branch was the same
as in England – hospital training, maternity and district training with
lectures and practical lessons on hygiene, food and cooking lessons.[16]
As a representative of the Queen Victoria's Jubilee Institute for
Nurses at the Sanitary Institute congress held in Glasgow in 1904, she
stated that they were a more suitable agency for sanitary improvement
than sanitary inspectors and health missioners and tried to demonstrate it in a speech entitled 'District Nursing as a Hygiene Agency'. In
her correspondence with Miss Alice Leake, secretary of the Queen
Victoria's Jubilee Institute for Nurses in London, she regretted that
her paper was read at the end of the congress and that the audience
was small; however, she justified her attendance by explaining that
district nurses had enough training to give valuable instruction on
hygiene and sanitary subjects and that they were the agents who could
really work for people by knowing the real conditions.[17]

Wright's speech listed seven topics with which nurses might deal
when giving advice and instruction through their work – household
sanitation (drainage, disinfection, fresh air for families), incipient
consumption (preparation of the sickroom, obtaining nourishing milk
or eggs by contacting other agencies to combat disease in its early
stages), infectious illnesses (vaccination), care for the mother after
confinement (including asking family and neighbours to help her), the
newborn infant (feeding and clothing), young children's health (care
of teeth) and, finally, cooking instruction. Cookery lessons for poor
families given by district nurses were an effective way of raising living
and nutritional standards, even if only done rather hurriedly. It was
expected to be effective because nurses had 'an opportunity *teaching*

and *improving cooking*, not only for the sick, but for the other members of the family. ... Nurses can show that good cooking is not only cheaper than bad cooking, but also aids nutrition and is pleasant.'[18]

Hughes made similar comments when she became superintendent of the Queen Victoria's Jubilee Institute for Nurses. She stressed that teaching cookery to poor families would increase their knowledge and help them feed themselves more nutritious meals at no additional cost. The district nurses' educational functions would raise them from being simply medical doctors' assistants to acting as the health missioners Nightingale had envisaged.[19] Cookery advice at home on how to improve diet and nutrition could provide an adjunct to the nursing that bible women sometimes provided, although almsgiving and selling bibles were the primary objects of their visits. Although their work was also different from district nursing, the 'Pudding Ladies', later to merge into the National Food Reform Association, were established in 1908 to enlighten schools, hospitals, the armed services and wider public on matters of diet.[20] Unlike health visitors, who were limited to maternity and childcare work, district nurses had to manage the broad remit of sanitation and understand the work of other charitable bodies. They were never inclined only to hand out food but rather to introduce people to progressive ideas and act as spurs for health improvement. Direct instruction from district nurses had a stronger impact than any other home visiting, as one district nurse, Greta Allen, asserted in her book for health visitors: because the district nurse's influence spread into the community far beyond an individual's home it was more effective than club activities, health lectures, coal funds or clothing funds.[21]

It is possible, therefore, to conclude that it was often the nurses who worked in the districts and at the homes of the poor who spread health and nutritional education throughout society. From the 1880s, the national education system supported domestic subjects with grants; nevertheless, instruction for many girls at home, and for their mothers, was considered more trustworthy if medical professionals delivered it and, through a nurse's understanding of the case in question, adapted it to each family's conditions. Even after an interest in food reform had developed among the upper echelons of society, real difficulties were encountered in delivery to the lower levels where, of course, the mass of those who needed both the information and the food lived. The nutritional value of poor people's diets, as well as the levels of infection and sanitary conditions in their homes hardly altered, even if the local health authorities had checked their sewerage system and other essential facilities. The social reforms continued and numerous public lectures were delivered on these topics, but they were not always immediately practical. Nightingale had always claimed the importance of direct instruction for people, for a lecturer's message should reach the household of every member of the audience. 'Did they practice the lecture in their own homes afterwards? Did they really apply themselves to household health and the means of improving it? Is anything better worth practising for mothers than the health of their families?'[22]

Unfortunately, her questions were not only appropriate for the poor; even in private nursing, basic instruction for the sick was some-times necessary in more affluent homes. Nonetheless, given the limited numbers of district and private nurses available, not all sick people at home could access their services and the very poor were generally sent to the poor infirmaries. In 1890 the Metropolitan and National Association had 50 nurses in London who could each attend eight cases a day, while the East London Nursing Society had 27 nurses divided into four divisions with a matron in each.[23] Hence, it was difficult to supply help for all the sick poor across London. To understand just what could be achieved, however, it is essential to look too at the work of private nurses, significant evidence of which is available from the records of the London Hospital.

Compared with the main object of district nursing, private nursing offered medical care to those who were not exactly poor. Such patients did not usually obtain free treatment at the voluntary hospitals, so their options were private nursing or general prac-titioners; a paying patients' ward at some voluntary hospitals would also be accessible. In London, district nursing by both the Metropolitan and National Association and the East London Nursing Society was based on the principle of nursing the sick poor without payment; other associations in many parts of the country had adopted the same policy from the outset, though there were some exceptions. One illustration of an overlap was the case of a barrister whose circumstances made him unable to board or lodge a private nurse. Occasionally, therefore, he would ask the district nursing association for help,[24] but since it was not always possible to receive help from them, private nursing institutions would play a part in providing the necessary assistance.

Private nursing might thereby supply extra income to support a hospital's voluntary provision if a private nursing institution were attached to it. No institution, however, ever had enough nurses and since the women needed to have holidays for the sake of their health, the number working at the same time was always slightly lower than the total. According to the metropolitan hospitals' report, 50 private nurses were attached to Guy's, 70 to the Westminster and 25 to the London.[25] The London Hospital formed a trained nurses' institution for the provision of private nursing in 1886 to give the nurses who had trained there an alternative work opportunity. Lückes started this private nursing, but not only to give financial support to the hospital. She considered it as part of their extended nursing care to all in society who needed their help; in fact, she had noticed that 'the sick rich were not as well looked after as the sick poor.'[26]

Her idea was to keep private nursing staff working in the hospital wards with other nurses when they were not undertaking private work. She felt they could update their skills, knowledge and new information on treatment through working at the hospital with medical doctors, while, possibly, their independence through private work would have a beneficial influence on the hospital nurses during their regular duty. Furthermore, it was an alternative workplace for nurses who were not very strong and could not work regularly as hospital staff.[27] This was also reflected in the sickroom cookery training for those working with private patients Lückes recommended from time to time in the matron's annual letters. Understandably, private nursing was profitable for the hospital financially, but it was also thought that by providing a high quality of medical treatment a satisfactory nurse would be 'an excellent advertisement' for the hospital to which she belonged. This 'advertisement' also meant encouraging donations and material support, such as 'secure fresh subscriptions, presents of games &c., and in enlisting a general, kindly interest in the various needs of the patients in the London Hospital'.[28]

The London Hospital's private nursing institution charged two guineas a week (for infectious cases) or one and a half guineas (its lowest rate); this was an average charge for private nursing. There were also commercial associations for private nurses in London. For example, the London Association of Nurses, started in 1873 with nurses with an average of seven or eight years' hospital experience, charged between one and four guineas a week. The fee for private practitioners was a little lower – on average 2/– to 2/6d for a visit to a working-class home and a little more to a middle-class one.[29] According to Booth's survey, very poor people on low and irregular incomes whom he defined as the lower classes (categorized as classes A, B, C and D in the survey) could not afford two guineas a week; they had to depend on voluntary hospitals, district nursing, or the infirmaries. Private practitioners or Metropolitan and National Association nurses might possibly sometimes care for people who lived in 'solid working-class comfort'. The latter helped small tradespeople and artisans who might be able to afford five or ten shillings a week from their average income of about 25–35 shillings a week (classes E, F and G below the wealthy classes, with groups F, G and H earning more than 40–70 shillings a week).[30] Private nurses, then, provided services for people whose diet was different from that of the poor; nevertheless, they were not free from illness and not all of them had proper knowledge and practical skills regarding personal or domestic hygiene and care of a sickroom. They could often afford to lodge a nurse for the sick and they were possibly well educated, though unfortunately not always in respect of hygiene and sanitation.

Understandably, even though there was progress in training sanitary inspectors and medical professionals, many reformers were more interested in public health from a non-scientific position as part of wider social issues. While there were many publications and lectures, it was difficult to judge how effectively knowledge was being spread to individual homes. This concern can be seen in the diary of Miss Wilby Hart, who worked as a private staff member of the London Hospital in the 1900s. She kept a record from the time of her arrival at the hospital for training, of her working days as private staff and then of her later work as a sister at the London

Hospital with details about the patients for whom she cared and her experiences of training young nurses at the hospital. On visiting one family to tend their sick, Hart needed to change the whole room because it was packed with furniture, interior decorations and carpets. Nurses might find that sunlight from windows was often ignored and that the sickroom remained dim and without enough ventilation. These were general problems Dacre Craven and Lückes came across in district and private nursing. Hart experienced similar problems at wealthy private patients' homes with ordinary rooms and sickrooms filled with ornaments and furniture. Furthermore, feather beds had to be avoided in home nursing because they were unhygienic, because it was difficult to remain in a comfortable position in them and because they interfered with a doctor's examination. Hart faced this problem in one wealthy patient's sickroom and had to move her patient to another bed.[31] Preparing a sickroom, even in a better-off home, required basic understanding of the sanitary system and ventilation – indeed, without experienced medical advice from outside the home, all they might do was make their sick weaker. Some might have learnt about the need for ventilation to aid recovery from disease from publications, a doctor's advice or from their friends; clearly, however, a private nurse could deliver this information as a support for the family more quickly than anyone else.

Interestingly, Hart recorded the case of a Mrs B who suffered from fibroids and was about 45 years old. She was in a very weak condition and the doctor who accompanied Hart to the lady's home told her the patient was going to die. He said she became very ill if she ate eggs in any form, although he asked Hart to try to build her up with at least two eggs a day. Hart tried to do this through experiments; because of the patient's obvious dislike of egg she mixed them in other foods. First, Hart mixed them with milk and gave them to the patient using a feeder in which she could not see the colour of the contents. Then Hart tried the same method with puddings, soups and custards flavoured with Bovril. Her trial did the trick and by the time the lady discovered she had been fed eggs, she was in a fairly good condition, could eat whatever she liked and recovered quickly. This clearly showed the benefit of the London Hospital's sickroom/cookery training; its nurses had no trouble feeding patients at home during private work. Hart continued her work on cooking with the patient's sister who stayed there and, as one of the medical professionals supporting the family, probably imparted useful instruction on sick cookery.[32] Mrs B clearly enjoyed a better living standard: she could have many eggs and could take anything she wished as nourishment instead of eggs. For someone in this position, nurses did not need to ask for support from any other organization regarding the patient's food or worry about cooking utensils and facilities in the kitchen, usually important matters in district nursing. From some of Hart's cases, it is possible to understand the requirements and opportunities Lückes mentioned for proper nursing among 'the sick rich', for visiting by nurses could improve their condition – as for the poor.

To 'feed up' and make patients strong enough to recover from disease was one of the main objectives of nursing; in hospitals, of course, an inpatient's condition was likely to be more serious and complex than that of a private or district patient, so his or her diet was sometimes arranged specially according to the doctor's suggestions. Naturally, feeding patients was linked to medical theory, as in fever cases where they had to be fed easily digested fluid diets prepared to refresh their thirst at hourly intervals. Doctors and nurses needed to collaborate to keep to exact dietary orders. According to nurses' recollections of feeding patients at hospitals, however, it is difficult to confirm that all nurses were able to consider the nutritional and dietetic aspects of each meal as carefully as their district and private counterparts. Hospital nurses had to manage many meals at the same time, whereas nurses attending cases outside hospital possibly only needed to prepare one meal for each home visit. Although hospital nurses had opportunities to prepare a limited amount of sick cookery for patients by themselves if necessary, it was not possible for all cases on the ward.

At St Thomas', one lady probationer remembered meals for patients from 1895 to 1903. It was a probationer's duty to carry all mugs with heavy trays in the ward and this was 'a backbreaking job'. She cited examples of general diets during that period. Patients had breakfast at 6 a.m. with bread and butter, or a boiled egg; at 9.30 they had lunch with hot milk, cocoa or beef tea and at noon the dinner of the day was supplied. The sister of the ward carried joints and fowl followed by milk pudding; a roast, chicken or game, were favourite diets. At 4 p.m. patients had tea, along with bread and butter, and at 7 p.m. milk was given for supper. Convalescents could not enjoy the same meals as others, so one physician allowed his typhoid patient to take two chocolate creams a day.[33] In the hospital wards it was impossible for nurses to examine the dietetics of meals along with the instructions on diet during busy meal times. However, even busy nurses could learn something about diet and disease.

Even in serious cases, nurses were required to feed patients with a little preparation in the ward kitchen. Hart's diary at the London Hospital suggests that in every case feeding was in the nurses' hands. One evening, after she became a sister at the London, she had to feed three patients (two males and a baby) at the same time using nasal catheters and unless the food reached their stomachs properly they would die from pneumonia.[34] To feed an adult patient with a tongue problem she also taught a nurse how to prepare the mixture of milk and egg ordered by the doctor. Hart warned that she had to calculate suitable amounts for the patient per feeding time by herself, for the diet sheet on the board only showed the total quantity for a day.[35]

Inpatient cases were effectively practical lessons for nurses, as they were for medical students, and only if patients were stable enough to receive visits and food from their friends did nurses have a good opportunity to educate them about diet, especially if they suffered from a food-related illness. Furthermore, nurses never had enough time to instruct their many patients on nutrition and diet, or on the important points they needed to remember about sanitary and hygiene practices once they left hospital to await a full recovery: had the nurses been able to give this kind of instruction, their patients might have been restored to health and been ready to work again more quickly. These inpatient cases, of course, were examined by medical doctors for their research on dietetics, though such studies were not mentioned directly to patients and were only reflected in their feeding and in later medical education. This connection in the hospitals between medical doctors and dietary issues must also be examined to demonstrate how the hospital actually delivered its educational influence on health and diet to patients.

It is not easy to trace a typical patient's diet in late nineteenth-

century London hospitals, despite complaints about it, consideration
of it when refurbishing the kitchen, and the problem of increasing
cost, as found in the records of St Thomas' and Guy's hospitals.[36] The
quality of a patient's diet depended on the hospital management,
unless research on dietetics, conducted by individual doctors, was in
progress. In Britain, dietetics and studies in nutrition were sometimes
included in practical medical education or chemistry, and sometimes
formed part of women's higher education, such as the course at
King's College for Women. Generally, though, doctors tried to solve
problems relating to diet and disease through discovering suitable
treatments and nurses who understood the system within the hospital
were then appointed to support them, as in the case of sister dietitians
from the 1920s. The later birth of dietitians in Britain than in America
was one reason for this rather fragmented and complicated hospital
catering system. In any case, hospital treatment was not the main
provider of healthcare in nineteenth-century London and not until the
Second World War and rationing did hospitals even become responsible for all their patients' food.[37]

Food in hospitals was examined in the three investigations of
metropolitan hospitals the House of Lords carried out between 1890
and 1892. Evidence on the comfort of patients was drawn largely
from their opportunities to complain about problems arising from
their diet both while they were in and on leaving the hospital. Yet,
even though a number of questions were asked, the quality of their
food could not be ascertained. In large hospitals, the sister usually
wrote up the diet sheets for each patient, following the doctor's
orders, and it was her duty to check whether or not patients were
supplied with proper meals. At the same time, gifts from patients'
friends formed an important part of hospital diets.[38] Looking through
the evidence collected for the three reports (chiefly for the four large
hospitals with nursing schools: the London Hospital, St Thomas',
Guy's and King's College Hospital), even though the food supply of
the hospitals were major items in their finances, all of them did want
to be responsible for everything related to hospital food.[39]

Witnesses said that if staff could resolve that issue, it would be a
great support for the management; instruction in that area, however,
had to wait until 1951 when the King's Fund started a specific scheme

for hospital catering. Until then, hospital caterers' responsibilities remained wide ranging. They had to draw up contracts with traders, examine the food they brought in before it was cooked, appoint cooks, maintain the kitchen and oversee the quality of cooked diets (complaints from patients or hospital staff included). In fact, since every hospital had to divide the above work into so many sections, in the late nineteenth and early twentieth centuries there was little room left to consider the nourishment of the diet for patients. Generally, a storekeeper or housekeeper under the steward examined the food brought into the hospital. Sometimes the steward himself would check the quality of the meat in the kitchen, while milk was often strictly checked for its storage method.[40]

It is true that when the 1890–92 investigations were held there was no widespread management of patients' diet from either a quality or financial aspect and that meals were usually supplied free of charge. This was understandable given that most patients in general hospitals were from the poorer classes. One general practitioner told the metropolitan hospitals' committee that a patient's diet in London was excessive compared with those at hospitals in Paris and Vienna, although admittedly the percentage of cure in London was higher. He claimed that the same results could be obtained if they reduced portions and changed to a simpler diet, because he thought that 'they are very freely given', just for the comfort of patients who neither appreciated the quality nor understood the hospital's financial problems.[41] Contemporaries were well aware of the very poor home circumstances of inpatients; one London Hospital nurse indeed observed that the standard of diet was very good considering the patients' great poverty.[42] Under such conditions, even when staff heard occasional complaints about the patients' diet they were neither seriously considered nor held to be representative of every medical institute. Investigations by the House of Lords committee therefore could obtain few worthwhile opinions about the quality of the patients' diet when presented with such vague evidence.

In these sometimes chaotic circumstances, each hospital tried to change its diet tables for patients for financial and medical reasons. Reforms of diet tables were done regularly: at King's College in 1885, the sister matron prepared a new diet table for discussion by the hospital's medical committee, while at St Thomas' the diet table, as it pertained to modes of cooking and serving meals, was revised under Buckmaster of the National Training School of Cookery.[43] One doctor's findings at the London Hospital merit analysis. As at other hospitals, feeding patients was a nurse's duty: doctors basically ordered the food and left the cooking arrangements to others. Stephen Mackenzie, a visiting physician and lecturer at the London Hospital's medical school, commented that he did not think that medical men even occasionally checked the quality of cooking and diet supplied for patients.[44] Nonetheless, the house governor and doctors at the London Hospital frequently considered the question of diet reform. William Nixon, the house governor, tried to introduce reforms after the 1870s when the refurbishment of the hospital kitchen promised to provide better food at lower cost. Hospital doctors Hutchison and Henry Head, who were experts on nutrition, continued the reforms as part of their dietetic studies after 1900.[45]

Research on food for patients was always of medical concern and most doctors awaited progress. One of the earliest examples was an instruction pamphlet from the British Hospital for Diseases of the Skin in 1872 concerning the relationship between specific diet and treatment. This guide for patients with skin diseases showed careful instructions on daily diet and cautioned against intake of salted meats and preserved meat and fish, cheese, potatoes, uncooked vegetables and fruit. The model diet table suggested consisted of bread and butter, eggs, fish, poultry and cooked green vegetables, and had to follow directions from the surgeon in attendance.[46]

In 1889 a discussion on food suitable for invalids and infants at the pharmacology and therapeutics section of the annual meeting of the British Medical Association was led by Isaac Yeo, a physician of King's College Hospital and professor of clinical therapeutics. He stated that feeding patients who suffered from fever needed to be reconsidered: because nurses could not easily change a doctor's diet order, even fever patients who just wanted cold water rather than beef tea could not be casually supplied by a nurse. Furthermore, port wine when added to that beef tea was of unimaginably poor quality. Yeo suggested that doctors had to adopt an alternative diet for patients instead of strong beef tea, such as digestible mutton, veal or chicken broth, or clear soup with added vegetable juices. He argued that doctors had to pay more attention to the quality and suitable quantity of food for patients because feeding patients in large hospitals was more typically routine than individual work and 'more of predetermination than discrimination'.[47] Even when research on dietetics was done by medical men, it was impossible for them to administer the whole regime of feeding patients at a hospital.

The reform of hospital diet at the London Hospital showed similar progress to that at other hospitals, though diet there was shared with the nursing department through dietetics lectures and training in sick cookery. Furthermore, there had been cooperation there between dietetics research and hospital management since the 1870s. Its house governor, Nixon, investigated the question of 'the apparently extravagant orders for patients' diets' and he recognized that confusion over the various diets and extras usually ordered by doctors could be avoided if remodelling the diet table proved successful. He claimed that it was necessary to supply the whole staff, especially the medical men, with the new diet table to aid their understanding of its role. House physicians, surgeons and visiting staff 'who are virtually the practical agents in the Dieting of patients', would likewise assist 'the economical cooking of the Hospital by exact recording of the diets on the prescription boards'. This was finally approved and copies were sent to all staff. The new diet table of the 1880s also started special diets, such as those for diabetic patients.[48] With the diet reform, Nixon also introduced a new hospital kitchen, adapting the gas and cooking system in place since 1871 to make it more economical. With 4400 meals a year being served to inpatients, the roasting and baking ovens had needed repair since 1869; the change to the new system saved expense and also a waste of meat during cooking.[49] As these records showed, only the house governor could manage the hospital diet economically. Once both the house committee and medical council of the hospital had approved the new diet table, the management came to consider nutritional value as more important.

In 1901 Hutchison and Head reported on diet reform for discussion at these two committees. As part of their review of the pharmacopoeia section of the hospital, they had been asked to investigate the diet table and they now recommended rapid reform for 'the present system of dieting in vogue at the Hospital'. They compared the nutritive value of the hospital diets, suggested altering the calories of energy required daily and asked house physicians to check on extra diet every week to avoid any increase. Furthermore, the diet cooking had to be simplified for 'the medical, nursing and lay authorities to see at a glance and to check any tendency to extravagance'.[50] Following these investigations Hutchison delivered lectures on dietetics to medical school students at the London Hospital, referring them to his 1900 book *Food and the Principles of Dietetics*. Adding new research results to later editions, Hutchison's text soon became a standard reference for the medical profession, including nurses, and had a wide circulation.

The interesting point was that he not only analysed the nutritional value of food but also explained how scientific knowledge of it would be useful for both doctors and their patients, especially when the latter were from the poorer classes. He referred to this as 'a knowledge of the economic value of food', because if doctors knew that then they could recommend the cheapest source of protein or fat for those patients who could afford to purchase fish, the cheaper cuts of meat, cheese, pulses, margarine and dripping but not more expensive chicken or cream with the same nutritional value. These articles were 'within the reach of almost everybody'. He required poor patients to acquire basic knowledge about food values because in general half a working man's wage was spend on food. Hutchison therefore claimed the vital need for 'popular instruction' on this subject.[51]

A number of suggestions could be found in his book, such as the economic cost of meat, vegetables, fish, cream, butter, margarine or jam in terms of their nutritive values and the possibilities therefore for their consumption by poorer people. However, he left discussion of the importance of cookery instruction to others; he focused mainly on the alternation of foods via heat and their chemical constitutions.[52] This was possibly because he saw nurses as more concerned than doctors about feeding and sickroom cookery. In any case, Hutchison did not think it necessary to include cookery in his research on dietetics at that time. He simply claimed that it was important for everybody to know about nutrition. On the whole, his objective was to ensure that doctors could provide suitable information about nutrition to their patients – especially outpatients or inpatients about to leave hospital – so that this knowledge would be effective when preparing suitable meals for convalescents. Hutchison's work clearly showed that he understood the need to educate the poor about nutrition. Nevertheless, it was always difficult to explain and demonstrate the value of nutritious meals and even doctors like Hutchison, who wanted to provide everyday knowledge on health and diet, found it a real problem to get their message over to their patients. Some poor people could take a nutritious diet if they became inpatients or could be taught by doctors as outpatients. However, patients did not always understand the advice. Nurses could at least support inpatients while they were in hospital, but it was almost impossible to look after outpatients or patients who had left hospital, irrespective of whether health instruction at the hospital had helped them or not. Apart from the opportunities district nurses had to visit people's homes ('the best weapons' Amy Hughes claimed for such work) to offer support and advice on cleaning, maintaining healthy homes and providing appetizing food, because they had so many patients, doctors had very few chances to give instruction about diet or healthcare in any detail.[53]

Since outpatients' departments at the London Hospital were usually packed, even the waiting rooms, medical doctors, supported by charitable organizations, asked for administrative changes to be made to limit outpatients to the numbers required for the purposes of training medical students. Between 1890 and 1892, the committee of metropolitan hospitals discussed the proposal, but some hospital doctors and private practitioners questioned its validity on the grounds that many patients needed food rather than medicine or medical treatment.[54] So, even under these conditions, doctors were trying to provide health instruction. For example, the outpatients' department of Guy's Hospital supplied a guide on infant feeding. It consisted of a printed slip about infant care that was meant to be kept in suitable boxes for use at the outpatients' department in 1892. Prepared by the medical committee for the benefit of outpatients, it contained suitable diets for infants of every age and easy recipes for barley water, lime water and meat juice.[55] This was an interesting trial case of direct healthcare from the hospital without medicine. It would be effective if the leaflet were handed to a person who wanted such a guide, either from need or interest. On the other hand, as Nightingale had always warned, without individual instruction it was not easy to understand such advice in practice.

Besides leaflets, hospitals could provide information to help outpatients recover from illness via an invalid kitchen scheme. The kitchen would be attached to the hospital and its purpose would be to issue nourishing meals. Ideally, it would be a sort of educational place, which indeed was planned, but its educational value could not be expected to flow simply from its work: after all, if poor patients could just feed themselves for free then that was all that would happen. The kitchens soon turned into soup kitchens, supported by hospitals only for their outpatients with a doctor's recommendation, but with the problem of how to deliver their educational aim to the poor unresolved. In 1884 Lord Brabazon announced to *The Times*, alongside Dr Bedford Fenwick of St Bartholomew's Hospital, that one effective way to tackle the general problem of poor nutritional standards would be to establish invalid kitchens near hospitals in east London for recommended outpatients and to charge a small sum for each meal. More importantly, he suggested that trained young women at each kitchen would save the expense of labour and 'also be a means of spreading a better knowledge of invalid cookery'.[56]

After this letter appeared, a new society named 'The Invalid Kitchens of London', which the Duchess of Somerset supported, started work in Southwark in 1905. After its success at Southwark, and similar successes by hospitals like Guy's and by district nursing organizations, the society extended its area of operations and established many kitchens in south and east London. The society's objective was the same as Brabazon's, namely to limit the supply of invalid cookery to those with a medical professional's recommendation. However, although they only supplied food, they did hope that mothers could learn about appetizing meals through visiting the kitchen.[57] Because there was no specific instruction on nutrition or cookery it was hardly a form of educational activity and would scarcely raise the standard of living of the poor. Such kitchens were exactly the same as the 'invalid's dinner table', which also looked like a soup kitchen, attached to University College Hospital for its outpatients. Charles Loch of the Charity Organization Society raised an objection to them at the committee of metropolitan hospitals in 1891, claiming that this kind of work by hospitals should be avoided, even if general relief was one of the hospital's objectives.[58]

With the progress of sickroom cookery in their training and in their district work outside hospitals, nurses attempted to convey information on health and diet into patients' homes. This could be effective, with practical methods, and even a little hygiene could change people's lives. At the same time, doctors continued their research on diet and disease and then treated inpatients with new methods, although it was not always possible to deliver basic knowledge about health from the hospitals to outpatients and discharged inpatients and they could not provide support to a patient afterwards. While busy and crowded outpatients' departments made it difficult for doctors to give individual care, invalid kitchens were not expected to be of much educational value to the poor. When it came to discussions about the medical profession delivering health and nutritional knowledge to a wider society, it seems clear that doctors' dietetic studies or chemists' food science were delivered to ordinary people by nurses: doctors lectured nurses on dietetics and hygiene and their theory and knowledge were then strengthened by practical training in sickroom cookery. Ultimately, it was nurses who translated professional knowledge and vocabulary into more common words understandable by everybody. It seemed modest work, but it was a huge support for developments in medicine and improvement in people's health.

Nursing and healthcare in the nineteenth century was part of women's work, along with domestic economy education. With these subjects, and with childcare, girls and women had more opportunities for health education from nurses or health visitors. But boys and men were also part of society and knowledge of health, nutrition and cooking could be equally important for their lives, even though they did not have domestic economy or cookery classes at school. Instead of such subjects, boys had drills to strengthen their bodies. But one of their greatest chances to learn about health, food and cookery would be in military service, which, of course, was a male preserve. I shall look at these opportunities in the following chapters.

Chapter 6

Cooking and the Health of the Army: From the Crimea to the Great War

Males undertook every job in military service in the nineteenth century, including nursing, healthcare, washing and catering, which were female preserves in civilian life and generally unfamiliar roles for men. Long after the Crimean War, soldiers continued to serve under harsh conditions. Nonetheless, for those who remained on home stations, the dwellings the British Army provided had fitted accommodation with modern sanitary appliances, there was cleaning and catering laid on for large numbers of men, and with hospitals for healthcare, the sanitary conditions were often considerably better than those commonly found in town residences. When they were overseas, however, the troops had to do everything in unfamiliar climates and in fear of local diseases; in fact, without suitable instructions it was impossible to prepare hygienic camp sites and to solve such daily problems as examining the water, purchasing extra food locally and taking proper care of latrines. Clearly, it was difficult to prepare for these tasks with knowledge derived solely from experience. Improvements in military sanitation and hygiene called for educational training for the men and medical research for that branch of the military service that undertook instruction in these areas.

To cover all aspects of hygiene, instruction would need to be made compulsory with the men taught healthcare through systematic training. Healthcare was thus incorporated into army regulations and the instruction the men received from medical officers was expected to translate into useful common sense after the men returned to civilian life. Historical research into army health and nutrition has revealed several works on rations and on the supply side of army food: Crowdy has analysed soldiers' diets, while Fortescue, Furse and Slade have written on canteens, provisioning and private contractors respectively.[1] The army's educational activities with respect to instructing cooks on the personal healthcare of soldiers have not, however, been emphasized. Yet this area is important if one is to illustrate how much concern there was for the health and sanitary standards of these men, especially given that an interest and knowledge in those fields are not always revealed by more general studies of British society.

The late nineteenth century was a period of reorganization for the British military medical service. Its area of responsibility was broadened and supported by research within military science, such as in hygiene, bacteriology, pathology and tropical medicine, which related to various kinds of diseases outside Britain. Issues of sanitation and diet within military service became strongly linked to the medical department. From recruitment until retirement of the men, the medical department acquired responsibility for food, dwellings, clothing and healthcare, along with general medical inspections and treatment. Providing instruction on sanitation and hygiene for the service became a more important area for medical officers.

With postings to places such as India, Egypt and South Africa between the 1870s and the early 1900s, the question of better sanitary care increased in importance, especially given that further investigation was required into the causes and more effective prevention of tropical diseases. The number of soldiers in the army rose from 113,221 in 1870 to 153,483 in 1890; and then the army's strength further increased during the Boer War from 231,851 in 1899 to 397,682 in 1902. It is clear that medical officers were required to give ever more attention to sanitary matters, both to maintain the healthy condition of troops and to teach them how to practise healthcare by themselves.

According to annual records of army recruitment, many of the men were in their twenties or thirties and came from working-class backgrounds. Quoting the views of Professor James Notter of the army medical school, Cantlie mentions that there was a decrease in patients with venereal disease in the army because the Education Act of 1873 provided elementary education for prostitutes and troops.[2]

The ability to read and write was clearly a key factor in health improvement, especially when instructing adults. Although it was not easy to alter their long-term habits quickly, the men could learn to apply what they had learnt to their present lives rather than just to some hypothetical view of a future life. Basic educational skills therefore assisted understanding. Nonetheless, healthcare instruction in the army developed slowly throughout the overseas campaigns in every decade after the Crimea. There was a shortage of professional nurses with specialized training in military service; moreover, there were no opportunities for those nurses to work like district nurses, regularly checking and instructing small groups about sanitary conditions and acting as reliable healthcare agents in areas ranging from dietetics to personal hygiene.

One early reform, when the tragedies of the Crimea were still fresh in everyone's memory, was to establish an army medical school. This was followed by a reorganization of the whole medical department. Cookery reform in the army started in the 1860s and was, of course, supported by Nightingale. Cookery reform progressed in two ways: hospital cookery and cookery for healthy soldiers. First, an explanation of reform in hospital cookery is necessary since this was the starting point of healthcare after the Crimean War. Then it is worth considering how the army started to feed troops to make them healthy rather than just fill their stomachs; from the 1880s onwards troops were required to cook for themselves as part of their personal healthcare. With these changes, from the late 1890s the army started to pay more attention to personal hygiene and everything related to health became an important educational matter. Notwithstanding its military character, from a purely educational aspect, health instruction in the army was an excellent opportunity for adult men to learn how to maintain good health and sanitary conditions.

Reforming army hospital cooking

Military hospitals were not the same as civilian hospitals; even the characters of doctors and patients were different. Medical officers worked in different conditions from civilian surgeons: they were responsible for the medical treatment of the sick and wounded and for the internal management and domestic economy of the whole hospital. They also had to act as matrons for orderlies and nursing departments and as stewards who solved hospital diet and house-keeping problems. Patients in military hospitals were not necessarily under stricter regimes or suffering more severe illnesses than those in civilian hospitals, so it was possible for them to move out of their beds, though naturally hospital orderlies were required to control and look after them.[3] However, even if there was not much difference between military and civilian patients in peacetime, if troops had to stay in hospital during war it meant, of course, that they became fighting men removed from the front line.

During the Crimean War the British Army realized that it was necessary to reform its medical organization, its sanitary standards and its ineffective supply transportation system. Among these urgent reforms, hospital cooking likewise had to be altered.[4] In the terrible conditions that prevailed, nursing support had also become significant for patients, as one soldier, George Williams, described in a letter written from a hospital ship. When women nurses started to help patients at hospitals, conditions there improved, though soldiers still had to wash their clothes and themselves even when helpless. On landing in the Crimea they became infested with lice and fleas, there was no proper treatment for the sick and wounded[5] and without nursing care it was difficult for sick or wounded soldiers to survive. Nightingale was in the East from November 1854 to July 1856 and her initial letters were full of demands for such supplies for hospitals as cleaning materials, cutlery, utensils, trained orderlies, systematic regulations and vegetables to prevent scurvy. It was under these circumstances that she prepared hospital kitchens for extra diets and in 1858 she wrote *Notes on Matters Affecting the Health, Efficiency, and Hospital Administration of the British Army, Founded Chiefly on the Experience of the Late War.*[6] She complained about defective hospital kitchens and stressed the importance of a nutritious diet. Her experiences influenced the training of gener-ations of nurses and set in motion the reform of army cooking.

Miss Margaret Goodman, formerly a Sister of Mercy at Devonport, recalled her experience as one of Nightingale's com-panions, from her departure to her time at Scutari, and she mentioned in particular Nightingale's reform of hospital food. She remembered cooking duty at Balaclava, which required some innovations. For example, she changed the cooking method to make the mutton palatable and frequently picked wild herbs to add flavour to soups. Faced with a lack of vegetables, one medical doctor discovered wild spinach, which was the only vegetable available in the Crimea.[7] It proved possible to prepare hospital diets if one were knowledgeable about ingredients and their nutritional value, though to do so perfectly required proper training as a nurse. Furthermore, in the military hospitals in war conditions, suitable cooking methods were needed to waste as few supplies and as little fuel as possible.

Yet, even in May 1855, Nightingale found that the hospital kitchen at the Balaclava General Hospital was not in ideal condition. It was organized by Mrs Elizabeth Davis, a Welsh nurse who worked under the army's chief medical officer, Inspector-General of Hospitals Sir John Hall. Davis was known to be critical of Nightingale and in her autobiography complained that every order she gave or attitude she expressed was difficult to understand. From February 1855 Davis managed an extra-diet kitchen at the Balaclava General Hospital, but because it had limited cooking appliances, she sent food to another kitchen where full diets for patients were cooked. She mainly prepared extra diets and hospital staff meals, and when Nightingale visited the premises Davis cooked her an arrowroot. Nightingale said it was good, though she thought it might be too thick for the men. Davis disagreed.[8] The episode does show, however, that nurses in this period could manage such necessities, even though training methods and systems were still developing.

Nightingale complained that insufficient attention was paid to diet and cooking in both military and civilian hospitals. She observed that sailors knew how to cook salted meat, whereas the army did not.[9] Naturally, she pointed out general improvements in army cookery in the context of her work with French chef Alexis Soyer and from 1855 introduced further ideas for setting up systematic and economical hospital kitchens and for cooking for large numbers of men. But she noted that even after the serious setbacks in the Crimea the variety of food and the importance of cooking were still neglected and that rations for soldiers, both healthy and sick, were little altered.[10] Cooking at the hospitals was poorly organized and patients got meals much later than the planned times. Until Nightingale introduced the extra diet kitchen there were no light diets in the Barrack Hospital at Scutari. Giving evidence later, the Revd Sidney Osborne confirmed that better cooks and provision for the sick had been needed under Nightingale.[11] Not only should the amount and quality of the ration be discussed: better cooking should also be introduced into the army.

Following the reforms instigated by Nightingale, the army medical department continued to reorganize up to the formation of the Royal Army Medical Corps in 1898. The army medical school was established in 1860 to instruct doctors selected for military service. This was achieved with the support of Sidney Herbert MP and Nightingale. Four professors for the school were chosen: Thomas Longmore for military surgery, Edmund Parkes for hygiene, William Aitken for pathology, and Alexander Maclean for military medicine. The school was located initially at Fort Pitt and then moved to the Royal Victoria Hospital at Netley in 1863, which thereafter became the medical centre for the army. Between 1871 and 1880 it was open to probationers from the navy when naval hygiene was also taught.[12]

Hygiene in particular was the new subject to be taught for military service. Parkes discussed the syllabus for his hygiene class with Nightingale, which he later compiled as an influential book: *A Manual of Practical Hygiene*. In it he explained the nutritional aspects of diet and dietetics along with his theory of sanitation for camp sites, barracks, dwellings, water supply and sewerage – areas that required attention in civil as in military life and that also impacted on district nursing training. Nightingale approved his plan and was delighted because all the details were those she had been eager to see medical officers satisfy in the Crimea.[13] The Nightingale-led reform of army sanitation undoubtedly broadened research opportunities both within military medicine and with respect to hygiene and nutrition. Parkes regarded cookery as a part of physiological chemistry and, as such, it should not be limited to culinary works.[14] Because the nutritional and economical value of food could only arise from good cookery, cookery was especially essential for soldiers whose strength depended on meals being prepared with good nutritional knowledge. Military cooks therefore acquired a responsibility to maintain the condition of troops.

Cookery instruction in the army progressed with respect to both hospital cookery and messing for troops. Instruction for hospital cooks started in 1860 with the preparation of suitable cookhouses for hospitals; more organized instruction developed from the early 1880s onwards. Hospital cooks, like hospital orderlies, were under the control of the medical department. Nineteenth-century civil hospital records reveal that several hospitals introduced women cooks into their kitchens to organize patient and staff meals; they were accustomed to contact with nurses and they worked under the matron. Some of them were employed for the nurses' homes, which probably expanded this area of work for women. The payment of hospital cooks varied between hospitals, though was generally the average salary for non medical staff.[15]

Hospital cooks were different from chefs in that the hospital required 'good plain cooks' who could prepare everyday meals and the kind of sick cookery that women could also prepare at home. In 1910 Miss E. M. Musson, matron of the General Hospital at Birmingham, pointed out that the small salaries paid did not attract experienced cooks. This often resulted in badly cooked meals being prepared by staff who lacked knowledge about food values, thereby making for an unpalatable diet. She suggested that employing a lady cook for the job would make a big difference, for successful results were already known about at other hospitals where their abilities to manage and supervise the catering were clearly shown. It remained difficult for individuals to learn better cookery by themselves because of the lack of good textbooks, so the shortcut to educate good cooks for civil hospitals had to be by proper training. From that point of view the systematic instruction given to army hospital cooks seemed an ideal method.[16] Training and qualifications for army hospital cooks in the 1894 standing orders for army medical staff stipulated that there were two examinations during the four months' course: candidates had the first examination mainly based on their instruction and then worked as hospital staff preparing all the hospital diet and extras before receiving first-class certificates as superintending cook in a military hospital and second-class as cook in a military hospital.[17] Since there was not any qualification for civilian hospital cooks, the army training model clearly offered advantages.

Influenced by Soyer and by the public attention now focused on army sanitation, the War Office published *Instructions to Military Hospital Cooks, in the Preparation of Diets for Sick Soldiers* in 1860. This was the first publication to show clearly how important it was for a military hospital diet to be based on nutritional research. It gave general directions and specified hygienic methods of preparing hospital food, such as cleaning the kitchen and cooking utensils, taking extra care to avoid using untinned copper boilers, never placing anything acidic onto glazed ironware, and using different strainers for greasy liquids like beef tea and refreshments like lemonade. Furthermore, cooks were strictly required to check and measure ingredients, as arranged by medical officers or according to Soyer's recipes, and then to prepare them in the time given, always sending meals to the wards in a hot and appetizing condition. The instructions included recipes for beef tea, for portions of vegetables and for the usage of egg powder – the same recipes were later taught to nurses as practical training for sickroom cookery in civilian hospitals.[18] Basic in their attention to cooking as these requirements were, according to Soyer, ignorance of them had been the real problem in the Crimea.[19]

Even before these instructions were devised, the Army Hospital Corps had been formed in 1857 with quartermasters, warrant and non-commissioned officers, and men working under officers of the army medical department. It was attached to the army medical school and its depot moved to Aldershot.[20] However, the Army Hospital Service Inquiry Committee's report in 1883 made plain that it was not only poor nursing skills that caused problems. The main purpose of this committee was to improve the army hospital system for active service, though the need to raise the whole level of health and sanitary care in the army both at home and overseas also influenced it. Orderlies needed sufficient training to be able to work as good nurses or good cooks during active service when conditions would be more chaotic than for normal hospital duties. The committee recommended attaching schools for hospital cooks to the large military hospitals at Netley and Woolwich. It also suggested that when examining medical officers for promotion, hospital administration (nursing, ward management, purveying, cooking and sanitary matters) should be included, along with basic skills in medical care and surgery, on account of the special character of a military hospital.[21]

It had been plain that the training of hospital cooks was not taken seriously enough in the 1870s when the Ashanti expedition had increased demands on the hospital corps. After this, the army planned the cookery course to include training for field duties and hospital wards and, beyond that, allowed men who had ability in cookery to continue further training so that the corps could provide trained cooks whenever necessary. In addition, they were planning to provide instruction in field cookery to all men in the future.[22] Most of this became a reality after the 1882 Egyptian campaign, though it took longer to introduce suitable instruction in field cookery for every soldier. Equally important, in 1883 Sir Garnet Wolseley also acknowledged the great assistance rendered by women nurses based on their practical trained skills. The training of orderlies could now be altered to provide better nursing care. Formerly, it had been normal for old men in the regiment to care for the sick as if part of their family. There was little complaint about this; indeed young orderlies only a few years in service often caused trouble. Their carelessness meant that sick soldiers had to fetch water themselves, that sometimes they were given other patients' medicine and that food cooked might be indigestible. This was why Wolseley proposed that at least a proper training school for hospital cooks must be opened soon to improve the medical arrangement of the army.[23]

As witnesses to the 1883 committee, Surgeon-Major William Johnston, of the army medical department and Surgeon Henry Bradford, an instructor at the Army Hospital Corps in Aldershot, commented that there was no special training system for hospital cooks and that only a limited course was given to regiments at Aldershot. Bradford said that, until just before the committee enquiring into training hospital cooks was set up, there was not even a practical textbook on military cookery. Bradford wanted a training school for cooks and hospital orderlies that would issue certificates; in addition, he claimed that ideally every man in the army should have an opportunity to learn cooking and that, as far as was practical, establishing cooks as a professional section would be far more useful for the whole organization of the hospital corps.[24]

Using a woman instructor, from 1884 onwards the army medical department began to train members of the medical staff corps at

Netley on how to prepare meals for patients. This was reported in the annual reports of health until 1890, though in fact the training continued after that date.[25] An outside body, the National Training School of Cookery, undertook the instruction. Sir Thomas Crawford, the director-general of the medical department from 1882 to 1889, started to correspond with Nightingale in 1882 about dispatching her nurses during the Egyptian campaign. He also discussed reforming the army's nursing department with her, not only by introducing female nurses but also regarding the instructions and regulations governing the hospital orderlies who worked with them.[26] Furthermore, these exchanges between Crawford and Nightingale significantly influenced the training of hospital cooks. The National Training School of Cookery communicated both with William Mackinnon, surgeon-general of the army medical department, and with Crawford, and it is clear that reforms for hospital cooks relied heavily on instruction provided by the school, which was Nightingale's doing. It was because the school was providing cookery training for nurses at St Thomas' Hospital in 1881 that Crawford had turned to Nightingale for advice on this, as on nursing and reforming the army hospital system.

In its 1887 report the National Training School of Cookery mentioned two years of work instructing non-commissioned officers and men of the Army Hospital Corps in sickroom cookery at the military hospitals of Aldershot, Woolwich and Netley.[27] In September 1883, when the War Office requested teachers for the new cookery classes at these three depots, the school's executive committee agreed to send one teacher to each and to instruct 12 men at any one time. When the lady superintendent, Edith Clarke, contacted Mackinnon, who was mainly in charge of the scheme, to discuss salaries for teachers, she informed him that the school would reduce its charges as they were sending teachers at the War Office's request – £2.10s a week would therefore be charged, though the War Office was required to supply assistants at 30s a week each, along with accommodation and railway fares. The following March Clarke reported on her visits to Aldershot, Woolwich and Netley to confirm what type of cookery instruction was required. Training at the three locations continued satisfactorily and the school awarded certificates (first and second class for good cookery and demonstration; third class for theory only). The War

Office subsequently asked the school to continue classes only at Netley and Woolwich because large numbers of troops from Aldershot were away on active service.[28] Unfortunately, it was always those most on active service who were unable to continue training to improve their skills.

Cookery classes given by a teacher from the National Training School of Cookery continued at the Netley hospital. In 1904 the War Office again requested lessons at Netley and in the camp at Aldershot, while in July the school accepted four superintending cooks from the Royal Army Medical Corps as pupils on their high-class cooks certificate course.[29] This would form a part of nursing reform within the corps in 1905, which in turn began to influence the status and employment of male nurses more widely in society. The advisory board of the medical department proposed to divide non-commissioned officers' work into nursing or cooking, with general duties retained within each specialized section. In the cookery section, it was planned to spend three months on hospital cooking in the charge of medical officers at the Cambridge hospital, Aldershot, followed by bakery at the Army Service Corps. One month's field cookery training was proposed as essential. The grading system already used in the navy was also added.[30] This move came after the establishment in 1902 of the Queen Alexandra's Imperial Military Nursing Service, which introduced more women nurses. For some men, systematic cookery training would be useful for obtaining work as hospital cooks in civilian hospitals after leaving the armed service, or as male nurses, who began to be accepted as properly trained for the care of patients and for sickroom cookery. From 1907 they were supported by a navy and army male nursing association.[31]

The process of training army cooks was recorded in a 1905 lecture notebook from the Army School of Cookery written by Felix Hadingue, who joined the Royal Artillery as a cook. It noted several methods of preparing a field kitchen, using mess tins and ovens at the camp area, with illustrations, and recipes suitable for soldiers' daily dinners from soup to puddings. More interesting still, it also included notes from a lecture on sickroom cookery accompanied by some recipes for such sick cookery as beef tea or apple water. The lecture clearly explained that cooks had to learn sickroom cookery with extra care because they had to support medical officers unquestioningly, strictly following a doctor's order.[32] Hadingue's remarks show that army cooks had a responsibility to prepare sick cookery if required. Their level of training was undoubtedly raised by attending instruction from an outside school. In 1910 the National School of Cookery opened classes for military cooks under agreed conditions and funded by the War Office, accepting eight army cooks to be trained specially for the high-class cookery certificate courses. The course lasted for six weeks and comprised ten lessons (40 hours) in each of plain and high-class cookery alongside other students of the school.[33]

Improvements in soldiers' diet therefore continued during this period on account of experiences at home and on foreign stations. Some improvements related to systems of supply, transportation and packing methods. Cooking, however, was one of the most important factors. Acquiring cooking skills and learning about the nutritional values of food became a necessity for soldiers before and between active service in the field; because unhygienic risks always surrounded cooking conditions in the field, soldiers had to take care in every sanitary matter. Where to set up cookhouses or kitchens in the trenches by digging soil, preparing mess tins, sewerage, and disposing of sticky grease after washing up were the main problems of the camp: knowledge of sanitary engineering was required along with personal hygiene. It was vital for soldiers to be able to feed themselves without any trouble and those skills helped keep camps free from epidemic diseases, especially during overseas campaigns. Medical officers had investigated suitable ways of instructing men about their healthcare and a focus on cookery proved to be one of the breakthroughs. An interest in cooking easily related to personal sanitation and hygiene, which had frequently been neglected because of their former habits in civilian life. If health matters derived from cooking were widely understood then there would be less difficulty controlling the spread of disease among the troops.

Cooking in the field
In 1862 Aitken, of the army medical school, wrote about British Army recruits: if the men were trained in unhealthy conditions then they were just wasting public funds and, after being discharged from the

service, a soldier might have to live with damaged organs for the rest of his life. Military service in Britain was voluntary. Men chose to join up and they therefore had to be kept in good condition for the sake of the country.[34] To do this, it was necessary to consider a better system of cooking along with health instruction. The Crimean experience had required a re-examination of supplies and nutrition, but the real turning point was the Egyptian campaign when hospital orderlies were seriously challenged. Soldiers' food was obviously connected with improvements in sanitation and cooking because, even if better rations were provided, they still had to be cooked hygienically. With the developments in military hygiene in 1880–90, troops were to learn cooking themselves both for sanitary reasons and to facilitate mobility.

Scarce supplies for the troops, often consisting of under half or even quarter rations of badly transported food, were widely reported during the Crimean War and lack of cooking skills and utensils made conditions yet worse. Because no field cookery was taught to soldiers and because camp kettles were the only cooking utensils with which they were provided until Soyer introduced his mobile oven, it was impossible to prepare a large quantity of food at any one time.[35] These problems began as soon as the British Army landed, for its troops, already burdened with a load of 63 lbs a man, tended to discard even such essentials as camp kettles.[36] Also, supplies were poor. With limes reaching the Crimea in bad condition and with no vegetables supplied for their meals, soldiers had to try to find them locally. If soldiers had been educated about nutrition and known more about cookery they might have withstood the severe conditions better. Men also had to adapt to unfamiliar cooking requirements. One of the rations, rice, was cooked by the men with good results. Boiling it required little fuel and it was a staple ingredient for the sick in the form of rice pudding.[37] However, being issued raw coffee beans, the men had to roast them and, in the absence of other utensils, would resort to using the lids of their mess kettles; also, even when the men cooked meals, they usually ate them cold.[38] French soldiers had better pots, a better mess system (including greater knowledge of cooking) and they collected herbs.[39] In Bulgaria, men who liked cooking but had no training were appointed as cooks. Before Sebastopol, however, the men were expected to cook for themselves and were supplied with raw rations, even though they knew nothing about how to cook them. For most, there were no facilities for cooking. There were no vegetables in the trenches, so the men had salt pork and rum.[40]

Even officers found it difficult. Major Daniel Lysons complained in letters to his mother and sister that his servant was not much use and that he had to do everything himself. In camp at Scutari, he was provided with a tough sort of buffalo beef and a small lump of brown bread. He got a cheap cauliflower there and a few potatoes for a stew, but later when medical officers examined the buffalo beef they condemned it on the grounds that it might carry a risk of cholera and replaced it with mutton. Lysons also made puddings using good local eggs, but in camp at Aladyn he had to go about six miles to reach a village to acquire them. He also complained about the lack of vegetables. Gradually, however, his cooking improved and at the camp before Sebastopol he even managed to build cookhouses with ovens using hand-made bricks.[41] He encouraged others to build cookhouses by showing them his model kitchen; clearly he had learnt a great deal about diet and cookery in the field.

Apart from Soyer's work, another move was made to improve the soldiers' diet and cooking facilities when Captain John Grant planned a new cookery system for barracks. He considered that since British Army rations were better than those of the European armies, the problem could readily be solved by giving soldiers a school of cookery, which he believed to be as necessary as a school of musketry. His cooking appliance was first introduced at Aldershot in April 1855.[42] A contemporary of his, Major Robert Bell, said that Grant's appliance was recognized as an effective invention, and not only for boiling meat, which always reduced its nutritional quality. It could also bake meat and easily prepare vegetables at the same time. Bell explained that in September 1856 a report confirmed its effectiveness; furthermore, when Grant's travel kitchen wagon was tested in China in 1861 it required very little fuel (120 lbs of coal for 500 men's dinners) and was effective for marching.[43] Demonstrably, some officers, like Bell, recognized the value of food.

Grant called the government's attention to this, claiming it was important for soldiers to teach cookery and not to have to depend on instruction from civilian cooks like Soyer. A cookery school run by non-commissioned officers was therefore proposed. Captain Albert Ross, a superintendent of army cooking at Aldershot and elsewhere in the country, said he preferred Grant's cooking appliance to other gadgets. It was convenient and economic in that it needed very little fuel and could cook potatoes in the upper part of the boiler and meat in the lower part at the same time. Ross did mention, however, that inexperienced soldiers preferred to use a single steel boiler for a little frying or stewing.[44] A commission set up in 1861 to improve sanitary conditions in barracks and hospitals recommended training cooks properly, particularly for active service. Cookery instruction was expected to help regiments and hospitals; training all men was ideal, though training specialists was preferred for economical and practical reasons.[45]

After the instruction kitchen was established at Aldershot in 1863, trained sergeants were appointed to regiments to give tuition. This became the central body for cooks' training and experiments on cooking fuels also took place. In 1883 the kitchen was relocated and later extended; in 1891 it was renamed the Army School of Cookery. Of course, Grant's experiments were tied up with the supply division of the army rather than with its medical department; indeed, his work would prove to be the origin of the Army Catering Corps, which was finally formed in 1941, with its Army School of Catering dating from 1920 and into which the army canteen was merged in later years.[46] The instruction kitchen also authorized publication of manuals on military cooking for use both at barracks and in the field using the rations provided. These volumes contained general information on cooking and described work by cooks and assistants while giving an example of company diet for a week combined with important advice on cooking methods based on rations. A sergeant-cook had responsibility as storekeeper, and as the supervisor and instructor of cooks under him.[47] For field cookery especially, after 1910 manuals advised that every soldier should learn to cook rapidly and in 1915 soldiers were even required to butcher their own meat rations.[48]

With a view to reforming soldiers' diets, questions were raised in Parliament in 1888 and a committee was set up to find out what changes should be made. The whole system of supply needed to be carefully revised and, as committee members recognized on a visit to the kitchens and cookhouses at Aldershot, further improvements in cookery were also necessary.[49] Cooking appliances and equipment in the barracks and regimental cookhouses were deemed satisfactory, but the committee recommended more instruction on cooking and more trained cooks in every unit to ensure a variety of good meals. Colonel Charles Burnett explained that he tried to provide nourishment for his men and avoid wasting rations by making soup from the discarded bones or heads of the slaughtered animals. He also reduced the amount of bread and purchased nourishing extras such as butter, jam, eggs, bacon or herrings for breakfast use. Furthermore, he arranged for the orderly of the barracks to do a little cooking to save work for the cooks, thus enabling the cooks to serve hot extras to the men and be more effective in conveying an understanding of cooking methods. Notter, professor of military hygiene at the army medical school, proved that Burnett's system was effective, even though it was based only on the latter's practical experience in the army.[50] The interest of a senior non-medical officer like Burnett helped maintain the focus on better nutrition for soldiers and on cooking.

The idea that all troops should learn cooking and baking for their field service had been mentioned soon after the Crimean War. As a witness at the commission on army sanitation in 1857–58, Major-General Sir Richard Airey stated that, aside from their regular daily meals, soldiers already cooked their rations for themselves in the batteries of barracks, which had fitted ranges; additional frying pans or utensils enabled them to cook their meat rations more palatably than merely boiling them with the coppers provided. Thomas Alexander, deputy inspector-general of hospitals in the Crimea, who later worked with Nightingale on the idea of an army medical school, mentioned that suitable rations and diets were necessary for soldiers' labour and that there was still scope for improvement in cookery methods. He asserted that the ideal way to teach cookery to young soldiers would be to employ two professional cooks in each regiment for both catering and teaching purposes.[51]

In his 1864 book, Parkes, at the army school, approved of the commencement of instruction for cooks at Aldershot. To save time and transport, the government should in future supply prepared and cooked food, but since this was not always possible he said that soldiers must be trained in cookery. Furthermore, medical officers must take a greater interest in the subject.[52] Some soldiers enjoyed cooking and many young soldiers liked to learn the 'art of cooking'. Better barrack kitchens also encouraged more use and increased the opportunities for soldiers to practise cooking. The bakers' training of the French army was recommended for adoption: currently only men who preferred baking work volunteered for the duty, but if every man was taught baking it would be useful in the field and some of them could earn a living as bakers when they returned to civilian life.[53] Already in the 1857–58 commission, the idea of introducing a third daily meal for soldiers, which would prevent them wasting money purchasing meals outside, was discussed. This was also advocated because of health risks from food that was not supervised or guaranteed by the army. This problem was still being considered as part of the army canteen system in 1903. Around that time third daily meals were finally provided.[54]

The need to teach ordinary soldiers to cook their rations became an army priority in the 1880s. It attracted the attention of such men as Surgeon Arthur Davies, assistant professor of hygiene at Netley, and Brigade Surgeon Lieutenant-Colonel George Evatt of the army medical department. They led the trend towards soldiers on overseas stations cooking for themselves for sanitary reasons and in the early 1900s reconsidered the nursing division of the Royal Army Medical Corps. As a medical professional, Davies complained that cooking remained unsystematic. He wished to introduce cookery training in barracks as a preparation for field service where soldiers would need to do everything, adding that if such training were successful, 'the British Soldier could go anywhere and do anything'. He encouraged soldiers to learn cooking, as they learnt to shoot and fight fatigue.[55] Notter agreed that soldiers should be taught cooking for better digestion and nutrition, with less waste.[56] Evatt pointed out that the proper feeding of soldiers meant less drunkenness and kept them fit for service. Nonetheless, even at Woolwich the preparation of meals by soldiers was still done in barrack rooms. Meanwhile, sergeant-cooks trained at Aldershot who could only look after the coal rather than do the cooking understandably complained that the teaching there was unsatisfactory.[57]

The new practice of soldiers cooking their own meals was consistent with medical officers' views on health and about paying more attention to the nutritional value of the rations. From the early 1890s medical officers in all districts and stations regularly reported how they instructed soldiers to protect themselves from enteric fever by boiling their milk, as well as their drinking and cooking water. The improvements medical officers in India, for example, saw after instructing soldiers on how to do more to protect themselves from disease, made a difference across the whole area of sanitation, including food. From the 1880s onwards, various handbooks and pamphlets on bacteriology written by Dr Ernest Hankin, who worked for the Indian government service, were widely influential. In particular, they directed surgeons to pay greater attention to sanitary details – in cookhouses, messes, personal cleanliness, food supply, sterilizing milk and water, keeping food off the ground and disinfecting wells. Commanding officers following Hankin's suggestions in the Punjab greatly altered the command's kitchen and hygiene practices, for the native cooks had not paid much attention to kitchen cleanliness and sometimes prepared meals on the ground, cutting up meat on a block placed directly there. Hankin explained how a cook's carelessness, dirty dishcloths and germ-filled water tubs provided infection routes for local disease.[58] Whether or not soldiers cooked for themselves varied from station to station, but in Bengal they did so to beneficial effect well into the 1900s, with marked improvements in their health, especially after proper cookhouses fitted with gauze doors to keep flies out became the norm. The best way to prevent enteric fever spreading to soldiers from the Indian population was to replace the native cooks and thus limit contact with the disease from outside.

A report in 1903 remarked that sanitary conditions among troops in India had improved over the previous three years, and it gave the fact that, in many regiments, soldiers prepared their own meals, both during the cold season and when they stayed at hill stations, as one reason for this. Further attention had also been paid to food storage and to maintaining clean kitchens and cooking utensils.[59] As the *Soldier's Small Book*, an official handbook of regulations issued to soldiers after recruitment, made clear, it had become common for soldiers to cook. There were instructions on the preparation of food during field service, care of mess tins, cooking methods, the use of preserved vegetables and pulses, and notes on firing. The booklet reaffirmed the importance of basic sanitary care and keeping the place tidy while cooking and avoiding using dirty mess tins or crockery, and gave instructions on how to clean these beforehand. However, apart from the army cookery school's handbooks, guides specifically on field cookery were not common in Britain: a rare example was Colonel Herbert James's translation from the French in 1912, which stipulated amounts for each company and suitable usages of mess tins.[60]

All the army's annual medical reports between 1870 and 1914 reflect an interest in improving soldiers' diets. The army tried to raise the standard of health among the troops and, of course, the soldiers' strength became a public concern after the outbreak of war. Several overseas expeditions and the growing interest of medical officers focused attention on the variety of rations and on methods of cooking during the 1880s. Both at home and abroad the amount and quality of rations were questioned. For example, in the hot climates of India, China or the Mediterranean, where the summer season required more appetizing meals to maintain the health of troops, the amount of meat in rations was decreased. Experiments were undertaken to assess the nutritional value of temporary supplies of portable foods like condensed soup and meat flour. The supply of vegetables was considered so important that in 1870 a medical officer in Ceylon advanced a plan to establish a farm to produce good meat and vegetables. When the nutritional value of preserved Australian meat was questioned in Gibraltar in the summer of 1875, fresh mutton was issued instead.[61] Nonetheless, the government ration remained at ¾ lb meat (with bone, uncooked) and 1 lb of bread a day, though those amounts and their quality were altered a little after the soldiers' dietary committee met in 1889. One idea for obtaining perishable vegetables overseas that was tried during this period was for soldiers to grow their own.

In the 1890s, experience and developments in medical research finally led to the decision to introduce cooking as part of healthcare. To avoid contaminative fevers and other diseases in tropical areas, soldiers had to stop buying food in local bazaars, which the army used to do when overseas in the 1870s and 1880s. Now regulations impacted too on military hygiene education and examinations for medical officers. When the Royal Army Medical Corps was founded in 1898 it drew up a new scheme for hygiene in the care of troops. Cooking individually and cooking in the field required more detailed instructions than training cooks for hospitals and barracks; individual cookery had to be more systematically taught and managed, even though this would require wider understanding of sanitary principles. Obviously, diseases not related to digestion or the climate, such as venereal disease, required yet further educational instruction for soldiers, but by the end of the nineteenth century improvement of a soldier's general health had come to include the whole of his lifestyle when in military service.

Cooking as part of healthcare education for soldiers

From the reorganization of the 1860s onwards, the army medical department's interest in health had begun to expand into related areas. The underlying principle, to prevent disease among troops, was based on an idea of healthcare concerned with 'how to keep fit' for military service rather than on how to restore health to weak infants or sickly patients. Medical developments in bacteriology influenced sanitary practices and living areas in camps were distanced from the latrines or ash pits: medical research confirmed the need for sanitary arrangements to be more scientific and it also justified informing soldiers that a poor understanding of health would put all at risk and in turn lead to the inferior condition of the whole army.

The necessity of healthcare, especially personal care, was acknowledged during the Crimean War, but took a long time to implement. Regulations devised in 1859 for the duties of medical inspector-general (and deputy inspector-general) created the position of army medical officer. Before then, army doctors had tended the sick and wounded but had not worked to preserve good health; now they had to advise on sanitation in barracks, food and clothing.[62] At the army sanitary commission, Parkes claimed that sanitary science instruction covering all aspects of hygiene was essential for young medical officers, especially on foreign service.[63]

Indeed, if the army really wished to raise health standards, it needed to reorganize the medical department and extend educational training. Healthcare instruction was thus incorporated into the work of medical officers who now had more responsibility for the soldiers' conditions. Because this related to the strength of the army and the defence of the empire, these movements became associated with the wider improvement of the people's health; Parkes even referred to this progress in state medicine as one of the silent social changes alongside the public health movement.[64] Over time, the benefits of progress in military medical science were delivered to civil society through the education provided for soldiers.

With ever more cases of disease in tropical areas, preventive medicine inevitably received much more attention from the 1870s. The developing role of medical officers in the 1880s was explained initially by Evatt and later by Dr James Cantlie, who considered that knowledge across the whole range of sanitary matters in hospitals was even more valuable for military than for civilian doctors.[65] Of course, Nightingale played a large part in these improvements. She acknowledged that civilian physicians would always be better advisers on family hygiene because they had more experience with sanitation in towns and buildings than military medical men who were always on the move with soldiers. On the other hand, she acknowledged, military practitioners were more specialized in the maintenance of personal hygiene (diet, clothing, camping) among soldiers. But, while army medical officers could perhaps care for personal hygiene and the topography of camps from their experience, even if they had received little education about them, such necessary branches of hygiene as drainage, water supply, cleansing and sanitary improvement in both barracks and hospitals had to be managed through scientific training.

For that instruction, Nightingale proposed a school of military hygiene, like the one already founded in France, where the subjects taught were wide-ranging but focused on personal hygiene, climate, diet, gymnastics, and cooking. Nightingale advised that hospital diets in particular must be worked out 'practically and scientifically' for use in the British Army. She urged that individuals paid attention to personal hygiene as a daily routine: for instance, soldiers should wash their own shirts as sailors were used to doing as a duty. Then she recommended introducing some instruction before soldiers were sent off on any overseas campaign.[66] More realistically, she pointed out the urgent need to give hospital orderlies a better training and to improve hospital catering. Referring to the instruction available for hospital cooks at military hospitals in the East, Nightingale noticed that sickroom cookery was never taught theoretically; men only learnt from experience, which was reflected in their poor understanding of healthcare.[67] There were of course soldiers' wives, but they could not be compared with women trained as nurses and could not play any part in instructive activities.

Some part of a medical officer's role in the army had therefore to be similar to that of district and private nurses in so far as they too combined sanitary matters with medical care when looking after the condition of soldiers. The scientific interest in hygiene that flourished in the army medical school when instructing medical officers, and the consequent concern for individual healthcare, basically depended on regimental medical officers. Evatt stressed this point in detail when comparing the army with other services, such as the police, whose health and sanitation were much better than they were for soldiers.[68] Even so, the Metropolitan Police Force suffered rheumatism from the climate and bad boots, despite also being informed about rules for good health, as was the army. In 1893, following the emergence of a police trade union, John Kempster tried to publicize such problems in *The Police Review*.[69] It was clearly a period of increasing attention to health both in civil and military organizations.

Providing basic information to soldiers started well before Lieutenant-Colonel Henry Allport of the Royal Army Medical Corps wrote a pamphlet on health for troops in 1906. Portable, small pamphlets on health matters for the army increased from the late 1890s onwards. The one by Allport, *Health Memoranda for Soldiers*, could be attached to the *Soldier's Small Book*, which also contained brief, though apparently insufficient, instructions on healthcare, basic attention to and care of boots, bathing and field cookery.[70] From the 1890s onwards, there was increasing mention of healthcare issues in the annual reports of each district and station.

Before that, since the 1860s, problems of sanitation were of course reported, but the 1890s was the real period of the army medical service's reorganization. The system of supply was another important question to be addressed and only after that did it become possible to draw up schemes for healthcare instruction as a priority. In the meantime, troops in camps were still at risk from disease and, to prevent this, practical instructions were issued for extra care to be paid to the usage of latrines and the cleanliness of cooking appliances. But these were not successful and those weak points continued to cause many problems and deaths overseas. To maintain a high level of hygiene in the camp it was necessary for troops to share a universal understanding of sanitation.

During the Boer War one young volunteer, Harry Neal, wrote vividly to his mother about the effect of the long marches on the state of his health. Soldiers sometimes had poor rations, though when they could stay at the same place they tried, through making local purchases, to cook additional nourishing food. When water was dear and only for drinking, he could not wash his hands.[71] He tried to pay attention to sanitation even in severe conditions of which he probably had no prior experience. Unfortunately, in February 1901 Neal died, probably from dysentery, which was very common among soldiers in Africa. The large number of deaths like his compelled the medical department to introduce urgent and further practical sanitary measures for soldiers.

A young officer called Captain Samuel Rowlandson also wrote home from South Africa referring to his daily duties and commenting on his food and health in a hot climate. Parcels sent by his parents had contained such items as socks, towels, soap, cholera belts, cakes and chocolate; his mother sent him remedies for his sunburnt face and he also suffered from sore feet.[72] He described to his mother the strict sanitary rules that operated in the camp, how boiled water was supplied and drinking unboiled water was strictly prohibited,[73] how the butter and cheese would melt in the heat, how they had fresh milk daily instead of condensed milk, and how they tried to get fresh eggs. Their cook was a poorly-skilled man who overcooked the meat and even served Welsh rarebit wrongly as melted cheese and tough toast on separate plates. Rowlandson managed to build a cookhouse with his men, but afterwards complained that the poor menus gave him a fever.[74] It is clear that the officers were better off compared with Neal, but their conditions were far from being satisfactory. Even so, after 1881 and during the South African War the Army Service Corps considerably improved army supplies.[75] An empty biscuit tin filled with potash and water would be left outside the hospital tent for soldiers to bathe their feet in so that they could continue marching when water was scarce. After hundreds of men had used it, however, it lost any curative effect and another method was required.[76] Such hazards due to climate and fatigue were the same for soldiers of every rank: all troops had to pay attention to maintaining their health.

A navy medical officer, Fleet-Surgeon James Porter, later director-general of the naval medical department from 1909 to 1913, served in South Africa with the naval brigade and observed carelessly run camp sites there. Because of the fatigue, soldiers did not prepare latrines and just allowed flies to infect them in filthy conditions. Porter mentioned that diseases such as malaria caused more deaths in South Africa than the enemy and urged that particular attention be paid to camp hygiene. Men drank boiled water on board ship, but not ashore where, through ignorance, many suffered from enteric fever. Porter was furious when given milk mixed with unboiled river water. The brigade's camp site was regularly changed to maintain healthy conditions.[77]

As army surgeon Chilley Pine experienced at Varna in 1854, when increased illness among the men necessitated moving camp, the medical and sanitary implications had to be judged carefully. During active service, it was necessary to consider problems arising from food supply, increasing work and fatigue.[78] The importance of finding sanitary sites was also significant in civil society and was referred to in public lectures.[79] Nightingale mentioned to army sanitary engineer Sir Douglas Galton that moving barracks and military hospitals to the hills of Hong Kong in 1896 had marked a 'principal point' in the outbreak of plague in the army.[80] As Porter reflected, the strict rules the navy maintained were generally enforced ashore as well, but the management of camp sites and men was always troublesome. On the whole, the navy's more familiar working environment at sea allowed its medical officers to implement sanitary regulations more effectively.

In the Crimea, Pine noted poor quality and insufficiently baked bread. Rations were 1 lb of meat and 1½ lbs of bread, but both baking and general cooking presented a problem.[81] However, more than forty years later in South Africa, Porter saw progress. When the naval brigade shared a camp with the Royal Berkshire Regiment at Stormberg, the armed forces built ovens to bake bread for 8000 men,[82] which was clear evidence of improved skills among soldiers since the Crimean period and of systematized cookery instruction. Porter went on to observe that the army's biscuit was better than the navy's, and that ideally tinned milk would be supplied rather than fresh. He found that the army rations the naval brigade received were of good quality, though sometimes the bread was sour. A stew was always served, even when on half rations, and other medical officers introduced him to a new and delicious portable supply of a German tinned variety that consisted of potatoes, sausage and French beans and only required heating using a lamp.[83] Although Porter's observations as a medical professional still showed how difficult it seemed to be to maintain sanitation ashore, the improvement in army food was nevertheless remarkable.

Even under such difficult conditions as immediately after the outbreak of an epidemic, it was the medical officer's duty to ensure that the loss of men was as small as possible; the quickest and best way to prevent tragedies was to give lessons in personal hygiene, which was what happened during an outbreak of plague in India in 1896.[84] This was vital if the army wanted both to revert to individual cooking and avoid the awful results witnessed in the Crimea. Individual cooking was convenient, especially in the field, and if the troops learnt about cooking and healthcare they could lower mortality and raise mobility. Cooking by native cooks in India had been accepted in the 1860s and 1870s. They were skilful and could prepare wonderful meals, even with only the old and primitive cooking appliances available, so the proposal to make soldiers do their own cooking was initially designed mainly to cut costs and avoid theft from stores.[85] It became clear, however, that a sudden change in climate caused many deaths, especially in the years soon after recruitment. In the six-year period up to 1870, for instance, 1307 young soldiers under the age of 24 had died and 1895 were invalided. Men in this age group were the main targets of disease.[86]

Handbooks on healthcare were published regularly after the Crimean War by members of the medical services and others who were individually interested in such matters. Wolseley published *The Soldier's Pocket-Book for Field Service* in which he mentioned the need to maintain cleanliness in camps and among soldiers themselves, with further observations on the preparation of meals and on diets during active service, explaining cooking appliances and methods.[87] Another guide published in 1890 by Surgeon-Major Robert Eaton paid even more attention to maintaining healthy conditions and to the danger of ignorance about the principles of health when at barracks and camps. Cookery was focused upon as promoting welfare and reducing intemperance.[88] However, these books were more theoretical than practical and, though worth reading for officers, they were not straightforwarded enough for most ordinary men.

The outbreak of plague in India also made medical officers realize the importance of minor sanitary details, especially those that related to cookhouses. Hankin asserted that the risk of contacting cholera microbes was increased by visiting local bazaars, so the cookhouses and their staff had to be strictly checked for the cleanliness of appliances and drains in the kitchen area.[89] Even where sanitation worked effectively in the barracks, soldiers still contracted enteric fever outside the barracks, often in the bazaars where medical officers could not provide any supervision. Young soldiers newly arrived in India were more frequently contaminated because of their curiosity and careless consumption of food and drinks.[90] The increased death rate of English troops from enteric fever in India during 1903 (1366 cases and 292 deaths and invalidings compared with 1012 cases and 260 deaths in 1902) was put down to ignorance of local sanitary conditions. A failure to eat and drink sensibly was also referred to as one of the causes of reduced natural immunity among officers and men. To protect soldiers from further illness, attention to personal health became a priority and all troops in India were given instructions on how to prevent outbreaks of enteric fever.[91]

Being alerted by the 1896 plague in India and the South African War, various pamphlets on personal hygiene were published: most dealt with knowledge and skills essential in the field and with an understanding of sanitary engineering. This last was more required than ever in creating hygienic camp sites and it had the effect of raising the whole level of army sanitation.[92] The handbooks about soldiers' health included notes on the nutritional value of various foods, an encouragement to attend ambulance classes, which would be invaluable in later civilian life, and hints on the care of feet and teeth along with bathing instructions.[93] They were easy to read and to learn by heart. In particular, Allport recommended that officers use his pamphlet as a textbook for sanitary lectures. For mobilization overseas they contained hints on how to prevent sunstroke or enteric fever, and gave advice on marching and morality. Furthermore, the habit of spitting was condemned because it increased the risk of spreading disease in barrack rooms and small tents. Allport reminded soldiers of their responsibility to prepare for future service through personal cleanliness, moderation, camp sanitation and a clean water supply. He concluded that pure air and self control were 'the watchwords' for fitness.[94]

Important as handling and cooking food had become, therefore, it was part of far-reaching improvements in healthcare in the British Army. Even two years before his 1906 pamphlet Allport had stressed the need for instruction on soldiers' personal hygiene, especially now that the formation of the army's medical corps made it possible to teach personal health systematically as 'an art neglected in civil life as well as in the army'. From his experience, the best method was to give lectures in simple language about soldiers' lives and habits. Care over fresh air, sunlight, food and drink, clothing, cleaning rooms, bathing and brushing teeth should all be covered. This instruction would then be followed by weekly inspections, as a practical support for the teaching and to ensure it was remembered at vaccination or in hospital when it was most necessary for men to maintain personal hygiene.[95]

This trend towards increasing sanitary instruction to troops was also being influenced from overseas; and one such influence was the Japanese army. Lieutenant-Colonel William MacPherson, who was attached to the Japanese army during the Russo–Japanese War, made it clear in his reports that the methods of healthcare the Japanese army employed were also useful for the British.[96] In 1905 MacPherson reported on the healthcare handbook printed for Japan's mobilization. According to Japanese army records, this was in print between 1904 and 1905 and 8750 volumes were initially supplied for the officer class of each regiment in Manchuria in February 1904. Its contents were almost the same as British Army healthcare handbooks, especially Allport's one. Printing continued as requested and by June 1905 more than 9550 volumes had been delivered to Japanese regiments to prevent illness, though mostly during the previous summer.[97] Lectures based on this handbook were also delivered along the same lines as in the British Army's healthcare scheme.

Sanitary lectures were being given to British troops in many places. In Bermuda in 1904, for example, non-commissioned officers were given 27 lectures along with practical demonstrations on the care of feet. For local plumbers, a lecture was also delivered on sanitary appliances. In India, greater care with respect to food was successfully accomplished after long years of suffering illness, though the careless use of latrines still caused dangers. Younger soldiers unfortunately paid less attention to food and they made slow progress in their instruction.[98] Lieutenant George Archer, of the Royal Army Medical Corps, pointed out how lectures in the 1900s mainly involved camp sanitation, accompanied by advice on personal hygiene, and how regimental officers were recommended to repeat them frequently to the men, if possible as a weekly routine. Handling food had to be taken very seriously to avoid enteric fever, as in South Africa, since flies carried germs from dead animals or latrines. He claimed that every man should have to carry out sanitary duty.[99] The annual reports of 1906 and 1907 contained clear evidence of progress in health instruction. Not only were lectures continued both at home and overseas but, to make the system more effective, the school of army sanitation was attached to the Royal Army Medical Corps in Aldershot to teach officers, non-commissioned officers and men of all branches. Examinations on sanitation became compulsory for promotion to captain, while publications about sanitary matters reinforced instruction for officers. Soldiers were not only provided with Allport's pamphlet but a small leaflet for use in the field was also issued to all on mobilization.[100]

Given that most soldiers came from a low wage-earning background and displayed a general lack of attention to personal hygiene before they entered the army, instruction during service certainly made some difference. Because soldiers were given lectures and practical instruction on a regular basis, and their understanding was checked frequently, sanitary matters became part of their routine. Compared with other employment, army service provided a significant advance in sanitary care. Time in the army was not just to make a man fit for military service: it 'should also turn him out a useful and healthy unit of society, when he leaves the army to return to civil life'.[101] The army described its hygiene instructions as 'trade sanitation' and expected educational benefits for the men.[102] Army instruction made it possible to prevent disease, which, of course, was much easier than curing it after contamination. It also began to alter habits and even morality.

From the late 1900s reports focused increasingly on dental care and instruction on tooth care became of much greater interest to medical officers. Young recruits from the Duke of York's School were noted as having significantly good teeth, thereby demonstrating that, to avoid costly treatment, care must stem from childhood habits. Despite all ranks of the army becoming familiar with sanitation, and with lectures and practical demonstrations being almost compulsory, 18 per cent of potential recruits were still being rejected in 1909 on account of bad teeth, even though they were otherwise basically healthy enough to join up.[103] Young men in society generally still had less opportunity to care for and receive instruction about their health than was common for serving soldiers.

It is safe to conclude that after the Boer War and the establishment of the Royal Army Medical Corps, healthcare was transformed for troops, especially where such matters had been neglected in their backgrounds. Ironically, although military service was always associated with a tragedy of some kind, being funded by the state it was one of the leading research laboratories for health science.

Without overseas campaigns the progress of research on tropical diseases would have taken longer and the need for organized cookery instruction and sanitary training would not have developed as it did. The late nineteenth century and the years before the First World War saw public health in Britain improve faster than in the early nineteenth century, in part because further attention was now devoted to preventing diseases and maintaining health in both the civil and military worlds and because scientists could often turn their theories into practice. Knowledge from other countries was also adopted, where suitable, to improve the British people's health.

It is difficult to ignore Nightingale's influence over every aspect of healthcare; even in the limited context of the army, she supported training hospital cooks and orderlies at a time when neither existed in civilian hospitals and she laid the foundations of healthcare instruction for men. It took almost thirty years after Nightingale first explained their importance to start systematic healthcare instruction and to train cooks. Learning about health, nutrition and cooking by joining the army became of enormous benefit for men. They not only had to practice these things after listening to the theory, but in the absence of any skilled help from women, which they could usually ask for in civilian life, they also had to do everything for themselves. For many young men in military service it was a precious opportunity to alter their unhealthy lifestyle, not only for the sake of the British Army but also for their own benefit and that of society at large.

In the next chapter I shall focus on similar developments among seamen, which had even more connections with civilian technical education in cookery than the army. Nightingale, no less, even in the 1850s, admired the navy for its cleanliness and hygienic conditions compared with those prevailing in the army. Given the limited working space aboard ships, such praise was indeed remarkable.

Chapter 7

Cooking in the Royal Navy

Maintaining good health among seamen was vital for the Royal Navy, for without it they could not continue sailing. Once they left land, the men always had to stay in a cramped environment and, on long voyages far from the shore, it was impossible for ships to summon help immediately. The men had to live on restricted amounts of food and in poor accommodation: they were confined to the vessel where they took rest on the lower decks. If one of them fell ill, the others had nowhere to go to get away from the disease. As a general regulation for military service, the navy, of course, selected its recruits from healthy men, but there were always unexpected dangers from epidemics at overseas ports or by way of unhygienic supplies during the voyage. The primary difference between the army and the navy was in their living circumstances, but for the latter it became an asset that hygienic conditions were maintained through habit and were based on medical officers' research.

This was probably why Nightingale claimed that the navy was generally in better health than the army. She said that the army should be able to adapt to the great sanitary improvements the navy had achieved, despite differences in their working conditions. The most notable of these was that a naval medical officer stayed with his men and carried out daily inspections to check causes of disease. Working closely with the men under familiar conditions helped him. The weak point of army medical officers was that they had to face different and unfamiliar circumstances, often with no experience and education to help cope with them. Nightingale spoke highly about the cleanliness of the ships, though less so about the seamen. Nevertheless, she recommended that the seamen's good habit of washing their own shirts should be introduced to the army as a part of personal healthcare.[1] She used such information to highlight the poor condition of the army in the Crimea, believing that the basic sanitary condition of the navy, reinforced by habit and managed by medical officers, provided ideal methods to maintain the health of a large number of men. Compared with the army, the size of the navy remained small. In 1850 the army was 99,128 men whereas the navy was only 39,000, and even in 1890 when the army became 153,483, and the size of the navy was increased as well, the navy was 68,800. It was one-third to half the size of the army throughout the years 1850–1914 and could perhaps more reasonably be expected to maintain healthcare.

Healthcare in the navy was already seen in the 1660s when hospital ships were introduced during the Second Anglo–Dutch War. Even though medical staff was on board, however, the sick diet was not cooked by a trained cook and the ration was inappropriate, mainly consisting of coarse, salted meat and fish.[2] A ship's surgeon held a lowly position, even in the late eighteenth century, although they improved their practical skills. Many of them tried to supply well-balanced fresh food for the men.[3] One medical officer at the time, Leonard Gillespie, had progressive views on naval medicine for hot climates. He referred to the importance of diet: fresh vegetables and orange or lime juices, fresh bread, reduced salted meat provisions and clean water. Maintaining personal health was also stressed.[4] The basic ration of the Georgian Navy was similar to that in the late nineteenth century. A new type of iron stove was produced that allowed different dishes to be cooked on board by baking or boiling ingredients. It was also replaceable when damaged. A mess cook, who was untrained, usually fetched and prepared rations and then handed them to the cook. Food for the sick contained some extras.[5] Expeditions and long voyages worked as medical experiments for keeping men in a healthy condition and had earlier led to the issue of lime and lemon juice. During long voyages it was necessary to obtain local products as additional rations for men, especially fresh food. As with soldiers overseas, seamen had opportunities to consume food at foreign ports and sometimes they too suffered accordingly.

Captain James Cook's contribution to naval medicine during his mid-eighteenth-century voyages, especially on HMS *Endeavour*, was remarkable. He eliminated scurvy by controlling rations and by issuing anti-scorbutic orange and lemon juice. He also reduced salt intake and issued malt. Wild celery was collected locally for flavouring, while vegetables were cooked with portable broth. Cook likewise supervised fresh water and personal cleanliness. He also oversaw the cleaning of the ship and found that using fire and smoke for disinfection was more efficient than using vinegar. Some 70 years later, Surgeon Robert Guthrie recorded in the South Atlantic that a midshipman shot a large albatross from the ship, which a seaman salted and cooked. It tasted like corned beef. Fishing overboard was a more familiar way for seamen to try to increase their food supply.[6]

Arctic and Antarctic expeditions from the early nineteenth century involved various scientific experiments related to diet and health. In the polar regions it was a great challenge to keep entire crews healthy for months or even a few years in the ice; their supplies had to be packed with extra attention to meet demands both during the voyage and when they had reached their destination. Portable foods and cookery utensils for sledge parties were also introduced. Scurvy was always expected: therefore, lemon juice and a number of preserved foods were prepared to overcome the lack of fresh supplies. Many naval captains and medical officers recorded such measures. For example, Surgeon John Richardson, who joined Sir John Franklin's 1840 expedition, proposed 'pemmican', the tinned processed beef with fats and currants, which was produced at the Royal Clarence Yard with himself in attendance. This afterwards became the basic supply for expeditions.[7] To survive in the Arctic during the voyage of HMS *Investigator* in 1850–53, which spent three winters in the ice, the men tried to supplement their meat supplies by hunting hares, reindeer and musk-ox. Assistant Surgeon Henry Piers complained of having too little fuel for cooking and not enough fresh meat, which was only available every four or five days, for the men.[8]

Even though the navy took precautions, some men still suffered from scurvy. Medical officers tried to prevent an outbreak by supervising the airing of bedding on a regular basis, along with routine cleaning. Patients had lemon juice and were issued extra vegetables whenever possible; growing mustard and cress on the ship was an inventive supplement in the Arctic. One of the earliest records of this interesting work was by Surgeon William Parry in 1820. He supplied vegetable soups, lemon juice, sugar, pickles, preserved currants and gooseberries to help a patient recover from scurvy; in addition, Parry fed the man a salad of mustard and cress he had grown in his cabin in a small box placed alongside the stovepipe. He found that it was possible to crop them in a week and that an ounce of salad could be supplied for two or three patients daily. The man, he hoped, would recover well after nine days.[9] Captain Robert Scott's voyages provide a very similar record from the early twentieth century. Techniques for tinning food had advanced by Scott's time, but the size, shape and paint on the tins still required attention, and medical officers inspected them regularly. Medical Officer Reginald Koettlitz also grew mustard and cress as an anti-scorbutic using Antarctic soil. Even under the limited skylight of the wardroom enough cress for the whole crew was cultivated. Traditionally, the officers and men who underwent voyages to the polar regions were less formal and often developed close relationships. This camaraderie, which might involve sharing the scrubbing, supported the smooth running of the ship and the main-tenance of sanitary conditions. This was important for good health and made the experimental diet easily acceptable for the whole crew.[10]

In the Antarctic expedition of 1910–13 an alternative way to grow yeast for bread was tried. It was prepared using malt, hops, bran and sugar instead of commonly sold German yeast. It kept well and was successfully used in the Antarctic for two years.[11] As well as this experimental work for cooking, scientific experiments on the nutritional value of food were also undertaken effectively – in accordance with the Royal Navy's now established attention to healthcare. Since 1825 surgeons had been responsible for issuing a suitable diet to the sick: for example, gruel or puddings with sugar and raisins. Beer, spirits or wine were also issued if necessary, with the captain's approval. Salt provisions were restricted. The surgeon had to organize all and recorded it in his journal.[12]

In the earliest report on the navy's health (1830–36), which was published in 1840 and which Surgeon John Wilson compiled, personal cleanliness for seamen was described with instructions to administer it as strictly for every man as it was for cleaning ships. It was clear that personal cleanliness, alongside the care of clothes and bedding, would be effective in preventing disease. Men were required to wash or scrub their clothes and change their shirts, frocks and duck trousers at least twice a week, and for their body care, bathing, shaving and combing were also done frequently. Their hammocks were scrubbed regularly and when the weather was fine they were aired with the bedding. Cooking appliances and mess places, with their utensils, were also to be kept clean.[13]

The regulated cleaning mentioned above so early in the nineteenth century is impressive when considering that the idea of personal cleanliness was not common at that time. Lack of facilities was often a problem in wider society. It also required a basic understanding of sanitary matters that was still confined to professionals and not yet spread widely in society as common sense. The navy, however, had to operate these measures compulsorily to maintain health in the service and its scientific approach to healthcare was always ahead of that in civil society and in the army. Even though it did not take any recognizable form of education, this attention to sanitary care was delivered by medical officers to seamen and if done from the youngest age, as with boys on training ships, these instructions could easily be turned into habits without any reluctance to perform them. This was why the cleanliness of the Royal Navy, which was well-known to contemporaries, made it possible for them to consider diet in the wider context of naval hygiene rather than as problems of the supply system or amounts of provisions.

Histories of naval medicine and victualling in modern Britain have developed as separate branches of study, although connections are always obvious. Lloyd and Coulter discuss these subjects, along with the administrative aspects of the navy's medical department, up to the early twentieth century, with reforms of the navy thereafter analysed from a more political perspective. Kemp covers reforms on the lower deck and greater welfare in the nineteenth century, while Rasor incorporates this into his work on medical progress between 1850 and 1880. Carew pointed out how payment, uniform and welfare run throughout the works of Lionel Yexley (James Woods). Bath, who referred to alterations in diet and cookery training in the navy before the early twentieth century, clarified the trend of victualling; Clayton, a contemporary who joined the victualling department in 1891, gives a brief summary of important reforms in cookery from

1870 to 1905. Watt has summarized the history of nutrition and of such maritime diseases as scurvy from the fifteenth to the twentieth centuries.[14] Healthcare for seamen can indeed be studied by looking at connections between the medical and victualling branches, most notably by way of cookery reforms, health related instructions for general seamen and those for boys before entering the service.

In this chapter I explore the progress of healthcare in the navy as part of naval hygiene, from the development of cookery for both healthy and sick seamen to the men understanding hygiene through training from the 1850s onwards. Introducing self-catering for sailors was discussed, as was the possible advantage for the service of abolishing the familiar savings system, which had been common since 1799.[15] The navy took one initiative by installing a cookery training scheme linked to the question of feeding its young boys healthy food. Training for boys was recognized as being important for the delivery of health and sanitary knowledge.

Sanitary conditions in the navy were never as dire as in the army, even in the Crimea, and the navy maintained progress independently, which it based on its own medical research. The victualling department was also interested in health reform; quantities of meat or bread rations were altered occasionally after medical officers had examined the reports. The navy's savings system was also an interesting aspect of feeding seamen: generally not fully satisfied with the government rations, seamen negotiated with officers to offer them money instead of some rations and then purchased whatever they favoured to make up their rations. Even though this system was common it was always far from perfect unless every man knew the nutritional value of food and understood how to eat healthily and hygienically. Seamen's health was not always incorporated into their educational activities in the same way as it was in the army, where more health lectures were given from the late nineteenth century onwards. By contrast, the navy passed on its research results on sanitation to the men from time to time via medical officers and in several forms.

Cooking and healthcare at sea
In the Royal Navy sick berth, men called 'loblolly boys' undertook nursing on board; the limited number of female nurses worked only

at hospitals onshore.[16] Men undertook almost every aspect of nursing and on overseas stations local cooks were employed for convenience. Basically, the medical officers provided a suitable diet for the sick. This was based on the standard ration, whether full, half or low diet, with extras, even in the 1830s. Sickroom cookery was not taught to sick-berth staff until systematic nursing training was introduced from 1884.

Aside from this special branch of the service, a general understanding of sanitation was learnt through daily instruction, especially for boys from training ships or at the Greenwich Hospital School who entered the Royal Navy after training aged around 15–16 years. It is clear that they soon knew every rule for life at sea. They experienced different climates during overseas voyages and, as part of regular duties, they had more opportunities to solve problems for themselves than ordinary boys in civil society – for example, in cleaning, cooking, washing and mending. Cooking on board was changed after cooks' ratings were set up in 1874, which required proper training for men as well as for boys, and gradually the men did not have to cook for their messes in turn. Formerly, cooks had been invalid sailors or boys and it was not a favourite occupation for able seamen; nonetheless, they were key people who had to manage the hygienic condition of everyday meals.

Merchant seamen also lived in similar conditions with limited accommodation while on board. Since the regulation for recruitment was not as strict as for the navy, boys from training ships who failed a naval recruitment examination could join the merchant service until their height or strength became suitable for Royal Navy recruits. Being a civilian trade, the occupation of merchant seamen was different from the navy regarding salary, employment structure and welfare. Charles Booth defined seamen as part of transportation labour. Moreover, food supplied for them became of more interest to wider society from the 1890s and related articles appeared in periodicals, encouraged by the trade union movement, followed by the establishment of cookery schools for sea cooks in many large ports.[17] Cookery training for merchant seamen was generally funded by county councils as part of technical education and there were some links and similarities between each school.

Better port sanitation, more hygienic conditions aboard ships, better-quality cooking appliances and systems of food storage, and the invention of preserved food improved seamen's welfare in both the Royal Navy and merchant service; improved diets and cookery training were supportive factors in maintaining the men's physique. Seamen's diseases were historically linked to their ranks and messes. In his 1830–36 report on navy health, Wilson explained there were five messes in every ship, for (1) the admiral or captain, (2) the ward-room mess master, (3) mates, midshipmen, assistant surgeons and clerks, (4) warrant officers, and (5) seamen and marines. Needless to say, there was a huge difference between the top two and those below. Naval victualling therefore had to be considered medically to avoid maladies caused by poor nutrition. Wilson considered that alterations in victualling from 1797 had brought significant advantages to the navy over other services in that naval health was more carefully monitored and disease among seamen was lower than among citizens in any climate. 'There it no doubt,' Wilson concluded, 'that for this striking and momentous change, humanity, and the country are chiefly indebted to abundance of wholesome, nutritious food.'[18]

Providing nutritious meals to crews was demonstrably part of the improvement in victualling and naval medicine. The Royal Navy's shocking experience of scurvy had mainly ended by 1800 – even though vitamin C was not identified until the early twentieth century. Beriberi, caused by a lack of vitamin B, had also been widespread among seamen in southeast Asia. These were like unknown epidemics until sailors were given lime juice, fruit and additional vegetables for scurvy and wheat or animal protein, such as eggs, for beriberi.[19] Living conditions on self-contained vessels required a general understanding of sanitation and hygiene: it was the responsibility of captains and medical officers to conduct and lead men properly in aspects of both public health and personal cleanliness. In 1844, for example, one ship's cook always put unwashed and unsteeped salt beef and pork in the coppers. Surgeon Maurice West then requested a tub in which to put salt meat to steep overnight and the cases of phlegmon (inflammation of bronchial tissue) diminished. As late as 1911, Porter attributed a

case of plague to cutting up infected rabbit-meat.[20] Poor food handling was obviously a vehicle for infection. If a trained person
handled it, however, that would be easier to prevent.

Richard Behenna, a farmer's son from Cornwall, left a record of
life at sea. He started his career on a merchant ship when he was
about 20 years old. As an untrained cook on a cargo ship during the
winter of 1853 (a general position for able seamen at that time), he
described vividly some typical conditions. Aboard *Bellona*, which was
taking government stores to Malta in 1854, he remembered the
accommodation being both unhygienic and, due to bad weather, in
limited supply on the return to London. The men collected rain for
their scarce drinking water; rats on the ship bit their toe nails while
they were in bed and they lived on one biscuit and a pint of water
for nine days until they reached Queenstown to obtain supplies.
They were almost starved and had received no water with which to
wash themselves for two weeks. On another journey to Bombay
from London that October, despite the water being full of little red
worms and maggots the men could not wait for it to be boiled, even
though they knew this was not allowed. Behenna reveals that there
was at least some hygiene instruction on ships relating to food consumption.[21] His experiences nonetheless expose the difficulties that
were common at sea until innovative storage facilities came into
general use; as a result, medical officers or captains had to conduct
frequent and strict inspections of both men and ships.

During the second half of the nineteenth century medical
officers wrote several books on naval hygiene that were published
for the benefit of the navy and merchant service. Their contents, of
course, depended on information available at the time of publication. However, the important points discussed in them were
roughly the same: the necessity of ventilation, care for the cleanliness of ships, personal cleanliness of crews to prevent epidemics,
treatment of common diseases and first aid methods, and, of course,
sanitation and medicine related to diet. Authors from the Royal
Navy encouraged officers in the merchant service to use their books
and they compared conditions: Surgeon William M'Kenzie Saunders,
Deputy Inspector-General Alexander Armstrong and Dr Gavin
Milroy all explained that a merchant seaman's medical comfort was

below the standard of a Royal Navy seaman's, especially because attention to preventing disease was insufficient due to poorer provisions and a less balanced diet. Milroy believed that a merchant ship's hygiene should be of much concern as a public health issue because more unexamined men were employed in that service.[22] Saunders's book was pocket-sized, as was *The Ship Captain's Medical Guide*, which was an official handbook from the Board of Trade for life at sea. It cited practical ways to maintain men's health based on the cleanliness of ships, personal cleanliness and proper provisions.[23] Naval hygiene in the nineteenth century was designed for men in a specific age range whose working environment had to be strictly regulated.[24]

The navy had the advantage of being able to test its medical officers' theoretical analyses of diseases and hygienic discoveries empirically. The daily instructions on cleaning ships in the medical handbooks of the 1860s and 1870s were thus very similar to those in the revised and more advanced editions of the 1880s and 1890s. The latter, however, paid more detailed attention to cleanliness and the care of food as important elements in preventive medicine. Such works would be influenced far more by further understanding of and research into tropical medicine and naval hygiene after the 1890s.[25]

Long-term interest in food was therefore not limited to providing suitable quality and quantity for the men: medical research also improved methods of storage and the role of the cook evolved as a sanitary and hygiene agent – both in the Royal Navy and for merchant seamen. In 1900 Thomas Adkins, instructor in nautical cookery at the Nautical Cookery School in London, observed that sea cooks for HM ships and the merchant service were generally much in demand because a clean and capable cook could do a lot at sea to keep men in good health and good spirits. Dissatisfaction among crews was less about the bad quality of food than about the dirty and slovenly way in which it was cooked and served.[26] Eventually, following the navy's example and a growing public interest in improving food for merchant seamen, a proposal to train cooks for the merchant service was agreed. With new preserving methods and improved storage to keep provisions in a better condition, along with additional rations being allowed, the service became eager to acquire a proper knowledge of cooking. Since the main object of cookery reform in the navy was to supply nutritious meals to men, evidence for success must be examined from several aspects – training for cooks, victualling for boys on training ships or at the Greenwich Hospital School, and wider training related to health matters.

Cookery training: 1850s to 1870s

Since early times seamen had taken turns to prepare meals in their messes and in some cases cooks attached to ships were men who were physically unable to fight or young boys, which meant that unskilled and untrained people probably just learnt by experience. In 1824 midshipman Henry Keppel had to do cooking while their steward was on the sick list.[27] Nevertheless, cookery was a useful skill for seamen, especially during war, as the naval brigade proved in the Crimea. Compared with the soldiers, they were well fed and the provision of fresh meat, vegetables and warm clothing kept them in good health. The navy camp was better organized than the army and its size and water supply were ideal. Not only was the food supply more suitable but cooking was at a far more advanced level. The brigade's ratio of death from disease between October 1854 and August 1856 was only 44 per 1000: there were only eight deaths among 1200 men during the winter of 1854–55. Cooperation between medical officers and men ensured hygienic living conditions and the care of diseases.[28]

The naval brigade was supplied with fresh meat and vegetables for longer periods than soldiers. Their health in the Crimea was thus also based on their victualling system (such as regular issue of anti-scorbutic lemon juice). In the Crimea the navy supplied fresh lemons and oranges as salad with a little sugar, as well as dried vegetables, which proved good ingredients for cooking.[29] Their health also depended on the cooking arrangements of each mess, where 18 men cooked in turn. One advantage the seamen had over other corps was their initial familiarity with this work. Undoubtedly, the naval brigade's superior sanitary condition owed much to its mess system.

In the medical returns of the Baltic and Black Sea fleets, William Smart, the brigade hospital surgeon, mentioned several experiments with cookery equipment. Because the cookery attachments on board were too small for all men to prepare food at one time and soon wore out through frequent use, in October 1854 the men tried to collect utensils locally. Most of these, however, were also too small. Then, in early December, they were sent kettles that were similar to large iron barrels cut in half, large enough to hold meals for everybody and with iron handles and wooden covers. The men could now cook safely with suitable utensils and always had warm meals available whether on day or night duty. Such an ideal cooking system boosted the seamen's mental condition as well – Smart explained that when the men took their rations to the batteries to prepare meals, 'it was not unusual to observe them offering cups of hot cocoa to the naval and military officers, and soldiers who happened to be near them in the batteries.'[30] If supplies had been scarce and without a proper cookery system none of the men could have shown such generosity. Clearly, it was a significant advantage to have knowledge of cooking for maintaining healthy companies, both physically and mentally. Henceforth, devising new cookery systems and training would be encouraged throughout the navy.

In his report on naval hygiene, Dr Gavin Milroy discussed the prevention of sickness and stressed how handling food and drink carelessly, especially in an unfamiliar climate, caused illness and dysentery. He also pointed out the need for thorough examination of cooking water. He explained that while clean and airy accommodation for crews and proper clothing, food and medical supplies all seemed very simple, they were major factors in making progress.[31] Milroy urged that every executive officer should be taught sanitary science to understand its importance. These measures go far to explain the Royal Navy's better health and welfare record over that of the merchant service, which, despite its important role in the economy, suffered more illness in unhygienic conditions.[32] Milroy referred to humidity in ships as 'a great promoter of sickness'; unless medical officers paid attention to it, then dampness, especially on the lower decks, would always cause trouble. John Macdonald, inspector-general of hospitals and fleets and professor of naval hygiene at the army medical school, Netley, thought the same as Milroy. Every day British seamen spent at least

three hours cleaning the main and quarter decks with water, with the
lower deck washed on the great cleaning days twice a week. Due to
the lack of natural ventilation to remove extra moisture, Macdonald
advocated scrubbing with dry sand and sprinkling as little water as
possible.[33] Again, this method seemed almost too simple, but it was
effective both for cleaning and controlling dampness.

Furthermore, *The Queen's Regulations and Admiralty Instructions Bearing
on the Province of 'Naval Hygiene'* of 1879 sets out the captain's role as a
sanitary organizer responsible for maintaining public health and personal cleanliness. He had to check the men's clothing, suggest proper
care for moustaches, beards and hair, conduct ventilation and cleanliness checks and, what is more, ensure that men could bathe as 'a part
of the daily routine'.[34] Together, then, the captain's role, progress in
naval hygiene, better victualling, improved ventilation and innovation
in cookery systems all contributed to the health and welfare of
seamen. Cooks trained at naval cookery schools ensured better
cooking on board. Ironically, the establishment of the first school of
cookery at Portsmouth in 1873 had some connection with cookery
instruction in the army, which had, of course, so tragically failed to
feed its men during the Crimean War.

Commander Frederick Warren, whose experiments gave the Royal
Navy an opportunity to improve its cookery system and training,
invented a new type of cooking pot. As mentioned in the previous
chapter, there were similar trials in the army, like Captain Grant's
appliance and Soyer's oven. Indeed, both branches of the military
took an interest in Warren's appliance, which he tried out in April
1865 at the army's Cambridge barracks, Portsmouth, under Sir
Richard Airey. It was a tin boiler consisting of a pot within a pot with
the outer pot provided heat to the inner one via the boiling water in
the lining between them. Meat placed in the inner pot was thereby
kept away from direct contact with steam or water while being
cooked. The experiment showed that Warren's cooking pot could be
easily used to prepare men's rations in barracks and in the field; its
further strong point was that it preserved the nutritive value of food.[35]

A contemporary of Warren, Letheby, and a little later, Sir Henry
Thompson, also a popular advocate of paying more attention to
diet, praised Warren's appliance as ideal for economical cookery.

Even as late as 1900 Warren's pot was still seen as valuable for slow cooking and Hutchison of the London Hospital continued to recommend it . He included it among other cooking appliances that were easy to use economically and had proven nutritional advantages.[36] In 1868 the navy recognized Warren's pot as an effective way of improving the nutritional value of food and decided to manufacture it on a larger scale for 120 men, or two companies that could cook separate dishes for six messes (with 20 men in each). Baked meat and vegetables, pie and vegetables, meat and soup, stew, 'warrenized' meat (meat cooked in steam without water, the main asset of Warren's system), meat puddings, 130 lbs of potatoes in the potato steamer and a dish known as sea pie, consisting of meat and paste in layers, could, for example, all be cooked in the same appliance.[37]

In correspondence with the secretary of the Admiralty in July 1868 Warren explained that his pot could prepare meat without the loss generally incurred by boiling and he proposed incorporating a modified version into every galley. Furthermore, he recommended replacing salt meat with preserved meat and issuing haricot beans and preserved vegetables to make the men's diet more nutritious. Even though Warren was not a medical professional he was keen to improve diet from a scientific point of view. There is a report of a trial of his appliance, with 15 kettles preparing varieties of meals using steam, on HMS *Pembroke* in June 1868. The ship's officers mentioned three strong points – the ship's company particularly liked the flavour of the delicately cooked meat in the sea pies and soups, they found that all food had a better flavour than when cooked in the old galley, and that it produced food 'in a most nourishing and palatable condition'. Introducing Warren's appliance would therefore clearly enhance the health and comfort of their men.[38] Based on information from Warren, the medical director-general, Alexander Bryson, and the comptroller of victualling, Charles Champ prepared a joint report in July 1868. They advised the Admiralty that at least six months of trials using Warren's system on seagoing ships would prove that the greater varieties of dishes and lower consumption of fuel would make it suitable for use in ships' galleys. Another point they mentioned was the faster cooking by this system, which reduced the time needed to prepare meals.[39]

As these comments show, cookery and food in a seaman's life were always linked to better health and were therefore addressed accordingly. For the Royal Navy, the 1870s was a turning point in thinking about food for its men, not only in terms of victualling but also by making medical officers the agents for naval hygiene. Bryson and Champ's report was examined and in 1870 the savings committee extended the amount of attention given to cooking on ships. It also encouraged the Admiralty to establish a school of cookery at Portsmouth on board the training ship *St Vincent*. The committee examined the current condition of cooks, their abilities and, after the 'universal satisfaction' expressed at the trial of Warren's appliance on *Pembroke*, the need for a new galley. Bryson's successor as medical director-general, Alexander Armstrong, and deputy inspector-general of hospitals and fleets, Alexander Mackay, felt that the old and long familiar savings system was generally harmful to the men's health. Armstrong believed that sick, invalid and death rates among the men would decrease only if the savings system were abolished. Mackay expressed his objection to the old system by arguing how on long voyages, when men had to keep themselves in the highest state of fitness for their duties, the unbalanced diet that the provision of salt meat and other foods of less nutritional value introduced made them weak and liable to suffer more from boils and abscesses.[40]

Medical officers' reports mentioned adjusting the diet to make the men healthier: more preserved than salt meat should be issued (more than every fourth day and with a better quality and quantity of vegetable rations) and, if possible, spirits should be forbidden to avoid misbehaviour on ships. The savings system, whereby men could select whatever they wished to eat and which they certainly considered their right, had, through habit and tradition, provided an alternative to the government ration. Armstrong and Mackay did not abolish it as anticipated because that would not be accepted by the men and eventually the committee decided to continue with it.[41] It was assumed, however, that the introduction of a systematic training for ships' cooks and qualifications for their rating would alter general habits and organization. However, even when better rations and more acceptable meal hours were introduced, on the suggestion of medical officers, poor cooking would often fail to make them effective alternatives. Whether within the savings system, in the hands of ships' cooks, or cooking for the mess, which was routine for seamen, food preparation was an important factor. The chairman of the committee on savings, Captain William Stewart, thought that preparing puddings and sea pies as kettle mess duties, as in the naval brigade, would help the men learn 'general knowledge of the preparation of food', which in turn would make lower-deck life more comfortable. He claimed that it was a 'useful part of a sailor's education' and extolled it as an ideal since it had proved itself in the Crimea. Cooking meals for themselves was recognized as an advantage that enhanced seamen's mobility.[42] For these reasons, the idea of educational training for cooking on board was introduced to training-ship boys.

Analysis of cooking by ordinary seamen showed that self-catering encouraged self-reliance and made the men ready for any eventuality. Merchant seamen were also required to learn cookery in the event of an unexpected emergency. In the Royal Navy, the 'cook of the mess' prepared sea pies and plum duffs (puddings), though if undertaken by untrained, amateur cooks the disadvantage was that it introduced inequalities between the self-catering abilities of each ship. The savings system had the advantage of being familiar but was 'clumsy' – it only worked because of long-time custom. Paymaster George Martin recommended introducing men with professional skills into the navy for curing instead of salting meat, which meant upgrading a person with additional skill for feeding the service.[43] There were opinions in favour of training professional cooks to ensure that these duties ran smoothly; seamen preparing meals by themselves had advantages but the work had to be combined with a better understanding of hygiene and sanitation.

Improving ships' cooks, in practice, was thus a slow process. Generally, their ability was unknown and it was often said they had no knowledge. Even when they were sent to naval hospitals for training, the cookery appliance there was different from that of the ships' galleys, so they too required the sort of special training given to the army. Plain and wholesome food prepared at convict establishments, which accommodated large numbers of people, offered one model that could be adapted to a ship's cooking, for rations like cocoa, soft bread and nutrious soups were suitable for the navy as well.[44] While the advantages and disadvantages of creating the formal position of a ship's cook were being debated, the fact remained that 'cooks of the mess' had evolved as suiting the navy, even if this arrangement did not always guarantee healthy meals. Nonetheless, professionally trained cooks could supply fully-cooked meals in hygienic conditions in the galley better than amateurs, with only a vague understanding of hygiene, who took turns and often in far less suitable cooking places. Cooks could raise sanitary standards aboard ship and thus be effective in preventing disease. This, therefore, eventually became the new policy for the navy's cooking.

Following the savings committee's recommendation, in 1873 Warren implemented the idea of a school of cookery at Portsmouth with himself as superintendent. The successful results of the experiments with his cooking pot in 1865 had made him an authority on new naval cooking. In 1872 Rear-Admiral Lord John Hay decided to introduce Warren's pot on account of the variety of dishes it could cook. Meanwhile, the training of cooks and methods of storing food on board were also considered. During a trial of the school on *St Vincent* Warren proposed that training should be done without any interfering boys, using such cookery appliance as was suitable for ships.[45] He also mentioned that payment and age limits must be taken into account when promoting men to a cook's position.

According to Warren, as in the army an instructional kitchen should be used to introduce the improved system of cooking. Cooks should be divided into two classes: first-class for vessels of 300 men and upwards and second-class for vessels below that number, with payment planned at £25 and £20 respectively. After three months' probational training men would be issued a second-class cook's certificate. Candidates to become cooks should be more than 25 years old, though training-ship boys were accepted as pupils at the instructional kitchen. Marines and marine artillery cooks who attended would, like army cooks, learn trench cookery. Training for the latter was influenced by the regime at Aldershot, where 13 marine and marine artillery cooks were taught in 1865, though this transfer was discontinued after the navy started its own instruction. Several trials confirmed the economical value of Warren's appliance in using less fuel. The introduction of new ovens for baking bread, as in the French navy, was also recommended effectively to provide the 'best class food', especially for boys on training vessels. These views were sufficiently persuasive to make the navy alter its cooking arrangements aboard ships, especially after testing Warren's scheme on *St Vincent* and given Hay's support for commencing cookery training. Hay was asked to prepare suitable plans for training using both Warren's and ordinary cooking appliances; however, baking bread as proposed by Warren, was rejected because it was impractical at that time.[46]

In January 1872, Commander Robert Molyneux confirmed there was no difficulty installing the experimental galley on *St Vincent*: it would not interfere with the boys' training and drills.[47] The *St Vincent* trial was extended to three other ships and in 1873 Captain Henry Glyn of HMS *Duke of Wellington*, Commander Alfred Markham of *Boscawen* and Commander Henry Cleveland of *Excellent* submitted a report on the cooking galleys and the new system for cooks to Commander-in-Chief, Portsmouth, Sir Rodney Mundy. They had considered the results of all the experiments with cooking appliances and concluded that Blakes's galleys (not Warren's appliance) won their final approval as the most suitable appliance for the service. Although all accepted cookery training, they only wished to recruit men with a proper knowledge and good understanding of a seaman's life and working environment, preferably aged between 28 and 35, with six months' training at the school of cookery for a certificate. Cooks' mates, who supported cooks, should finish at least 28 days' training with a certificate before working on board; the three officers wished to make this a qualification and a cookery school procedure.[48]

The report from *Duke of Wellington* endorsed the ruling that ships' cooks and cooks' mates should be trained at the cookery school on board the flagship at Portsmouth. This directive also stipulated that pensioners were prohibited, that ships carrying more than 250 men qualified to have cooks' mates and that cooks must obtain certificates from the school. Promotion was possible only after six months' training for cooks and three months for cooks' mates and they could have pensions after retirement.[49] Even though the three training ships did not in the end choose his appliance as the most suitable, Warren's contribution to the navy remained important. He gave important advice on preparing nutritious meals for the men that went beyond that recommended by contemporary civilian scientists like Letheby, and even more than thirty years later Hutchison proved that Warren's hypotheses were still being used. The advice the Admiralty adopted as being most suitable both for the organization and for training cooks was built on Warren's views and on several of his experiments.

A report by the surgeon Alexander Rattray argued in favour of training cooks from a medical point of view. In 1871, while he was on HMS *Bristol*, a training ship for cadets that sailed from Portsmouth to the Cape of Good Hope, then on to the West Indies and back, he spoke about issuing and cooking preserved meat. More than half the voyage was in a tropical climate and it ended up with a large number on the sick list. Several problems affected the crew's health, most notably overcrowding on a lengthy voyage, working in tropical heat and diet. The men spent 199 of the 233 days in the tropics and were issued salt meat for 123 days with vegetables so scarce as to cause scurvy. Rattray analysed the sickness, blamed the diet, and proposed to reduce issuing salt meat. Cooking the preserved meat by another method could also make the rations more nutritious.

For hygienic reasons, Rattray considered issuing preserved meat more frequently, even although it was difficult for untrained cooks to make it palatable. It was also not an ideal way either to teach cookery to seamen or to encourage more highly skilled cooks than those currently in the service to come and work aboard HM ships. Rattray's plan to feed men economically and healthily first of all involved introducing a clear and easy method for cooking preserved meat – his experiments using sick-berth stewards had convinced him that there were several ways of cooking preserved meat that could make it tasty for both healthy and sick men. He recognized that the value of a good cook who could prepare 'presentable savoury – nourishing – digestible dishes' for health and comfort among all the men was 'inestimable', both afloat and onshore. Rattray recommended conducting further experiments on other seagoing ships.[50] He regarded improvements in cookery as medically important and his report provided another incentive to establish a training system for navy cooks.

Both victualling and medical departments thus supported the

establishment of a cookery school. A hygienic and economical cooking galley was also considered, though, unlike the army when it started its hospital cooks' training in 1860, a training handbook was not issued. In fact, only in 1905 did the committee on naval cookery devise the first specifically naval cookery handbook; until that time the army school's handbook was used for training. In 1894 the Admiralty examined a sea cookery book, *Cookery for Seamen*, to see whether its dishes were suitable for seamen. Its authors were Alexander Quinlan, an instructor in seamen's cookery at Liverpool, and Miss Mann, the head teacher of the Liverpool Training School of Cookery, and it was based on training merchant seamen in cooperation with the Liverpool Shipowners' Association. Their book was a good example of the work of nautical cookery schools all over the country and it was widely circulated at institutes that provided training for ships' cooks.[51]

Special training in cookery was also introduced to merchant service training ships. William Collingridge, medical officer of health at the port of London, praised it because the instructions given to training-ship boys on cleanliness and victualling improved hygienic conditions on the ships.[52] With medical officers eager to deliver their professional understanding of sanitation and hygiene in general terms and as routine cleanliness, cookery training that incorporated healthcare for the boys thus had a wider educational purpose.

Food and healthcare for young seamen

Medical officers looked after the boys on training ships and at the Greenwich Hospital School. In 1846 there were complaints about their quality and requests for more careful medical inspection to ensure that only healthy and strong boys were selected. Young officers and men in the service then had to grow up receiving appropriate food for 'athletic frames' and stamina. Airy accommodation was also necessary to maintain good sleeping conditions.[53] Seaton Wade, staff surgeon of HMS *Impregnable*, stressed the advantage of medical care from a young age, especially since most boys who entered the service aged between 14½ and 16½ were from the lowest classes in the community. Even the Greenwich School could send only a few boys to the navy, despite being thought of as a nursery for the service. This meant that medical care had to become a priority during their training, for it was recognized that it had the potential to upgrade the health of the whole navy. Because smallpox could become a serious problem on board, revaccination was introduced for boys from 1871 onwards.[54]

Fleet Surgeon Thomas Williams claimed that good medical care for boys would show up in the better health of future recruits and would avoid later waste. If this were done properly then boys would be fully developed and in good health by virtue of their suitable diet and physical training, unlike the young recruits who had grown up in civilian society without professional healthcare.[55] This would be advantageous for the strength of the navy and, of course, an understanding of the hygienic principles necessary for sea life would be developed better if seamen had trained from an early age. As a supplier of able seamen, the Greenwich Hospital School's records show what approaches the school adopted to keep boys healthy throughout their training period.

The Greenwich report of 1859 referred to the healthcare of boys, especially those below the age of 12, who should be carefully watched with respect to their cleanliness. They should clean themselves and their hair via instruction and be expected to maintain this as a habit.[56] While examining school conditions, the medical director-general, Sir John Liddell, and the medical inspector of Greenwich Hospital, John Wilson, both claimed that the boys' personal cleanliness was quite good though there was still room for improvement in the care of bedding, which should be aired and dried, and in the issue of sheets rather than just using blankets, which were usually washed only once a year. Boys were expected to follow strict rules of healthcare even though at that time the baths did not supply hot water in winter.[57] Changing boys' habits by such discipline was not confined to Greenwich Hospital and similar practices were adopted at training ships open to boys from wider backgrounds and ages. Training methodologies had similarities, of course, in that general sanitary measures affecting ventilation and the prevention of disease were always basic for the accommodation of a large number of people.

Boys' training and health appeared on their daily routine schedule alongside educational subjects such as seamanship. Generally, instructors and teachers on training ships included retired naval officers, which meant that the traditional daily routine would be carried out under them. Boys in good physique could join the Royal Navy, not only the merchant service: learning about cleaning ships and how to look after their own health was an advantage for either service. The 1870s' training ship schedule shows that cleaning and washing were included in the daily routine along with sail drills and swimming. During the summer, cleaning occurred at least once or twice a week in particular places, from the upper-deck to lower storerooms, while the lower deck was cleaned daily. Mending and washing clothes and airing bedding took place once a week, boys bathed twice a week and hammocks were scrubbed once a month. In winter, some of these tasks were reduced in frequency though those related to personal cleanliness remained the same as in summer. This daily timetable was the same as that of *Impregnable*, even fifty years later, which introduced hygiene lectures and instruction about alcohol.[58] Gunner Thomas Holman recalled washing day on *St Vincent* with soaps, tubs and clothes then hung up to dry; instructors usually assisted boys who had just joined the service.[59]

Because of overcrowding, the Royal Navy transferred the training from ships to shore in about 1903. One ship, HMS *Ganges*, was set up for this purpose at Shotley in 1903. It accommodated 1600 boys sent from the old training ships (*Boscawen*, *St Vincent* and *Caledonia*). Boys had hygiene lectures during the first month of the training and the diet supplied there was clearly effective because the boys gained weight and their physiques improved. Likewise, in the course of nine months the young cooks on *St Vincent* provided the 700 boys in their charge with enough fresh vegetables daily to put on eight to ten pounds in weight and two to three inches in height.[60] Surgeon Captain Richard Munday referred to these developments in his attempt to improve the training environment for boys, which was the naval medical department's responsibility. Munday was concerned about the large numbers of boys infected with diseases like tuberculosis even after having passed a strict medical examination on entry. From his experience at the Greenwich Hospital School, Munday recommended alterations to the shore establishments. However, his ideas were not fully put into practice because of the First World War.[61]

Whether or not the boys understood the sanitary and hygiene benefits of their routine, they clearly recognized that it taught them important lessons for life. Learning the principles of naval hygiene, public health and personal hygiene made it possible for them to pass the strict tests for recruitment into the Royal Navy. They faced similar dangers as soldiers of contracting diseases overseas by consuming unhygienic food or drink. With their additional overseas campaigns, however, the army received more health instruction and lectures than the navy from the 1890s onwards. Unlike the army, the navy did not of course need to set up camp, which involved preparing sanitary systems from latrines to cookhouses. Except when the navy sent men ashore, as in the Crimean naval brigade, sailors lived on familiar ships, the sanitary weaknesses of which had been thoroughly investigated and the cleanliness of which was routinely maintained.

For life at sea, once cleanliness was understood as vital then diet and food became the other factor necessary to maintain the men's strength. Seamen needed suitable amounts of good quality provisions, combining preserved food with fresh supplies. Cooking was essential to turn these ingredients into palatable meals with minimum waste. From this viewpoint, food was a medical and not simply a victualling issue. Following the savings committee of 1870, a further committee in 1872 reconsidered both the financial and medical aspects of victualling for boys on training ships to determine suitable amounts and better value. A reduction in salt meat and a daily issue of soft bread were recommended as being beneficial to the boys' growth. Ordinary rations were judged too much for boys, so these alterations would also avoid waste. After a medical officer's inspection cheese, though economical, was taken off the menu on the grounds that it caused indigestion and diarrhoea. However, the boys' lack of cooking knowledge presented a problem in that they could not prepare their sea pies or puddings and could not therefore obtain maximum benefit from the improved diet.[62]

The paymaster of *Impregnable*, John Hayward, mentioned at the committee that seamen instructed boys on how to prepare sea pies and plum puddings and surmised that 'they soon learned to cook'. Alfred Martin, paymaster of *Implacable*, also commented that seamen instructors and petty officers, though not ships' cooks, regularly instructed boys on how to cook sea pies and puddings. Commander Dashwood Tandy, former lieutenant of *Martin*, stated that boys mixed puddings and cooked sea pies. Hugh Pullen, paymaster of *Boscawen*, nonetheless advised that boys needed teaching and an additional cook was requested for that purpose. Commander Andrew Kennedy of *Implacable* later pointed out that, using the scale of diet, boys could derive more nutrition from vegetables and pearl barley.[63]

These findings inevitably persuaded the Greenwich Hospital School to reconsider its diet, which medical officers and the superintendent there had long considered a healthcare priority. The 1860 Greenwich Hospital School committee addressed the issue, following which Wilson and Liddell devised new dietary scales. The health of Greenwich boys had to be improved because the navy was rejecting too many as undersize. It was of national importance to make boys strong as future seamen for the Royal Navy; therefore they were provided with 8 oz of meat and potatoes, vegetable and meat soup and 4 oz of bread as typical rations.[64] Investigation on *Implacable* at Devonport had suggested a new scheme for boys' victualling in January 1873 and the Greenwich Hospital records reveal that the school superintendent, Staff Commander Charles Burney, experimented with cooking sea pies using more vegetables. To satisfy the boys' hunger, he also proposed increasing the daily bread ration to 1½ lbs and reducing the meat from 6 oz to 4 oz, which meant that he supplied a smaller portion than for adult seamen but well balanced by additional vegetables.[65]

The dietary question was discussed again in 1882 from a medical officer's perspective. A new Greenwich Hospital School committee was set up to discuss boys' admission, their employment afterwards (whether to Mercantile Marine or Royal Naval Reserve), and their physical condition with reference to the diet scale. As early as 1860 Professor Robert Christison considered a nutritious diet essential to boys' proper growth and to fulfil the energy requirements for training activities. The 1882 committee therefore recommended a more nutritious scale, with fresh foods for boys entering the school aged between 10½ and 13 who would be eligible to enter the Royal Navy at 13 or 14.[66] Greenwich was compared with other schools and considered to be providing a diet for 'the development of boys'. At the committee Henry Hadlow, fleet surgeon of *Impregnable*, drew up the new diet and John Reid, medical director-general, commented on it and added that an alteration of meal hours would also be beneficial.

According to Medical Officer George Armstrong, the three-month trial at the Greenwich School was very successful and the boys looked much better than before: 'their general appearance' was improved even though it was tried for only a short period. Armstrong urged Superintendent Burney to divide messes into two according to boys' ages in order to provide accurate amounts of food to each group.[67]

Burney sent the final report of his three-month trial to the Admiralty: in the trial he had altered the amounts of bread and other items while supplying onion and lettuce as salads, with vinegar for the meat dish; and the boys liked it more than stew or soups. Issuing butter for tea was another of his recommendations, along with altering cooking methods to make the food more appetizing.[68] Hadlow relayed its obvious result in November – less waste and more palatable meals. Furthermore, dividing the mess by age improved the boys' eating habits. He found they looked stouter and healthier, and the superintendent and resident officers at Greenwich fully accepted Armstrong's scheme. Fleet Surgeon William Lloyd likewise reported to Reid that he had witnessed the boys in better physique, although they would have to wait to see whether they could pass the examination for the navy. The superintendent and officers of the school constantly reported to Reid on the scheme.[69]

Apart from the Greenwich Hospital School and the navy's training ships, charity-run training ships across the country also trained seamen from a young age for the Mercantile Marine and Royal Navy. Although the Admiralty started its training ship system in 1854 and by 1863 had established five training ships, these were not always filled: in 1865 *St Vincent* accommodated only 317 boys out of a potential 650. However, public interest in training ships grew during the 1860s and 1870s as part of a movement led by charitable organizations for poor boys. The earliest movement, in fact, the Marine Society, dated back to 1756. The movement aimed to provide training on seamanship and elementary education along with a general understanding of the rules for life at sea, as well as serve as an agent for finding occupations for boys. The training included instruction in carpentry, painting, tailoring, cooking and washing, which were necessary aboard ships but also of course useful even if the boys could not obtain a berth at sea afterwards. Between 1856 and 1885, the Home Office ran

14 sea training ships as reformatories and industrial schools, while six more were organized, including two for officer cadets. Although they were not always able to provide candidates for the Royal Navy, or even employment at sea, about half of the industrial training ships' boys were nonetheless placed in the latter category.[70]

One of those ships, *Exmouth*, had an interesting identity in that the Metropolitan Asylums Board supervised it for pauper boys, which meant that the medical section of the Local Government Board ran it. Here, great attention was paid to the boys' diet and their training in health and cookery. *Exmouth* was moored in the Thames off Grays in Essex and between 1875 and 1929 it was more successful in sending boys to the Royal Navy than any other mercantile training ship. It could accommodate up to 600 boys aged between 12 and 17. The ship's captain superintendent was a retired Royal Navy officer. In total, *Exmouth* sent 4624 boys to the Royal Navy and 6386 to the merchant marine. More specifically, between 1876 and 1914, 3758 boys (from a total 11,328) were discharged to the Royal Navy and 4512 to the merchant marine. Between 1865 and 1870 *Exmouth* had about the same amount of accommodation as the naval training ships *St Vincent* and *Impregnable*. Commenting on *Exmouth*'s spectacular results, Admiral Day Bosanquet, the registrar-general of seamen, said that every port should have poor-law training ships.[71]

Many of the boys were originally from very poor backgrounds – it goes without saying therefore that the ship's discipline would be important to allow them to develop a good physique and to provide them with opportunities to learn skills for work on board. They also had aftercare from a member of the ship after leaving and boys visited the ship or wrote to the superintendent to inform him of their recent rating at sea or onshore. The boys were well looked after during training and the seamanship classes, drills and cleaning learnt constituted useful knowledge for their future life. The Local Government Board and the admiral superintendent of naval reserves regularly inspected their health and education; they also had a number of visits from local parishes, from guardians and even from overseas. Officers of the Imperial Japanese Navy visited from 1909 onwards and were very satisfied with the boys' conditions and their employment.[72]

In such circumstances, cookery was of course one aspect of the training that allowed boys to become ships' cooks, stewards on board, or cooks onshore. From 1878 the management committee started to record this training in *Exmouth*'s annual report. In the 1890s it became part of a national movement for more technical education, but even then no particular curriculum was drawn up until, at an HMI's suggestion, it became necessary to introduce a more systematic training. In 1878, 40 boys received instruction from cooks alongside other subjects on *Exmouth* and a number of them entered the navy as officers' servants, with some accepted as cooks' mates. Robert Mallan from Wandsworth, for example, discharged to *Impregnable* in January 1881, was drafted to *Duke of Wellington* and qualified as a cook's mate in October 1883. A. Rodman from Holborn worked as a cook's mate on *Pembroke* in September 1892 and became first-class cook on the same ship in October. He was still in that position the following November and reported to be doing very well. Records of the boys' careers after training show others employed as cooks in the Mercantile Marine and as mates of officers' cooks in the Royal Navy. In addition, some of them became sick-berth stewards after 1883.

Those who failed to reach the standard to become blue jacket boys entered as these ratings and then obtained opportunities to train, with payment, until 17–18 years old to make themselves strong and fit.[73] Royal Navy cooks required training for promotion to first-class cooks after 1874, which meant that boys from *Exmouth* had an advantage in this technical subject compared with the gunnery training that was so esteemed among boys who entered the navy's own training ships. Skills learnt on *Exmouth* with respect to cookery, washing and the general habit of maintaining personal cleanliness would prove to be foundational benefits for those pauper boys who joined the sea service alongside their stronger counterparts.

From the early 1900s more attention was paid to cooking in the training on *Exmouth* and the washing system was also changed. The chief cook was required to instruct boys to a higher level now that the captain superintendent, Reginald Colmore, former commander of HM training ship *Black Prince*, wanted to supply them as cooks for the Royal Navy. The boys learnt to wash their clothing and bedding on board, unpick and recover their beds and also make cap covers. All these were economical as well as useful instructions for the boys.[74]

Following visits by HMI Miss M. Nicholson in 1908 and 1909 to inspect the cookery training, further methodological instruction was requested to improve the boys' real cooking skills rather than just letting them help by peeling vegetables. Boys could now maintain clean kitchens and were expected to become good cooks in the future. At the same time, on Nicholson's advice, cookery books, especially Quinlan and Mann's, were purchased.[75] But even after these changes the standard of cooking remained unsatisfactory. The cook was deemed unsuitable as an instructor because he kept the boys acting as assistants rather than teaching them plain cooking skills like stewing, roasting, boiling and baking. In the end, boys were sent to the nautical cookery school in London for cookery training.[76]

The trials on *Exmouth* clearly showed that the boys' training, which retired naval officers to some degree influenced, gave the many boys sent into the service from there a good preparation for sea life; also, by being under Metropolitan Asylums Board management, much attention was paid to health-related matters. Inevitably, the instruction for boys on washing and cooking was not always successful, but it was nonetheless a good opportunity for them to learn cookery and domestic economy like girls of their own age.

The research that medical officers carried out on naval medicine and hygiene was delivered to seamen and boys as 'cleanliness'. Even though the audience might have been unfamiliar with the scientific research findings, the theory of sanitation could be learnt via that general concept. Professional knowledge was thereby converted into common understanding. The careful introduction of new methods of cookery and healthcare through practical experiments on board ships made such schemes more adaptable for the service. Experiments on ships had an advantage for naval medicine over experiments conducted elsewhere because the restricted accommodation provided more closely controlled conditions.

As part of healthcare, the reform of navy diets started in the 1860s. Unlike the army, this was not just because of the Crimean experience, for the navy had taken an interest in this issue even before then, but more and more attention was being given to providing a nutritious diet for the men. Once it was accepted that the regime aboard training ships could have a beneficial effect on the seamen's overall health, the boys' victualling was adjusted accordingly. The increased demand for skilled cooks by the Royal Navy and merchant service also affected cookery instruction. The start of the navy's cookery school in 1873 was early evidence of this, for ships' cooks and cooks' mates needed qualifications, especially if they were to join the Royal Navy. When sick-berth attendants became properly trained from 1884 onwards they too strengthened their capacity to organize themselves as a skilled and professional group. Cookery skills for this last class of men will be investigated in the next chapter.

Chapter 8

Naval Hospital and Sick-berth Cookery before 1914

From the 1860s and 1870s the navy began to train selected men for a specific branch of cookery designed for invalids. In this chapter I shall focus on these men's educational training and on how from the 1880s onwards cookery reform related to the medical service. This reform involved significant changes in the nursing service and among these, for example, was the introduction of sick-berth staff. Furthermore, improvements in hospital catering brought great benefits, while the establishment of the school of cookery ensured that patients were given better diets, which, in turn, brought down the incidence of food related diseases and contributed to a healthier service. After the Crimean War the medical officer's responsibility for the care of seamen on board increased and this was accompanied by scientific progress in bacteriology, which had a beneficial effect on both water and food analysis.[1] Communication with outside bodies also introduced fresh ideas on how to improve the navy's medical service.

One important naval reform relating to diet in the 1900s came as a directive from the victualling department. It was the decision to instruct paymasters who, even though they did not actually undertake any cooking, had to attend a short course in cookery training at the National School of Cookery. It was now considered necessary for officers who controlled food supplies to understand the basics of cooking so that they could manage the men who worked under them. Constructing a systematic scheme for cookery training, and for officers to conduct their own trials, would likewise confirm cooking as one of the important strategies for better healthcare in the navy.

Cookery reform at the naval hospitals: 1880s and 1890s
In 1927 Commander Charles Dawe, a surgeon, drew attention to the
link between diet and disease in the navy that had been ascertained
through factual analysis since the 1880s. 'Sickness only' rates almost
halved between 1882 and 1923. He pointed out that about 60 per
cent of this reduction was attributable to improvement of the skin
and digestive system associated with issuing more varieties of food:
vegetables, milk and jam. Then, with the introduction of the canteen
system in 1901 (reformed 1907), seamen were allowed to purchase
food as they liked. Furthermore, modernized cooking helped them
to make appetizing meals, while the abolition of salt beef in 1905
was another factor in decreasing diseases.

Dawe described how seamen's living conditions had likewise
improved with a better diet, more comfortable accommodation and
fewer hours of labour than had been common on the small steamships with poor ventilation on the lower deck. Seeing that the army
based onshore found it physically easier to obtain fresh food than the
navy when ashore, he stated that further improvement of naval
victualling was necessary. Even though the rations consisted of fat,
protein and carbohydrates, in general their diet remained ill-balanced,
with few fresh vegetables, and the cooking arrangements were still
primitive. He claimed that nutrition and 'the wellbeing of the body'
were essential to maintain physical energy. Dawe also mentioned that
the general messing system still operating in the 1920s no longer
required any additional purchase of food by the men since cold
storage and bakeries on board made diet less troublesome. This
system was started as an experiment on HMS *Dreadnought* in 1907,
which required some alteration of the ship's accommodation into
galleys and serving rooms. It was introduced more extensively after
the First World War, with allowance for the necessary storage and
cooking facilities, and half the navy was on this system by the 1930s.[2]
That was a significant change from the late nineteenth century.

Diseases caused by polluted water or food continued after 1910
even though they were significantly reduced. Annual reports on the
navy's health between the 1860s and 1910s show that generally the
attention given to sanitation and a hygienic diet remained much the
same, though some differences can be found in the records from each

decade. In fact, the health matters referred to in those reports are largely divided into two areas – public health, which includes port sanitation, local epidemics and revaccination, and health matters that relate specifically to life at sea. The 1911 report includes a table for the whole service showing the decrease in the death rate since 1856, which halved in the two decades between 1856 and 1876: the ratio of death from disease per 1000 seamen fell from 12.1 to 5.99, and then remained the same until 1884. Thereafter it gradually decreased by 20 per cent every ten years until 1911 when it was recorded as 2.22.[3] The crucial reform period was thus before the 1870s; what came after can be regarded as a more advanced reform period for the navy's health. The first type of public health problems mentioned occurred at home ports and overseas: at Portsmouth, for instance, the harbour had bad drainage with offensive smells that were unhygienic for seamen's dwellings close by. Overseas, conditions were sometimes harmful, such as during smallpox epidemics in China when ships offshore tried to limit their contact with the locals to avoid disease. Reports on the origin of food-related disease became more detailed in the 1880s; food poisoning from poorly preserved food or local supplies required routine analysis by officers.[4]

In the 1860s and 1870s, along with reports on fevers and such other ailments as venereal diseases, a number of problems arising from food were also cited. In response to special reports from medical officers, altering the seamen's diet was considered: here, reports by Rattray and Staff Surgeon John Hunter in 1867 and 1871 were especially significant. In the 1860s there were troubles with food-related diseases: for example, drinking bad water on the China station, consuming poisoned fish in North American and West Indian waters, or tapeworm cases in the Mediterranean. It was obvious that more hygienic and better food would improve health and that avoiding uncooked vegetables and unclean fruit was necessary. Improvement of cookery was also discussed as a part of sanitary care for the men; in 1868 it was noted that eating raw beef caused tænia among the naval brigade in Abyssinia, at the Cape of Good Hope and on the East Indian station. This arose from the seamen's common habit of consuming uncooked salt pork. Because of tiredness they did not cook the beef and no native cooks were attached to help them.[5] While no doubt all seamen would benefit from having some cooking ability, to maintain a good standard of cooked meals support by skilled men would be more effective still.

Better cooking was also thought to help overcome digestive ailments caused by the men eating too quickly, not chewing enough or smoking soon after meals. Staff Surgeon John Cockin mentioned this in his reports on barrack sanitation in the Royal Marine artillery division, in which he claimed that by changing the men's habits it might be possible to prevent disease and perhaps even reduce death rates. Medical opinion recognized his comments as understanding the need to encourage extra cookery training because better cooking could effectively reduce diseases of the digestive system.[6]

As Cockin mentioned, the establishment of the cookery school in 1873 generated an interest in the early 1870s in cooking methods and training skilled men. Rattray insisted that progress in naval medicine should follow the doctrine 'prevention is better than cure'. He stated that new victualling supplies had produced remarkable effects on seamen's health and that food would support their wellbeing and fighting capacity. Proper diet, alongside other common hygienic agents on ships such as cleanliness, dryness and ventilation, would preserve their health and protect them from disease. These measures were so effective that, on comparing the average death rate with that of civilians, the amount of sickness in the navy was lower.

Of course, as stated earlier, the navy had always considered diet important and water tanks were introduced to seagoing ships from 1815. The purity of water depended not only on the distilling equipment for producing drinking water on board but also on how it was transported and handled for storage. Using distilled water for washing and cleaning also supported better hygiene on ships. In 1825 cocoa was provided for breakfast, in the 1850s the daily allowance of biscuit was increased to 1¼ lb and of salt meat to 1 lb, and in 1867 preserved meat replaced salt beef and pork. From 1871–72 the quality of preserved meat was carefully checked and meat was purchased from Australia, New Zealand or North and South America. The convenience of preserved food was recognized and various kinds were issued.[7] Self-raising flour, manufactured by Henry Jones, was introduced in 1855 for baking bread on board instead of unappetizing biscuits. *The Lancet* supported its health benefits, while merchant ships likewise provided satisfactory evidence of its use in tropical climates. The medical director-general, Sir William Burnett, had approved of Jones's flour since 1845. The Admiralty eventually accepted it with the expectation that its high nutritional value would help soldiers and sailors recover during the Crimean War. In 1854 Commander Charles Talbot recommended Moore's preserved concentrated milk to the Admiralty. This was after trials by surgeons on four ships had shown that even in the tropics it was sufficiently nutritious to use for rice puddings, rice milk or simply as a substitute for fresh milk. Only one report contradicted this evidence. Patients liked preserved potatoes and they were suitable for cooking on board. Unquestionably, early nineteenth-century experiments were introducing new food to the navy. Furthermore, supplying nutritious foods in different climates had always involved careful arrangements by medical officers and thinking up ever more innovative storage methods. Rattray, however, now paid attention to cooking, arguing that for easier preparation at sea, food must be selected carefully and primitive cooking methods avoided as much as possible. No longer would fresh meat be roasted only occasionally — this would all change with the introduction of a better class of cooks and better cooking appliances.[8]

As early as 1871, when comparing the Royal Navy diet with those of other navies, Hunter noted that a change of diet was needed in tropical areas and that the salt beef ration was a health hazard. The *British Medical Journal* reviewed Hunter's findings and agreed that salted rations caused a loss of teeth when accompanied by prolonged consumption of hard biscuits. Introducing soft bread, which became much easier to produce after the invention of better baking powders that could be used instead of yeast, reduced the problem.[9] Salting was useful for storage, but it had to be changed so as not to become a health hazard for more seamen.

It was an important part of naval medical care not only to keep men in good physique and to help boys grow up to be like them, but also to provide suitable diets for the sick, for mentally ill patients and for pensioners who attended the naval hospitals that functioned throughout the nineteenth century almost everywhere the Royal Navy was based. For example, until 1893 Haslar Hospital in

Portsmouth, with 1500 beds, was the largest hospital in Britain; the naval medical service thus had ample opportunity to engage in research and experiment.[10] Haslar was already in good sanitary condition in the late eighteenth century and employed women nurses. Its diet for patients, as recorded, was about the same as that Wilson mentioned in 1840.[11]

Even patients who could never again be fighting men had to be looked after sympathetically and given the best medical care science could provide. Wilson stressed the need to give nourishing food to the sick, for otherwise they would not be cured. The sick diet at sea was much improved compared with former times and had become similar to those in hospitals. The diet tables consisted of full, half, low and fever diets, the basic quantities of which were 1 lb bread, 1 lb meat, 1 lb potatoes, as well as greens, fresh herbs, seasoning and tea. Extras such as rice pudding or fish were provided only on a medical officer's order.[12] Not only did the food supplied at naval hospitals receive attention, but the medical department also specifically considered the use of suitable cooking utensils, especially when manufacturers introduced cookware specifically for hospital use in 1854.[13] Until the early nineteenth century many naval surgeons were responsible for the health and medical care of detainees on convict ships for the long voyages from England to New South Wales. They had to control sanitary conditions aboard as well as care for sick prisoners, especially those who suffered from scurvy. Naturally, following earlier reforms on emigrant ships and warships, attention was paid to such matters as providing lemon and lime juice.[14]

The navy had indeed long been keen to provide a range of sick diets for the care of patients in hospitals and on ships. To treat scurvy on board, the surgeon Maurice West prescribed lemonade, and suggested eating more fresh meat and vegetables,[15] with sago and arrowroot regarded as useful medical standbys. For example, a diarrhoea patient would be issued arrowroot with port wine, light rice pudding with eggs and rice water.[16] In his report, James Allan, acting surgeon at the temporary Naval Hospital in Macao in 1842, which at the time accommodated 70 patients, regarded an adequate diet as being almost the same as for the sick on board (under naval medical instructions) but with various affordable animal and vegetable produce from the local market. A plentiful and nutritious full diet was provided three times a day and the amount shown on the diet table was divided into three – namely a full, half and low diet. The full diet was the same as the one contained in Wilson's 1830–36 report on the health of the navy: 1 lb bread, 1 lb fresh beef or other animal food, 1 pint broth with vegetables, 10 drams of barley or rice, seasonings such as salt, pot herbs and vinegar, tea and milk. Wine and beer were provided at the discretion of the medical officers. Local Chinese cooks who could make 'a great variety of rich and nutritious soups, and animal jellies' prepared the food.[17] However, when Assistant Surgeon Michael Cowan was ill at the Royal Naval Hospital, Malta, in 1856 he complained: 'Hospital fare dry toast and dish water!'[18] As these cases show, the quality of the hospital diet required standardization.

As medical inspector, Wilson explained in 1854 that mentally ill patients at the Haslar's lunatic department should never be treated as beyond recovery. Officers confined there had puddings for dinner and butter for breakfast and supper, in addition to the same quantity of seamen's meals, namely 12 oz meat (boiled or roasted), 12 oz–1 lb potatoes, 1 pint soup or broth, 3 oz bread and 1 pint beer. Mustard, pepper and vinegar were also supplied. Wilson emphasized the nutritive value of his diet tables, adding that vegetables should be palatable and augmented by supplies from the asylum garden. Seasonal fresh fruit should be added because of its positive benefits for mental disease.[19] Diet for pensioners was another question; it was necessary to provide carefully cooked food for the aged. In 1860 the Greenwich Hospital pensioners were reported to be successfully fed, though toughness of beef was complained about a little. Basically, the pensioners were given a nutritious cooked diet; however, when they suffered from scurvy in the summer 1858 it transpired that they had insufficient vegetables and had been issued bread in lieu of potatoes. Cabbage was introduced to their rations, which they liked very much, and eventually it was supplied daily.[20]

The records show that medical officers tried to ensure that every person in the navy, whether sick or healthy, boys or aged, were given a suitable diet. All diets had to be analysed and their nutritional values considered separately. As Allan revealed, even before the Crimean War the navy tried to support its sick with a balanced diet. The systematic sick diet training set up in 1884 showed how the navy tried to improve its feeding of the sick in a well-organized manner. Several practical problems were associated with the preparation of meals for sick and aged seamen in hospital. The contents and amounts of the diet table for the sick remained about the same during this period: 1 lb meat and 1 pint broth were the full diet basics as late as 1900 – accompanied by 1 lb bread, 1 lb potatoes or greens, 4 drams tea, 16 drams sugar and ⅓ pint milk for tea at home hospitals such as Haslar.[21] This was not significantly altered until after 1908 when Porter, as the new medical director-general, organized advanced nursing care and overall improvement of the medical service, including hospital catering.

By being trained properly, sick-berth staff could also raise the standard of medical care in naval hospitals. This would occur in collaboration with civilian institutions, such as the National Training School of Cookery and the London Hospital. A number of advantages to be gained thereby were considered as part of the preparation for any war; however, it is also possible to say that this was the moment when the long-term challenges faced by naval medicine attracted the widest public interest. Analyses by Wilson, Rattray and Hunter had shown that ideas about victualling methods based on medical research existed before the 1870s. These theoretical approaches to diet now became the foundation for cookery training and reforms for sick-berth staff in the nursing department of the navy. Those who were active in this field looked upon health as a food related question from the 1870s onwards.

There was a long tradition in the navy of having sick-berth attendants. By 1833 the qualification for the position was to be over 18 years old, to be able to read and write, to know how to keep accounts and to pass a fitness examination. Nevertheless, young boys and pensioners were included as candidates. In practice, they all worked under medical officers in the sickbay on board or as male nurses onshore. In 1830 one surgeon recorded the bad behaviour of a sick-berth attendant for ignoring his orders and neglecting his patient on board, and for this he was punished. There was no standard among them and surgeons always valued reliable sick-berth attendants.[22] Qualified female nurses were introduced into the navy after Eliza Mackenzie's successful work at the Therapia Hospital in 1855. Women nurses were officially recognized following the 1884 committee on naval nursing.

The naval hospital at Therapia was temporarily established in December 1853 to support the large naval hospital at Malta. In January 1855 the Admiralty asked Eliza Mackenzie, who had undertaken the nursing there and was the wife of Revd John Mackenzie, to act as matron. It was a small hospital, originally accommodating 50 patients, though its capacity was extended to about 100 and later to 150. Until Mackenzie arrived at Therapia one of the invalids was the hospital cook. In the 1850s even hospital cooks had low qualifications. However, because the hospital had to be enlarged, in March 1854 the surgeon in charge, John Davidson deemed it necessary to alter arrangements for both cookery and hospital stores. The deputy medical inspector at Malta, John Stewart, asked Admiral Houston Stewart to send Davidson economical cooking appliances, ideally something that could cater for 150 men, as some spare ranges were stored in the Malta dockyard.[23]

To maintain hospital care, even in a temporary hospital, it was recognized that the navy had to provide suitable cookery appliances that used economical amounts of fuel. The Therapia hospital could provide a full diet (1 lb meat, 1 lb bread, 1 pint broth, extras ordered by surgeons such as wine, fowls and rice pudding) though it suffered from choked drainage and badly fitted doors and windows. The navy's health became critical during bad weather between February and May 1854. Men kept at sea by fog suffered from scurvy on their salt beef diet and then, in August 1854, cholera struck. The commissariat's lack of management and poor transport caused more disease and deaths. David Deas, the medical inspector to the Black Sea fleet in 1854–55, urgently considered these problems. Support from female nurses who could provide skilled care for the sick and war wounded was requested and Mackenzie remained at Therapia from January until November 1855. She had no formal nursing training, so before leaving England she worked at the Middlesex Hospital for a short period. When Nightingale became ill Mackenzie looked after her at Therapia. Despite this obvious success the navy did not formally employ professional female nurses until 1884, and on board a hospital ship not until 1898 when four nursing sisters accompanied a naval force to Benin to care for patients with malaria.[24]

Basically, therefore, the service needed to see more improvements among male nurses. The home hospital instructions of 1866 referred to female nurses as widows of seamen and marines; there was nothing about any training for either female or male nurses, though work by sick-berth attendants clearly required some standard. In 1882 Admiral Sir Reginald Bacon stayed in a naval hospital that had no lady nurses and that employed only pensioners or seamen who had no interest in looking after patients. He recalled all this later as a horrible experience. Another admiral mentioned his experience at the same hospital 40 years later and he was looked after well, provided with good food and made very comfortable. Clearly, standardized staff provided better nursing care and it was the 1884 committee on sick-berth staff that brought that about.[25]

Undoubtedly, by setting up a systematic training scheme at land hospitals, especially if supported by professional female nurses, the overall standard of nursing skills and sick-berth attendant care would rise. In this respect sickroom cookery instruction and changes in hospital catering were both important, for medical officers' reports paid attention to these when considering the nutritional value of food delivered to patients. Training men as sick-berth staff was recognized as essential if the diet table for the sick on ships were to be carried out effectively. Only onshore did more skilled female nurses look after patients; and the positions they held at naval hospitals were the same as those who worked in the military hospitals as superintendents. This became clear from 1884 onwards when support training for sickroom cookery began from an external institute, as in the army, and when the National Training School of Cookery undertook cookery instruction for sick-berth staff. Because of the navy's medical appreciation of cooking, along with increased public interest in hygiene and sanitation, proper preparation skills were now required.

A new training plan and the 1884 committee on sick-berth staff questioned the hospitals' culinary arrangements and decided to introduce new appliances, a new dietary plan and cooks' training. Though partially connected to nursing work and needing therefore to be improved alongside basic sick-berth training, culinary issues at the hospitals were a management matter. Advice was forthcoming from civilian hospitals such as Guy's, St Thomas' and the London. The Netley hospital and the Army Hospital Corps depot in Aldershot also contributed to this attempt to improve sick-berth staff.[26] The 18-month sick-berth training course already included limited sick cookery, but it was now proposed to introduce instruction by teachers from the National Training School of Cookery. The latter, at Nightingale's request, had run a class for nurses at St Thomas' Hospital since 1881, had afterwards provided teachers for the army, and from 1895 had frequent contact with the navy. This was after Lückes had begun to collaborate with the school in 1893 over sickroom cookery training for nurses and when the same scheme was introduced for sick-berth staff training. Haslar Hospital was a good example of the growing interest in hospital catering: in 1886 its hospital kitchen was refurbished and put on the top floor to avoid spreading the smell of cooking from the kitchen. Despite some initial difficulty, a new gas appliance was installed at Haslar after the manufacturer had instructed the hospital cook on how to use it and it did give satisfactory results.[27] A surgeon checked the kitchen at Haslar daily and the food cooked there was examined before being sent to the wards. The inspector-general of the hospital, David Morgan, also inspected the kitchen and paid much attention to making it better.[28] The prior investigations of the 1884 committee had influenced these improvements.

In an attempt to improve sometimes unsatisfactory and inadequate standards of nursing, dressing, cookery and dispensing, a number of medical officers urged a better training for sick-berth staff. All except dispensing were compulsory subjects for female nurses training at civilian hospitals and cookery was also considered useful for sick-berth staff. One witness at the 1884 committee, sick-berth attendant aboard HMS *Royal Adelaide*, Thomas Reed, said that when he became a sick-berth attendant in 1872 he had received no prior instruction about nursing, either at land hospitals or on ships, and that all he had done was cleaning under a nurse's supervision; he was then employed as cooks' mate at Plymouth Hospital. He agreed that the young staff should have cookery training for the sick, especially for service afloat. He recommended it also be given to first or second petty officers with catering responsibilities. William Parkhurst, sickbay steward from HMS *President*, also mentioned that cookery training at the hospitals should take priority under the new training system.[29]

Under these circumstances, Haslar Hospital started to train sick-berth staff. The committee's records for 1884 show that the hospital cook and not an instructor from the National Training School of Cookery, which the committee had wanted, had introduced sick cookery for probationers. The committee did, however, ask the school's superintendent, Edith Clarke, for advice about instruction. Francis Clark, the secretary of the 1884 sick-berth staff committee, claimed to have been told during an interview with Clarke that there was no space at the school to instruct men from the navy alongside other women pupils. Clark therefore proposed she send a teacher instead, which was agreeable to her. Later records indicate that Clarke responded positively to preparations for the course in 1894– 95 when further reform of sick-berth staff training was introduced, but thought that sick-berth staff needed more basic training before being introduced to the sickroom cookery programme the London Hospital used.[30] Had the cookery school carried out regular systematic training at Haslar soon after the 1884 committee met, then Clarke's comment in 1894 might well have been different. Even so, by 1895 the school had become more confident after running its successful training course at the London Hospital for the nursing profession. The school's records show a fairly regular correspondence between Clarke and the medical department of the Admiralty after 1894, among which were several enquiries from the shipping federation about training cooks in the Mercantile Marine.

Although Haslar's own cooks led its cookery training for sick-berth staff in the hospital kitchens, for general diet, and especially for sickroom cookery extras, nursing sisters gave instructions on how to prepare specialities like arrowroot, poached eggs and lemonade. Thereafter, new sick-berth staff commenced work after probational training and certainly were able to improve cookery in the navy from a medical perspective.[31] Nonetheless, about ten years later, the Admiralty decided to set up a cookery course at Haslar to improve the sick diet afloat; the medical director-general, James Dick, and one of the Lords of the Admiralty agreed that this would be appropriate for sick-berth staff with more advanced skills. If possible, the course should be open to ships' cooks as well as to those onshore at the time, and enquiries were made to the National Training School of Cookery about sending teachers to advise on the curriculum.

Clarke, as superintendent of the school, first sent staff to investigate the cooking system aboard HM ships and then discussed the scheme with Clark. Since it would be difficult to adapt the training given to the London Hospital nurses for the needs of sick-berth staff, she recommended that the men should have plain cookery lessons in advance. After trials conducted for 36 pupils, these lessons were extended from three to four weeks. It was then planned to extend the lessons to the Royal Naval Hospital at Plymouth in 1903.[32] The higher rating of instructor on cookery was also established in 1895, which meant that proper instruction by the navy itself now became available; Sergeant Major John Laverty, army instructor in cooking from Aldershot, was now replaced by M. Thomas Wyatt, chief cook of the Royal Navy. Communication between the National Training School of Cookery and the Admiralty continued thereafter and, to maintain the quality of hospital catering, in 1903 the cookery teacher at Haslar Hospital was ordered to be inspected for her efficiency.[33]

The introduction of a training course for naval medical officers in 1881 increased the attention paid to maintaining sanitary conditions on board ships and to hygienic checks on food supplies, especially overseas. This began with the establishment of the training school at Haslar; officers had earlier attended the army course at Netley hospital. Making Haslar a medical centre for the navy would obviously benefit sick-berth staff training. Special knowledge among medical officers was necessary for the service – as Porter mentioned in 1891. When there was a danger from the shore water supply he had proposed replacing the water distiller on board and mentioned the oily and unpalatable water produced from the ship's inadequate type of distiller. However, even though he was a medical officer with training in food hygiene, he complained that the captain and officers never sought his opinion.[34]

Porter's comment shows how slow was the progress made in accepting professional knowledge, even when medical officers were authorities in this field. Nonetheless, such training for medical officers continued. In 1899 new subjects were added for those who worked on foreign stations, while lectures on local diseases, bacteriology and food and water analysis were adopted for those ashore.[35] Patrick Manson, medical adviser to the Colonial Office and physician of the Royal Albert Dock Hospital, described the course on tropical diseases in his neighbourhood to the 1899 committee. He recommended using a branch of the *Dreadnought* seamen's hospital at Greenwich (the Royal Albert Dock Hospital), which had a useful attachment to the new school of tropical medicine, for conducting the special training on naval hygiene and analysis.[36]

Along with these reforms in training medical officers and nursing staff, a significant change occurred in the recruitment of sick-berth staff. Before the 1899 committee met, Robert Grant, deputy inspector-general at the Royal Naval Hospital, Chatham, had commented to the medical director-general, Sir Henry Norbury, that if payment for sick-berth staff could be raised to two shillings a day it would be possible to recruit better educated candidates. By this time, sisters were already instructing probational sick-berth staff in all branches of practical nursing. Miss Louisa Hogg, head sister at Haslar, explained that the instruction given to staff in the medical and surgical wards was almost the same as the practical instruction given to probational nurses.[37] At the time of the 1884 committee, sick-berth recruits had frequently been boys with a basic training in seamanship from the Greenwich Hospital School or training ships. In 1889 men from the Royal Marines and civilians were introduced and after 1893 most of the candidates were civilians. Yet, even though staff numbers doubled between 1884 and 1899, from fewer than 300 to more than 700, their payment and prospects remained the same. The 1899 committee on training medical staff proposed lowering the age range of entry from the present 21–25 to 18–22.[38] By the beginning of the twentieth century, naval sick-berth staff had gradually become more professional and had secured a more skilled status. An important element of their enhanced skill was their knowledge of cookery.

Cookery reform for seamen and in the sick berth after 1900

From 1890 onwards, the navy and merchant seamen were provided with extra cookery instruction, especially the latter whose welfare had been attracting public attention. The Royal Navy had recorded considerable progress since 1873, with better hospital catering and, since the 1880s, supported by sick-berth staff tutored by the National Training School of Cookery. Further instruction for sick cookery was arranged from 1894 and after the foundation of more cookery schools in 1902. The committee on naval cookery that met in 1905 could be seen as marking a milestone for systematic cookery and for reform of victualling in the early twentieth century. Alongside these reforms, two committees were formed, in 1901 and 1907, to oversee the navy's canteen system. The navy tried to raise the level of the men's welfare both by supplying them with better rations and by paying attention to general victualling and hospital care for the sick.

Although general attention to naval health and hygiene continued to concentrate on ventilation, supplies and moderate exercise on board, the main change at this time was that ships' cooks gained professional recognition. On board, the men no longer cooked for themselves and it was now expected that professional cooks would prepare their food. Though the canteen committee still seemed concerned about supplies, there was no doubt that properly trained chefs maintained hygienic conditions at sea. Unlike the army's policy of self-catering by soldiers when overseas, to which medical officers had paid much attention in the late nineteenth century, the navy had switched from self-catering via the mess to professional catering by ships' cooks — albeit with a slight fear that by altering the system the seamen might lose some of their abilities and self-reliance. However, as a number of experiences proved, crews welcomed the more hygienic diet.

The Portsmouth cookery school reported successful results in 1901 from its 97 entries for training in 1900 (of which 63 were for cooks' mates). The chief cook acted as an instructor and provided training ranging from introducing pupils to the ship's galley through to cooking meals for the men. To provide opportunities for training at all ports, two more schools for ships' cooks were planned for Chatham and Devonport. This would make each port more self-supporting in cooks' training, for it was necessary to increase the number of cooks as a preparation for any war. It was planned to train them in the galley to cook plain food and bake bread. Issuing a handbook was considered and supplying copies of the Army School of Cookery's manual on military cooking was also suggested.[39]

Compared with cooks' training in the merchant service, both for the benefit of seamen and as a necessity for passengers, the Royal Navy's training should be seen as part of medical reform rather than general welfare. The two services, however, were influenced by each other and by increasing interest in public health and sanitation in the 1890s. Indeed, even before cookery classes for merchant seamen became popular in Liverpool in 1891, Dr William Spooner had questioned dietary scales in connection with the health of seamen at the naval and military hygiene section of the seventh International Congress of Hygiene and Demography held in London that August. He complained that the merchant seamen's general diet still contained too much salt meat and too few vegetables to maintain the men's health on board: the shipowners should add extras like vegetables or oatmeal even though they were not compulsory under Board of Trade regulations. Inevitably, it was difficult to maintain a check on how generous and medically acceptable any diet given to seamen was at that time.[40] Nonetheless, around this period victualling and provision for men at sea was under closer scrutiny.

In 1894 medical officers Collingridge from the port of London and Henry Armstrong from the River Tyne port authority delivered speeches on hygiene and reforms on merchant ships, which, from a public health, diet and cookery angle, the service badly needed. Collingridge mentioned there were 250,000 men in the merchant service, which meant a lot of health checks for officers to make on board. Even though there was a diet scale regulated by law, he argued that feeding men was still not properly controlled. It was necessary to establish cookery schools at every large port where seamen could learn skills before going on board. He also said that it made good economic sense to employ cooks on ships to preserve the crew's health. Armstrong pointed out that ship hygiene was a serious international issue to be considered by all nations. He urged that certified cooks be employed on every ship and that the Local Government Board rather than the Board of Trade supervise sanitary arrangements for mercantile ships, for the former would understand local conditions and problems better.[41]

These comments supported the opinions expressed by nautical cookery schools in such places as Liverpool, London and North Shields . Although merchant ships' cooks were regulated from 1906, until that time seamen generally claimed that 'anyone can cook' and were not interested in this skilled position. One witness, Miss Effie Bell, superintendent of the nautical cookery school in North Shields, reported this view to the Mercantile Marine's 1903 committee.[42] However, the position of cook became more respectable and skilled, as it had in the Royal Navy. Although the aims of each service were different, merchant seamen could become the naval reserve. This meant that the Admiralty had to keep an eye on their strength and health as part of the progress in naval and maritime hygiene designed to improve all sanitary matters at sea.

There was an interesting reference to supply differences between Royal Navy vessels and ocean liners, as a category of merchant ships. The 1901 navy canteen committee report referred to supplying butter and cheese to ocean steamship companies as being ideal. As civilian bodies, the companies had no traditional system of 'savings' as in the navy; also, they could manage their supplies better because they would be consumed by men with settled sailing routes who worked at regular intervals. They did not have to carry large stores in case of alternative destinations, which was common for voyages aboard warships. The big difference with ocean liners was that they had enough space for refrigerators and other appliances for preserving fresh supplies.[43] To overcome this, the canteen committee expected the navy to be as self-supporting as possible when it was abroad. As a result, medical officers were required to inspect food using the food analysis skills they had learnt in their training. To provide suitable food to keep the men in 'a fit state of health', either in peace or war, it became important to consider whether the standard of living of new recruits had risen. This would ensure that the victualling system was providing appropriate quality and variety.[44] Communication with civilian trades working in similar conditions again might provide fresh information on better victualling in the navy.

The Admiralty therefore set up the committee of naval cookery in 1905. After that, collaboration with the National Training School of Cookery for the further instruction of petty officers (as the 1884 committee had expected for sick-berth staff), cooks and sick-berth staff took place. It was part of general training, though it could be categorized also as an educational training to create professionals in the navy. The evidence to this committee threw up the following five points to be solved: general cookery arrangements afloat, organization of schools of cookery, pay and advancement for cooks' ratings, cookery appliances afloat and bread-making afloat. Improving storage using cold chambers in the modern steam navy was also considered, for that allowed smaller amounts of salted and preserved food compared with fresh provisions.

According to the 1905 report, cooks' training improved after the savings committee had drawn attention to their lack of ability in 1870 and following the commencement of the school of cookery at Portsmouth three years later; their systematic training, and that of ratings, clearly showed up in the good enough results to create 'the present class of well-trained competent' ships' cooks. However, untrained cooks still existed and because of them the traditional view persisted that the average seaman could cook better than a naval cook and that specialist cooks were of less value than a cook of the mess with no cookery training but familiar with the old custom of savings. Nonetheless, leaving the ration provided under the savings system and purchasing tinned food from the canteen was felt to be 'less wholesome'.[45] It was time therefore to consider again whether the cookery training and trials conducted among themselves, rather than those run by the National Training School of Cookery, were effective.

With a view to bringing about further improvement, the National Training School of Cookery agreed to examine the navy cooks and between 1905 and 1907 experiments on ships were also undertaken. These proved that trained cooks not only invariably provided better meals but that they were also more hygienic; also, the boys on ships showed greater strength when provided with better cookery.[46] Since cookery arrangements afloat clearly required reform, the committee considered three methods. The first idea was for the ship's company to prepare meals under the supervision of the ship's cook. This was dismissed on the grounds that the men's inadequate knowledge and extra duties would make it a health hazard. The next idea was to send all newly recruited men for cookery training. This might be an ideal solution, following the Crimean experience, but impractical over such a short period of training. Among 40 boys who had just enrolled at the Portsmouth cookery school only two had any knowledge of cookery and that was only because one was from a bakery and the other had worked in the chief petty officer's mess during convalescence; possibly some of them received a little training while they were training-ship boys, though clearly not enough for this special type of work. The third idea, which was eventually adopted, was to increase the cookery staff of each ship so they would not need to ask any assistance from the men while preparing meals.[47] This meant that naval cooks must be more professional than before and the large divergence from the army on this point started at this time. Sanitary problems on ships were, however, greatly reduced once the general health of seamen was managed by a centralized cookery system that was suited to the accommodation available aboard the ship.

Reforms were based on successful experiments on seagoing ships as well as on work conducted at the school of cookery at Portsmouth. As for experimental results, HMS *Narcissus* reported that the selected cook prepared palatable food with less waste and that a good cooking outcome was agreed throughout the mess. The report did caution that if this scheme were applied to the whole service there would be a danger that 'the seamen will lose all knowledge of preparing dinners and consequently lose some of the readiness of resource for which they are famous.' On this point, however, the committee concluded that the men's knowledge was so elementary that they could not possibly suffer any disadvantage; if required, it would be possible later to provide voluntary classes for men on ships along the lines of those at home ports. Cooks would be included as members of landing parties or of a naval brigade to support the company.[48]

To support training and a good standard of cookery on all vessels, the committee proposed compiling a handbook; this was because only newly-entered seamen went to established cookery schools, whereas all naval cooks on seagoing ships would in the future be expected to bake bread. The manual on naval cookery contained instructions for cooking in the galley and recipes based on rations; information about butchering meat would also be made available in the handbook, which it was planned to supply to all ships. After being first proposed in

1901 (when more cookery schools were established) and again at the 1905 committee, the *Handbook of Naval Cookery* was eventually published in 1914. It contained recipes for general meals and light dishes for convalescents, the latter being especially suitable for preparing on board ship. It contained many of the recipes taught to sick-berth staff, such as egg dishes, gruels and several broths or refreshments.[49] Not surprisingly, training was becoming more detailed.

After the 1905 committee, the director of victualling, William Greene, suggested further experiments to the treasury in September 1907. These were designed to improve the standard of cookery in the Royal Navy and involved experimental trials on ten ships – *King Edward VII, Cornwallis, Venerable, Carnarvon, Drake, Good Hope, Euryalus, Grafton, Endymion* and *Theseus* – and reports showed successful results. Greene also mentioned installing baking ovens on ships, which he felt would make a cook's rating and payment more attractive. Financial support for training officers and men was likewise essential. The commanding officers of the ships explained that introducing a new system to provide well-cooked food by skilled men 'under clean and hygienic conditions' was effective for 'not only the greater contentment and comfort, but also to the better health of the crews of His Majesty's Ships'.[50]

Support from the National Training School of Cookery was not limited to cooks' training: they also accepted three fleet paymasters, including a member of the 1905 committee. Fleet Paymaster Ernest Silk attended the course at the school and obtained information on training seamen. Margaret Pillow examined three officers, three cookery instructors and two ships' cooks. The cookery instructors were especially satisfactory. The ships' cooks also did well, demonstrating both their regular duties and how they prepared meals for large numbers of men. They were quite skilful and could use tinned and preserved food effectively.[51] After this, specialist sea cooks could receive instruction at the school on request. Even so, to control the untrained cooks who had entered the service before 1873, the committee should perhaps have been set up a little earlier. The traditional view of the cook of the mess, who, based on savings, might somehow provide better meals than properly trained cooks remained strong. If universal understanding of the value of trained cooks could be conveyed to the whole service, the benefit would reach the men more easily; it required a committee such as this to emphasize the usefulness of proper training through evidence from ships.

On behalf of the National Training School of Cookery, Pillow examined three naval officers, three cookery instructors and two ships' cooks in March 1905. For their practical examinations, the candidates were asked to prepare general courses from soups to puddings. Pillow then examined three chief cooks and seven ships' cooks after either eight or four weeks' training, though she commented that none fell below 80 per cent on the whole set of marks, so qualified for the school's first-class certificate. The men worked very satisfactorily in the time allowed – neatly, cleanly and quickly. They were given examination menus requiring verbal assessments by each candidate. The main difference was that the chief cooks also had to prepare a range of sickroom cookery to include beef tea, cauliflower mould or baked custard, along with the general course menus, while only beef tea was requested from the ships' cooks for this examination.[52]

Pillow produced a special report on the preserved and dried vegetables provided in ships' kitchens. It contained detailed remarks about every vegetable commonly used on board, including their nutritional values, general usage and most suitable cooking method. She analysed potatoes, shredded beans, haricot beans, compressed mixed vegetables, compressed carrots and onions, cabbage, loose and compressed spinach, and dried onions and peas. Some lacked a fresh taste, though by preparing them carefully they could be useful ingredients for soups and stews. Beans especially, which were very good in quality and valuable for the men's diet, and haricot beans were well understood from long experience as valuable sources of nitrogenous food. However, Pillow also recommended that the school teach cooks some better ways to prepare dried peas. She concluded her report by saying that the men examined showed good results and that they displayed a very good attitude in the kitchen, adding that there was probably a teacher at the navy cookery school who provided excellent instruction for the men.[53] From professional assessment and examination the Admiralty could be assured that the skill of its cooks had been independently proved by an outside body. They could provide a nutrious diet using naval supplies.

These actions by the 1905 naval cookery committee were followed by further experiments and the training of staff became standard practice. During his tenure as medical director-general, Porter extended the reforms of the 1880s and 1890s, including that of nursing by sick-berth staff. Although the introduction of advanced training for these men was an educational activity, it differed from the training given to female nursing sisters in the hospitals and in the Queen Alexandra's Royal Naval Nursing Service established in 1902. Sick-berth staff consisted only of male nurses and Porter's reforms turned this branch into a more professional group. His efforts to raise the profile of all medically-related work in the navy were to be found in various areas: for example, introducing a first aid course from the St John Ambulance Association for the men, establishing a new naval medical school for medical officers that would increase opportunities to research into tropical diseases (as part of the collaboration with the Royal Albert Dock Hospital suggested in 1899), and issuing the *Journal of the Royal Naval Medical Service*.[54] Among Porter's several reforms, those for sick-berth staff had the greatest link with civilian society.

After his retirement Porter spoke about the changes made in hospital provisioning and claimed that the men in the Royal Navy were in better health than in any other navy at the time. Despite a long tradition of salt meat rations and 'biscuits with maggots', it had improved significantly during Porter's career in the service. He spoke about hospital catering in the navy from the point of view of a medical professional and claimed that the food served to patients was carefully prepared to make it appetizing. He also mentioned that feeding arrangements and patient care at naval hospitals should be of the highest standard and that the instruction of sick-berth staff had shown highly satisfactory results alongside the reorganization of the female nursing service. The women who supervised male nurses instructed them practically, tended severe cases and became widely known for their specialism.[55]

As an example of Porter's influence on hospital food, a letter from Surgeon Donald Hoskyn at Haulbowline Naval Hospital near Cork refers to the new diet table Porter revised in April 1908. At that small hospital Hoskyn explained how patients now consumed the reduced portions at meals economically and without the large waste as before; a smaller and reduced richness of the rice pudding was also effective. Cheese issued with bread and butter for supper and chocolate were considered ideal for men doing no work. There was only one cook, though his work was very satisfactory. He had been an admiral's chef and could prepare several small dishes that were suitable for the captain who was convalescing from a gastric ulcer.[56]

As a young ship's surgeon in the 1880s Porter had recognized the poor quality and low status of sick-berth staff when one marine, ordered to help in the sickbay, engaged in other work aboard such as polishing the brass. In 1900 Porter was glad to hear that the medical department had decided to warrant sick-berth staff as petty officers.[57] Providing better nursing care was discussed in Porter's time at the 1909 naval medical service committee when, finally, the service tried to bring qualifications and training into line with what had been suggested at the 1884 and 1899 committees. This had not been done before because more consideration needed to be given to payment, physical standards and more advanced training. In addition, this 1909 committee required training in sickroom cookery, both at an advanced level and as part of the systematic training for overall nursing. Sick-berth ratings now had six months' training as probationers at Haslar Hospital before going on board. They learnt anatomy, physiology, first aid, nursing, dispensary work, cooking and ward work from sisters, followed by two weeks of physical training under an instructor. A woman from the National Training School of Cookery much expanded the instruction in sickroom cookery and it now ranged from a basic sickroom diet, such as beef tea or egg flip, to convalescent dishes of meat, fish and vegetables. It continued for three weeks. Sisters also instructed them on cooking jellies, custards, junkets and peptonizing milk for the sick, along with practical nursing skills.[58]

Porter also contacted the National Training School of Cookery about sick-berth staff training and, after that, the Admiralty asked the school to instruct two or three paymasters a month. Silk became responsible for matters related to this at the Admiralty. Under this scheme, 20 paymasters were sent to the school for four weeks of training between July 1909 and July 1910; two ships' cooks also sent during the same period had a six- or eight-week course. They were among 683 civilian pupils who attended short courses or evening classes at the school. Some paymasters did not train seriously and caused trouble in 1911.[59] Even so, the navy was clearly interested in training officers for victualling for both healthy men and the sick under treatment. Although the navy could train cooks by providing opportunities for officers to run their own course in the service, the training at the National School of Cookery remained valuable.

Lückes, still matron of the London Hospital, supported Porter's nursing reforms as a civilian adviser. The committee in charge of ordering, receiving, issuing and accounting for food supplies or other connected stores at the naval hospitals at Haslar, Plymouth and Chatham in 1910 received information about the catering system at the London Hospital, which was yet another influence on the navy medical service brought about by Porter's connection with Lückes. Porter later explained to the First Sea Lord that he had contacted Sydney Holland at the London Hospital to ask Lückes about the reorganization of naval nursing around 1908–9; this had both improved the Queen Alexandra's Royal Naval Nursing Service and influenced the reserve nursing staff for possible war service. Lückes had advised Porter that obtaining ladies with the best nursing qualifications would be necessary for a high standard of management and nursing care.[60] For war service, Porter was trying to establish a naval nursing reserve and while most civil hospitals were supportive not all matrons agreed with him. The support of King's College Hospital for supplying nurses for his scheme was the strongest. Applications from nurses greatly increased from 1911.[61] At Haslar Hospital there were disagreements between nursing sisters and other hospital staff about regulations. Lückes visited and became involved, though Porter did not always accept her opinions.[62]

This 1910 hospital stores committee set out to alter the rather vague system of food supply, which was different in each establishment. It clarified not only what provisions were valuable for patients but also how to serve them in appetizing ways – the latter was now held to be an important factor in helping sick men recover their health and in preventing the large amount of waste arising from unappetizing looking dishes. It was proposed that issuing a bread-cutting machine to each ward would reduce the waste of bread and that the London Hospital's delivery system of meals to the wards should be followed, whereby on leaving the kitchen hot water jackets and hot plates were used to keep the cooked dishes hot. If this were introduced to the naval hospitals it would reduce complaints: meals would admittedly be served warm, not hot – but warm was better than cold. Haslar already tried to deliver meals in good condition, especially after the refurbishment of its kitchen, though the London Hospital system was to be adopted there as well. The freshness of rations such as meat, milk and bread was to be checked and tested more frequently. Prevention of waste required some alteration in the preparation processes for each meal and, following close inspection of the kitchen at the London Hospital, the use of bones for soups or stock was recommended for naval hospitals. One committee witness, the head sister at Haslar, Miss Evangeline Harte, mentioned that the hospital was run like civilian hospitals; sisters were responsible for food and they checked quantities, ideally in the ward. She pointed out that it was also ideal if sisters had a list of the diets for each ward and prepared the diet sheets with doctors. Served meals were still not hot enough, though better than before. The ward kitchen was used for cooking eggs and cocoa at night.[63]

The London Hospital's steward and matron's assistant had carried out inspections of other infirmaries in 1905 to compare the cleanliness of kitchens and use of new cookery appliances. This was admittedly to help persuade the London Hospital management of these benefits and to provide reasons for new investment in the catering system under the control of the matron's nursing department.[64] Nevertheless, it was very useful for the naval hospitals to have such guidance from the London Hospital. Porter also asked Clarke at the National Training School of Cookery to provide further and extended training for sick-berth staff on sickroom cookery. This commenced in May 1912 and thereafter teachers were sent to the naval hospitals from time to time. The courses at Haslar and Plymouth were extended from three to four weeks and held every quarter; a course was also started at Chatham in June, costing three guineas a week. The financial report of the school that October shows that the tuition fee from the Admiralty was £155 for the three hospitals, which was a great profit for the school.[65] This instruction by the school was obviously an important basis for sickroom cookery training because *The Manual of Sick-berth Staff*, which was published two years later, included about 60 recipes that seemed no different from those for cooks and probationer nurses being trained at civilian hospitals. Such popular sick and convalescent meals as meat dishes (grilled, boiled, roasted and minced) and fish dishes (boiled, steamed and fried), peptonized or albumen milk were also included along with other common refreshments for the sick such as barley water.[66] The navy thus acquired highly skilled sick-berth staff through training under the National Training School of Cookery.

The friendship between Lückes and Porter, which had developed from their shared concern for better nursing and better hospital care, inevitably helped the reform of sick-berth staff. Porter conveyed her ideas on nursing reform to the First Sea Lord, who praised her remarkable personality and said she had achieved perfectly organized nursing, which, he added, would have been impossible for anyone else.[67] The 1911 regulations for Queen Alexandra's Royal Naval Nursing Service stipulated that ladies must be between 25 and 35 years' old and be properly trained. Sisters' status and payment were fixed; furthermore, nurses' responsibilities for ward work were to be the same as at civilian hospitals, namely maintaining the cleanliness of patients and preparing their diet and extras under orders from medical officers. Regarding handling patients, dressings, dispensary, diets and sickroom cookery, sisters, under a head or superintendent sister, assisted in providing practical nursing training for sick-berth staff.[68]

Lückes undoubtedly suggested introducing civilian-style nursing and hospital management, especially with respect to food supply, to the navy medical service, just as Nightingale had done for army sanitary reform half a century earlier. Several of the new systematic nursing methods that Lückes introduced for her nurses at the London Hospital were revolutionary: for example, the sickroom cookery training commenced in 1893 was soon recognized as a standard training for nurses and adopted by many nursing schools. It suited the new nursing requirements of the late nineteenth century based on Nightingale's foundational theory of nursing. Porter understood her systematized method as ideal for the instruction of sick-berth staff. It was adaptable for the naval medical service, which, although a special organization, paid great attention to the better welfare of its men and undertook extensive healthcare. Through his plans for advanced instruction and training for sick-berth staff, their status, welfare and comfort at work were much altered. This was acknowledged by the sick-berth staff themselves, as George Wilsmore, the head wardmaster at Haslar, indicated when Porter retired.[69]

His reforms notwithstanding, during his time as medical director-general, Porter had to recruit more medical officers because their numbers were dwindling. In addition, to acquaint naval medical officers with developments in tropical medicine since the late nineteenth century for service overseas, as part of their postgraduate instruction Porter worked to establish the new naval medical school at Greenwich, which had been mooted since 1899. Even though there was a course at Haslar to prepare medical officers for sea service, the demands of maintaining hygienic conditions on ships were always increasing. Food and water analysis were not taught properly at civilian medical schools, so while obviously any training in these was useful, further knowledge was certainly required. Because medical officers in the navy mainly had to work as 'sanitarians' to prevent disease, in 1899 it was suggested they attend the tropical medical school in the Royal Albert Dock Hospital. Since it was recognized as essential to have such extended instruction for naval medicine it was later planned to attach a naval medical school to the Royal Naval College to provide training in tropical medicine and naval hygiene, clinical pathology and bacteriology for five to six months. Because the navy had shore establishments all over the world, naval medical officers' duties now included sanitary care on land. Supervising food supplies was therefore necessary to avoid turning food and water into vehicles for spreading diseases, in conjunction with a number of other sanitary matters for the 'wellbeing of the men'.[70] These further tasks for medical officers led eventually to the establishment of the school at Greenwich in 1912.

Meanwhile, better organized nursing by sick-berth staff helped to achieve satisfactory care at hospitals and on hospital ships. The 1914 manual for sick-berth staff indicated that they undertook the sanitary arrangements necessary for camps if they became members of landing parties. There were many things to do: daily supervision of water and disinfectants, care of latrines and refuse, construction of places for washing and waste water disposal, and care of sanitation at cooking sites and in slaughter houses.[71] One effect of introducing systematic instruction is found in a recollection by W. Swalies, who had joined the navy as a steward in 1892 and then transferred to the sick-berth branch. He recalled that once when he was aboard a warship overseas a young assistant surgeon tried to supply fresh vegetables for the crew in the tropics by growing marrowfat peas using a wet blanket.[72] Surgeon Commander Christian Hamilton had successfully grown marrowfat peas on board, which made it possible to supply vegetables, during a shortage, served boiled. It was more palatable than the usual cooking method of peas.[73] Swalies's remark at least showed how both medical and sick-berth staff understood that having enough vegetables prevented scurvy.

Nursing training, including sick cookery, was of great advantage to sick-berth staff for the hygiene regime that now supported the medical officers' work: as with ships' cooks, practical training based on specific duties was of benefit to other men. Porter's contribution to the naval medical service was spelt out when, as chairman of the naval and military section, he referred to his detailed attention to the whole branch of naval hygiene and organization at the 75th annual meeting of the British Medical Association in 1907. He stated that a 'military doctor has to be an expert adviser'. Porter's influence in medical matters was always liberal.[74] He considered the naval medical service to be a professional medical organization, not only a military support, and he believed in educating professional men for the service.

Progress in naval hygiene thus professionalized the positions of cook and sick-berth staff. Traditionally, these jobs had been carried out by untrained and unskilled pensioners, men disabled by injuries and so unfit for normal service, or boys of weak physique who had just entered the service and knew nothing about life at sea. Although training-ship boys still had many opportunities to join the service in the 1900s, the training courses had by then begun to educate them professionally and the character of the position had changed. Their professionalism helped them maintain a high standard throughout the navy and its benefits gradually became apparent even in the merchant service. Advanced medical research into how to overcome whatever epidemics or common diseases might occur at overseas ports or on the ship had a further impact on the seamen's daily duties and long-term cleaning techniques. Teaching boys from a young age about how to prevent food-related diseases and ensuring that cooks and ships' officers could properly organize and check the supplies reinforced this trend. The National Training School of Cookery courses worked effectively from the perspective of everybody who had any dealings with food – whether they were officers, ships' cooks or sick-berth staff. Although the navy initially adopted its cooks' training from the army, it later tried to adapt it to its own service through a number of experiments ranging from Warren's pot to the establishment of schools of cookery for specially skilled cooks. Sick-berth staff then had the benefit of learning sickroom cooking from the civilian nursing training that Porter instigated and Lückes supported.

To achieve its systematized medical service the Royal Navy had to pay attention to cookery. Cooking involved more than just adopting a new technology for preserving food. In civil society the two generally progressed separately, but the navy operated as a self-contained unit. The research reports of medical officers concerned with food indicate that the theory of preventing food-related disease, in conjunction with naval hygiene, was introduced into the navy in the mid-nineteenth century and that this allowed naval hygiene to develop as a branch of public health alongside sick-berth reform and further instruction for medical officers. Even so, in 1907 Major Robert Blackham of the Royal Army Medical Corps compared the hygienic training in the navy unfavourably with that in the army at the time. He observed that although the navy's strict sanitary standards were obviously suitable for service at sea, more instruction on hygiene should be provided in the event of their men joining a landing party.[75] The navy eventually achieved this through instructing men in special branches.

As a publicly funded service it was also possible for the navy to introduce the latest inventions and technology for the men's welfare. One great virtue of the navy was that it always tried to maintain the highest standard of cleanliness and even if the men did not have much idea about hygiene or sanitation, cleanliness was regulated throughout the service. It was important to deliver medical knowledge to the men in accessible forms – such as enforcing daily habits in the hope of turning them into common sense, consistent with the principles of a seaman's healthy life. It seems there was no doubt that if young boys learnt these during their training period they would have become unquestioned habits by the time they had grown up or even left the service – practical understanding was highly effective for health and the service was an ideal opportunity for such practical training. Wide connections with the civilian world likewise provided great benefit to the naval medical service, which had a high reputation among the public. For instance, Warren's pot became a general slow-cooking appliance for making nutritious meals. Trained sick-berth staff would likely always find employment and even if they left the service they could continue their professional work under the aegis of the army and navy male nurses' cooperation.

It is possible to say therefore that the navy's contribution to the health of British society was important and contributed to a better understanding of basic ideas about cooking food and personal clean-liness that everyone could adopt. No doubt joining the navy provided opportunities for boys and men to learn about cookery and healthcare that were generally unavailable in civilian life; this was both through general training for the sea and by way of specific services that had educational aspects and, for some positions, professional training. In turn, professionally skilled men such as medical officers, sick-berth staff and cooks had an educational influence throughout the Royal Navy and increasingly in every aspect of its organization.

Conclusion

The late nineteenth and early twentieth centuries witnessed great advances in urban sanitation, with increased attention paid to providing elementary health instruction to the less privileged members of society. This was highly visible in cookery and domestic economy education, which aimed to bring identifiable improvements to people's daily lives. Unless this basic knowledge could be delivered, little would change and scientific research findings would fail to benefit the lives of ordinary people. Through analysing different areas and institutions, evidence emerges of the effective contribution of cookery training to this process. In particular, the efforts of professionals in nursing and in the armed services were influential with women instructors contributing significantly to progress in the broad area of health. The armed forces realized the importance of cookery and cooking instruction even before it was adopted in school education: indeed, both the army and navy conducted their own reforms. This study has been of such trends in Britain. In some instances, however, these trends were spread worldwide.

Although the men and women professionals who contributed to these activities did not usually initiate or play a leading part in the health legislation governments introduced, their perspective was not limited to their individual work. Records show that in trying to improve people's lives by introducing them to the importance of cookery they had a broad understanding of such reforms. There was an exchange of professional knowledge and experience between organizations, whether civilian or military. Married and unmarried women worked as cookery specialists and frequently there were no boundaries between the men and women who worked as professionals, for they all realized the need for reform through cookery and cooking instruction. Their work might be defined as having a grassroots character; their contribution was to fill the gap between medical science, governmental reforms and general progress in the community. They encouraged attention to cookery as the foundation for a healthier society and eventually made its benefits felt throughout.

Of course, in the context of governmentally organized sanitary reforms such as water and drainage systems, cookery was only one solution to the nation's health problems and it is impossible to determine whether it was the most influential. It is not possible even to judge whether it was the main influence in the declining death rate among the young, for cookery does not always appear in the statistics. The navy, for instance, while listing gunners and carpenters before 1914, did not distinguish cooks from other able seamen. The Board of Education only began to keep a card index of domestic subject teachers in 1906 and even this remained unreliable until 1911.[1] Therefore, it is difficult to set up specific dates from which to compare statistical information on cookery teachers, nurses and cooks in either the army or navy. Figures vary depending on the organization and do not cover the whole period (c.1860 to c.1914). It is possible to say, though, that the early twentieth century was a period when the skills and knowledge of cookery specialists were given a specific value and this was linked to their improved status in various organizations.

For schools, cookery teachers were lumped in among teachers of domestic subjects and were not identified in the annual educational statistics for public elementary schoolteachers – especially if they were only engaged in teaching 'special subjects'. Even when the statistics showed the number of certified teachers, they did not indicate whether or not they were actually employed.[2] In any case, not all newly-qualified teachers of domestic subjects from training schools were employed at elementary schools; there were not only insufficient vacancies for them but also some would teach at secondary schools or technical institutes. Others, of course, would marry and enter private life. There are some statistics on teachers of domestic subjects employed at elementary schools in 1906–12, which had a bearing on the reform of their training. On average 292 new graduates qualified each year and the total employed was 1424 in 1906–7; this increased annually to reach a total of 2153 by 1911–12.[3]

Of course there were differences between regions: for example, in 1912 there were 450 domestic subject teachers in London but only 36 in the northeast division.[4] Even so, compared with the figure Calder quoted to the Cross Commission in 1887 this was a large increase: she claimed that only 175 teachers from the Northern Union of Schools of Cookery at that time were properly qualified to work in England – an average, she suggested, of between ten and twenty schools per teacher.[5]

The number of hospital nursing staff and probationers who had sickroom cookery training at the London Hospital shows a similar trend, although, of course, not all of them regularly cooked sick diets at hospitals or in patients' homes as district or private nurses. In 1896 there were 158 (57 staff and 101 probationers), rising to 181 (25 staff and 156 probationers) in 1904. There were about 20,000 British nurses in 1892–93. In that context, therefore, it was not a dramatic increase.[6] In the trials started at the London Hospital, however, the number of new nurses with a distinctive understanding of the importance of cookery for nursing was maintained, which obviously opened a new field for women as dietitians.

In the Royal Navy, in the 1870s cooks and cooks' mates were included in the ranks of able, ordinary or second-class seamen. Later they were grouped among miscellaneous ratings or domestics. Generally, the only cooks appearing in the annual naval estimates were in temporary positions or cookery instructors. Nevertheless, there was a constant increase, along with plans to recruit more cooks and cooks' mates, following satisfactory experiments on boys' strength and regarding preparations for war. The 1905 naval cookery committee effectively established a 'cook' and 'instructor' status, while other records show the increasing number of cooks with training at the navy school of cookery. In January 1873, 12 cooks were ready for the navy's new system. Training for five cooks and eight cooks' mates was reported in 1874 and one report in the following year said that 12 men were being trained as cooks' mates. In 1895 the rating of instructor of cookery was established and there were cases of promotion for ten ships' cooks, 21 second ships' cooks and 19 cooks' mates.[7]

The navy suffered from a shortage of ratings of domestics,

including cooks, and considered abolishing this general title to attract recruits for the cookery branch with an additional allowance; indeed, cooks' mates were gradually increased from 67 men in 1903/4 to 124 in 1906/7 with a view to trying to fulfil the target of 340 for this rank. To expand the service both for peace and war and, of course, to cover the annual wastage of ratings, increasing the number of recruits was planned. Newly-entered cooks could receive instruction at three navy cookery schools from 1902 onwards: in 1904/5 there were 785 cooks, rising to 880 in September 1906, with a net increase of 100 men a year. In 1907, 919 cooks were in service and it was planned to have 1336 for war and 1293 in peacetime.[8] Cookery instructors had the rank of warrant officer in 1910 when three were appointed after experiments in cookery in 1907 showed better health and comfort among crews.[9] Navy cooks were finally recognized as essential and reliable professionals for the service.

The same is evident from the army's records. Because cooks were distributed among regiments their actual numbers remain unclear. In the statistics, though, the number of instructors at the Army School of Cookery was recorded separately. From 1887 onwards, a cookery superintendent was appointed as a warrant officer with three cookery instructors. Formerly, in the 1870s and 1880s, there had been only one instructor with one assistant.[10] In 1915, after the outbreak of war, it was planned to obtain 8000 cooks, for every 100,000 men needed 800 cooks. The army school yielded about 200 annual 'graduates', so it was necessary to meet the number by producing 80 cooks a fortnight (it would otherwise take four years to produce 8000 cooks). The importance of cooks for the army depended on their ability to use rations satisfactorily and to reduce unnecessary waste.[11]

As shown above, the purely statistical records relating to cookery do not obviously clarify its influence; they mainly indicate the gradual increase of professionals in this field who were recognized for their special knowledge across society. But, as a supportive factor for health improvements, the influence of cookery was arguably unique. Even if it did not play the leading part in health reform, it was a vital agent for translating medical knowledge into common sense. Progress in medical research on food-related disease and the transmission of disease via food consumption could not be delivered to large numbers of people without support from educational activity. Cookery instruction conveyed information via such forms as sickroom cookery and military cooking, and could combine it with instruction on personal hygiene. Prior to and during the development period of dietetics such ideas and methods were new to medicine. They should be recognized as a major innovation contributing to better health and sanitation across modern British society.

Cookery instruction at elementary schools took off in the 1880s. The subject was amenable to simple manual training while compulsory elementary education now provided the opportunity for children to learn the principles of health. Girls at poor law schools were perhaps the most obvious beneficiaries. The girls in one residential domestic training class in the metropolitan union had a particularly successful experience when they played out the roles in turn of cook, house and parlour maid, and general servant. When a girl was on duty as a cook she would purchase goods at the local shops and thereby learn the basic bookkeeping skills required for the homes in which they would either live or be employed. This method had both educational and technical objectives, for it targeted girls to become respectable adults in the future. As this example proved, cookery instruction was regarded as a key element in social improvement.

Women professionals in cookery education like Calder, and Henry Williams, a working-class witness at the Cross Commission in 1887, also demonstrated this point. Williams took an interest in his children's education and sent them to the Home and Colonial School in Gray's Inn Road, central London. He was pleased that his daughter could cook meals at home and discuss her cookery lessons. Indeed, many working-class parents welcomed cookery lessons for their daughters. Furthermore, Calder said that many doctors praised instruction in sickroom cookery and believed that it was more useful for common people than medicine. As these opinions suggest, knowledge of cookery delivered through education began to alter ordinary people's lives. Booth found that London schoolgirls often cooked meals for their families and imparted their knowledge about cleanliness and sanitation in kitchen work. It showed that cookery education was a successful agent for raising the standard of living. Girls' cleanliness, as reported by HMIs, was reinforced through habitual instruction to keep tidy and clean before cooking. Their experiences of making their own aprons in needlework classes and washing them in laundry lessons further encouraged hygienic habits.[12]

The introduction of mothercare instruction and school health inspections in the early twentieth century changed the character of cookery education and, for many contemporaries, diminished the status of cookery training. Unsurprisingly, though the Board of Education strongly encouraged the formation of a school medical service, its educational influence on children was nevertheless vague.[13] Medical officers were good at combating diseases, but they could not work in the same way as cookery teachers who had been trained how to instruct children. Although the instruction such teachers delivered was more relevant to people's daily lives, they came to be seen as non-medical amateurs, while medical doctors took the lead in controlling schoolchildren's health and physiques.

But cookery teachers were less useless at educating young girls about health as it sometimes suited the medical profession to claim. One district nurse mentioned how easily nurses could instruct a girl at home who could recall her knowledge from school.[14] The largest hazard facing cookery and health education for children was often the condition of their homes, which they could do nothing about. Without installing new cooking facilities or a bath, it was not always possible for the children to introduce their parents to what they had learnt at school. The instruction in schools might well be good, but, as the Ladies' Sanitary Association remarked in 1891, it took a long time for the information really to reach every household. As an organization that targeted the wider public, the association preferred to promote mothercare training rather than 'sowing sanitary seed' through instruction on cookery or needlework.[15] Sowing 'seed' via cookery at schools nevertheless was effective in expanding an interest in public health because, as Fanny Calder claimed, cookery was widely recognized as the ideal subject for promoting knowledge and values beneficial for raising living standards. Calder observed that even very poor people usually purchased rather than made their own clothes. With cookery, however, they could not take such a shortcut: food bought from shops could make people full but could not improve their health unless chosen with care, while the process of preparing food required self-control on hygiene, which was learnt from cookery instruction. Ella Pycroft likewise observed how instruction in cookery and related areas of domestic economy provided permanent benefit for people's everyday lives.[16]

Witnesses in London referred to the benefit ordinary people gained from cookery education. Mrs L. Humm, headmistress of Cook's Ground Council School, Chelsea, explained convincingly to the 1906 medical inspection and feeding committee why teaching domestic economy should be promoted much more. She stressed that through cookery lessons girls could learn how to prepare economical dishes and shopping skills. Furthermore, domestic economy schools after elementary school were beneficial because for some poor girls they would extend opportunities for education supported by scholarships. She pointed out that cookery classes in London helped the whole family. For example, an older sister who had cookery lessons had made the family's life healthier and her influence was apparent in her younger sibling.[17] Even if the influence on family life was not immediate, the knowledge obtained from cookery and domestic economy education could and would have long-term advantages.

Cookery instruction for nurses clearly affected the progress of medical care and dietetics and no one represented this movement more than Eva Lückes. Cookery teachers delivered sickroom cookery instruction to nurses smoothly and an understanding of the nutritive value of food and its preparation in a suitable form for each patient strengthened nursing skills. Sickroom cookery by nurses was an important medical treatment, especially for food-related diseases like diabetes. Research on food and diet by medical doctors like Hutchison strengthened the educational character of cookery instruction and provided a link between school education and instruction for specialists. Instruction and knowledge of sickroom cookery among nurses had a direct effect in that they could carry it out in practice. Sickroom cookery was not therefore something to be understood just for future use – unlike some cookery lessons in school, which could be a problem when educating inattentive schoolgirls.

The experience of teaching nurses also influenced cookery schools and their teachers in that they improved their instruction methods. Cookery books on diet were developed, while cooking methods and information about ingredients became more detailed. Of course, the readership was limited to wealthier households where books would reinforce a general understanding of cleanliness and sanitation. The poor had to rely on district nursing for sick care and cookery instruction as part of their general healthcare. Nurses did translate medical and scientific knowledge on sick diet, nutrition and hygiene into words that poor patients and their families would understand. Their contribution to improving people's health in civilian society was thus widely diffused. More specialized support by nurses, however, was found in military service, especially following its nursing reforms.

Unlike girls, only boys who lived in specific areas close to sea ports had cookery lessons at elementary school; also, most boys spent their lives differently from girls, not regularly attached to domestic duties. Booth described the typical lifestyle of working-class boys: soon after finishing school aged 13 or 14 they became money earners for the family. Younger boys handed their wages to their mothers and were sent out to work with food from home. Others would purchase food outside the home or lodge out by themselves, where they were usually charged for basic cooking and washing. Either way, the additional food and drink the boys consumed would be from cookshops or restaurants, and if a boy lived away from home he often had to find food to be cooked at his lodging.[18] There was no guarantee they could cook, select suitable food or keep their clothes clean unless they had some knowledge from school or some experience through helping their mothers or sisters at home. An analysis of healthcare in military service shows that men's knowledge of and attention to these matters developed throughout their career. It affected the broad area of health and sanitation from nursing to cooking, for both sick and healthy men. Progress in all areas was seen after the Crimean War. Advances in cookery and knowledge of hygiene among men cannot be discerned from analysing only civilian history.

It took many years to organize all reforms and to put them into practice. In the British Army the nutritional value of the ration was considered seriously. Instruction about army cookery commenced, first from hospital catering in 1860 and then at the first cookery school in Aldershot. The effectiveness of this cookery reform in the army should not be recognized only via the decrease in death rates from preventable diseases. Its value was confirmed by reforms within other armed forces. This was so in the Royal Navy and, internationally, in the Japanese navy and in the United States' army and navy. Other armed forces soon recognized the beneficial effects of cookery and healthcare education as significant advances for military medicine.[19]

The British Army's annual medical reports showed better trends in food consumption alongside overall health improvement among the men. In addition to the establishment of cookery schools, the idea of replacing native cooks overseas and using soldiers to cook and to prepare better cookhouses was successful in preventing enteric fever. The method of self-cooking allowed men to eat with reduced risk from local diseases. It encouraged hygienic food handling, which was linked to the introduction of personal cleanliness. The army was also keen to work out a new supply system. Baking was a major advance since the Crimean War and men even built bread baking ovens at campsites. The quality of the army ration in the late nineteenth century was judged to be as good as that of the navy, as Porter had mentioned with regard to the naval brigade in South Africa.[20]

In the Royal Navy medical knowledge relating to healthcare among seamen was delivered through training from a young age and supported by experiments conducted by medical officers. Advances in scientific research were usually soon introduced into the service. The problem of feeding men properly was approached from two angles: setting up an instruction scheme for cooks and concern about rations. Even before the establishment of the navy's school of cookery there were successful results from the naval brigade's cooking in the Crimea in 1854. The Admiralty also recognized the medical benefits of replacing the old cooks of the mess with trained cooks. Serious attention was paid to food and sanitation in the navy as both affected men's health in often cramped working environments. Introducing improved cookery systems and training was recognized as important. Surgeon William Smart later referred to the well-organized cookery among sailors during their time in the Black Sea. Knowledge of cookery saved men from irregular and unsatisfactory meals and kept them in good spirit, as was seen when they offered cups of cocoa to nearby army and navy officers and soldiers in the batteries before Sebastopol. This is evidence, perhaps, of another real contribution of cookery training to social improvement; a similar effect could be seen in poor people's homes from cookery by district nurses and instruction given to their daughters at school. Better meals could provide direct mental and physical comfort and raise the quality of life.

But more than that, boys under training actually showed better growth patterns because of improved cookery. Again, this illustrates the effectiveness of cooking and cookery education, for the young boys required sufficient food to grow up strong enough to become naval recruits. The Greenwich Hospital School therefore continued with its cookery and dining reforms designed to stimulate the boys' appetites and by 1882 the boys had become stouter and healthier. A similar improvement was reported among 700 boys at the *St Vincent*'s shore establishment where the cooks in charge provided them with fresh vegetables daily. As a result, in nine months the boys put on eight or ten pounds in weight and grew two to three inches taller. Trained cooks conducted several more experiments on board after the committee of naval cookery's 1905 meeting. The cooks could provide more hygienic and better prepared food and the boys duly put on weight. By increasing its trained cookery staff the navy became more confident about maintaining health by using a cookery system on board ship that was best suited to naval accommodation.[21] Naval medical officers proved that, through their fitness and growth, fully-accommodated navy boys really benefited from improvements in cookery. It was more difficult to judge the influence of cookery and health education on girls at elementary schools because their diet at home and after school hours was less easily observed.

Cookery, as an essential part of healthcare, also underwent far-reaching reforms in military hospitals. Generally, though, civilian hospitals had a wider influence in society because of the district and private nursing they provided. One clear area of progress came via sickroom cookery at civilian hospitals where the emergence of dietitians opened up a new area of medical treatment. It is possible, therefore, to say that sickroom cookery altered the relationship between patients and medical specialists, allowing the latter to enter more into the former's daily lives, which might hold the reasons for illness, perhaps due to the lack of sanitation at home or an insufficient knowledge of hygiene. Cookery training, both through its daily immediacy and when connected to medical treatment, delivered a variety of useful skills to both sick and healthy people: and dietitians, who became the new professionals in cookery and health instruction after the First World War, commended it.

Dietitians began this work from the 1920s onwards. In 1924, for instance, a discussion at the British Medical Association focused on the connection between diet and public health. In this period of progress for dietetics, food education was recognized as vital for a healthy population. William Savage, medical officer of health for Somerset, proposed using diet control as an instrument for better public health. It was already proved that mothers and infants enjoyed better health from proper feeding, that tuberculosis could be caused by lack of nutrition, and that well-fed people could better combat bacterial diseases. Above all, however, Savage emphasized the importance of knowledge. Such ideas had already been mentioned in earlier studies, including those by Booth and Rowntree, and research on the labouring classes' diet conducted by the physiology department of Glasgow University in 1913 concluded that better health would be slowly achieved as a result of proper teaching and training on cookery and food at schools.[22] Progress in nutritional science in the interwar period became more widely disseminated with the growing popularity of new nutritional knowledge, for example with the discovery of vitamins. Therefore, interest in food consumption shifted from just eating enough to choosing a suitable quality of diet; the Medical Research Council led this trend. Furthermore, international scientific research paid more attention to nutrition. One nutritional physiologist, John Boyd Orr, produced a significant dietary analysis in 1936 showing that only half of Britain's population had a good enough diet to maintain their health.[23] Of course, better healthcare was developing from the focus on cookery as a part of education. However, in 1937 Rose Simmonds, a former dietitian at the London Hospital, went further, urging that the treatment of diabetic patients necessarily involved considering their personal circumstances because the economic status of the family largely affected the diet treatment.[24]

In many ways the dietitian's role remained similar to that of the district or private nurse who had so frequently tried to alter the eating and hygiene habits of patients through their instruction. Ruth Pybus, who was appointed sister dietitian of the Royal Infirmary, Edinburgh, in 1924 also highlighted this continuing educational function. In a lecture to medical students in 1942, she pointed out how educating the general public about cookery would make them healthier and went on to discuss her findings on inspecting outpatients' records. Pybus instructed patients when they were ill, but the real problem was that they were not taught how to eat to stay healthy. As late as the Second World War, then, Pybus argued that better health was not dependent on the amount of food one ate: the key was knowledge of cookery. She accepted that good diet was not the only thing; however, she claimed that it would make a greater difference than any other factor. Generally, she asserted, poverty was the main cause of malnutrition even though, during the war, the government controlled the price of food and, in such circumstances, poverty was not recognized as the problem because rationing could provide basic food. Even if poverty were the main reason for malnutrition in peacetime, the problem did not end there. Pybus claimed that people's ignorance, laziness and food prejudices also caused the problem. 'It is not only in the poorest homes that dietary errors are to be found. Careless buying, bad cooking, and a total ignorance of food values can prove almost as disastrous as an inadequate income.' Some of Pybus's outpatients even suffered from scurvy. Some single women did not prepare meals for themselves because of laziness and did not wish to wash vegetables for the purpose. More cookery education must therefore be provided for the young. Cookery teaching had to change its target to make it more popular. The people who really needed the instruction did not always have the opportunity to learn it.[25]

All this was reminiscent of an earlier era. Pybus demonstrated most clearly the long-term problem of poor health caused by lack of knowledge. As a professional dietitian, she concluded that cookery education still had the capacity to alter people's lives. This was more than half a century after cookery instruction had been introduced at elementary schools and about a century after medical officers in the armed forces had been alerted to the need to protect men's health by focusing on cooking. Many efforts had since been made to deliver medical and scientific knowledge through cookery and cooking instruction and it had undoubtedly played a major role in public health improvement in its broadest sense. Such work had started following Nightingale's experience in the Crimea. According to Pybus, with Britain once again at war, the work of previous generations was still unfinished.

Notes

Introduction

1. Teaching at the School began in 1874. Helen Sillitoe, *A History of the Teaching of Domestic Subjects* (London, 1933, reprint 1966); Dorothy Stone, *The National: The Story of the Pioneer College, the National Training College of Domestic Subjects* (London, 1966) pp. 29–30. The National Training School of Cookery was renamed in 1931. For the Army and the Navy, see pp. 57–62, 94–9; Ailsa Yoxall, *A History of the Teaching of Domestic Economy: Written for the Association of Teachers of Domestic Subjects in Great Britain* (London, 1913, reprint 1965) p. 50.

2. Emily Briggs, 'Cookery', in Thomas Alfred Spalding, *The Work of the London School Board* (London, 1900) p. 227; Sir John Lubbock, *Addresses, Political and Educational* (London, 1879) pp. 74–5.

3. June Purvis, 'Domestic subjects since 1870', in Ivor F. Goodson (ed.) *Social Histories of the Secondary Curriculum: Subjects for Study* (London, 1985) p. 146.

4. For example, Lee Holcombe, *Victorian Ladies at Work: Middle-Class Working Women in England and Wales 1850–1914* (London, 1973) pp. 62–3; Annmarie Turnbull, 'An isolated missionary: the domestic subjects teacher in England, 1870–1914', *Women's History Review*, 3 (1994) pp. 81–100.

5. Nancy L. Blakestad, 'King's College of Household and Social Science and the origins of dietetics education', in David F. Smith (ed.) *Nutrition in Britain: Science, Scientists and Politics in the Twentieth Century* (London, 1997) pp. 75–98; Lynn K. Nyhart, 'Home economists in the hospital, 1900–1930', in Sarah Stage and Virginia B. Vincenti (eds) *Rethinking Home Economics: Women and the History of a Profession* (Ithaca, 1997) pp. 125–44.

6. Martha Vicinus, *Independent Women: Work and Community for Single Women 1850–1920* (London, 1985) pp. 211–46.

7. F. B. Smith, *The People's Health 1830–1910* (London, 1979); Anthony S. Wohl, *Endangered Lives: Public Health in Victorian Britain* (Cambridge, 1983). For the contribution made by scientists to public health policy through the improved purity of water and better knowledge of diseases, see Christopher Hamlin, *A Science of Impurity: Water Analysis in Nineteenth Century Britain* (Bristol, 1990).

8. George Barnsby, 'The standard of living in the Black Country during the nineteenth century', *Economic History Review*, 2nd series, 24 (1971) pp. 221–2, 233; Wohl, *Endangered Lives*, pp. 44–5.

9. Anne Hardy, *Health and Medicine in Britain since 1860* (Basingstoke, 2001) p. 29.

10. David McLean, *Public Health and Politics in the Age of Reform: Cholera, the State and the Royal Navy in Victorian Britain* (London, 2006) pp. 1–9.

11. Robert Millward and Sally Sheard, 'The urban fiscal problem, 1870–1914: government expenditure and finance in England and Wales', *Economic History Review*, 2nd series, 48 (1995) pp. 501–3, 526; J. A. Yelling, *Slums and Slum Clearance in Victorian London* (London, 1986) pp. 12–13; Also, E. H. Gibson, 'Baths and washhouses in the English public health agitation, 1839–48', *Journal of the History of Medicine and Allied Sciences*, IX (1954) pp. 392–3; Sally Sheard, 'Profit is a dirty word: the development of public baths and wash-houses in Britain 1847–1915', *Social History of Medicine*, 13 (2000) pp. 63–85.

12. Frances Bell and Robert Millward, 'Public health expenditures and mortality in England and Wales, 1870–1914', *Continuity and Change*, 13 (1998) pp. 225–6; Derek Matthews, 'Laissez-faire and the London gas industry in the nineteenth century: another look', *Economic History Review*, 2nd series, 39 (1986) p. 246.

13. *Longman's 'Ship' Series, Domestic Economy Readers*, Book 2 (London, 1900) pp. 88–92; Betty McNamee, 'Trends in meat consumption', in T. Barker, J. McKenzie and J. Yudkin (eds) *Our Changing Fare* (London, 1966) pp. 76–93; Derek J. Oddy, *From Plain Fare to Fusion Food: British Diet from the 1890s to the 1990s* (Woodbridge, Suffolk 2003) pp. 41–70.

14. John Burnett, *Plenty and Want: A Social History of Food in England from 1815 to the Present* (London, 1966); John Burnett, 'Trends in bread consumption', in T. Barker, J. McKenzie and J. Yudkin (eds) *Our Changing Fare* (London, 1966) pp. 61–75; Derek J. Oddy, 'Working-class diets in late nineteenth-century Britain', *Economic History Review*, 2nd series, 23 (1970) pp. 314–23; Derek J. Oddy, 'Food, drink and nutrition', in F. M. L. Thompson (ed.) *The Cambridge Social History of Britain 1750–1950* (Cambridge, 1990) II, pp. 251–78. For working-class women and food, see Joan Perkin, *Women and Marriage in Nineteenth-Century England* (London, 1989) pp. 143–55.

15. Kenneth J. Carpenter, *Protein and Energy: A Study of Changing Ideas in Nutrition* (Cambridge, 1994) pp. 46–8, 59–69, 103–24.

16. Roderick Floud, Kenneth Wachter and Annabel Gregory, *Height, Health and History: Nutritional Status in the United Kingdom, 1750–1930* (Cambridge, 1990) pp. 27–8, 286–7, 326–7.

17. Thomas McKeown, *The Modern Rise of Population* (London, 1976) pp. 42–3, 92, 127–9, 159.

18. Third annual report of the Local Government Board, 1873–74, Parliamentary Accounts and Papers (PP) XXV (1874) pp. 247–60; Report of the Inter-Departmental Committee on Medical Inspection and Feeding of Children attending Public Elementary School, PP XLVII (1906) (hereafter Report of Medical Inspection and Feeding Committee) II, pp. 203–4.

19. Simon Szreter, 'The importance of social intervention in Britain's mortality decline c.1850–1914: a re-interpretation of the role of public health', *Social History of Medicine*, 1 (1988) pp. 1–37.
20. P. J. Atkins, 'Sophistication detected: or, the adulteration of the milk supply, 1850–1914', *Social History*, 16 (1991) pp. 317–39; Michael French and Jim Phillips, *Cheated not Poisoned? Food Regulation in the United Kingdom, 1875–1938* (Manchester, 2000) pp. 33–65; Anne Hardy, 'Exorcizing Molly Malone: typhoid and shellfish consumption in urban Britain 1860–1960', *History Workshop Journal*, 55 (2003) pp. 73–90; Jim Phillips and Michael French, 'Adulteration and food law, 1899–1939', *Twentieth Century British History*, 9 (1998) pp. 350–69; Keir Waddington, '"Unfit for human consumption": tuberculosis and the problem of infected meat in late Victorian Britain', *Bulletin of the History of Medicine*, 77 (2003) pp. 636–61; Wohl, *Endangered Lives*, pp. 48–54. Even the legislation regulating the sale of food and the inspection system regarding food-poisoning bacteria could prove ineffective because it did not prevent unhygienic food handling. Educating the public about this at schools and in organizations such as the armed forces was also not always satisfactory because too often washbasins were not attached to lavatories. Unhygienic habits thereby continued into the interwar years and even into the late twentieth century. See Anne Hardy, 'Food, hygiene, and the laboratory: a short history of food poisoning in Britain, circa 1850–1950', *Social History of Medicine*, 12 (1999) pp. 302–7.
21. Matthew Hilton, '"Tabs", "fags" and the "boy labour problem" in late Victorian and Edwardian Britain', *Journal of Social History*, 28 (1995) pp. 587–607; Matthew Hilton, 'Retailing history as economic and cultural history: strategies of survival by specialist tobacconists in the mass market', *Business History*, 40 (1998) pp. 115–37; Matthew Hilton and Simon Nightingale, '"A microbe of the devil's own make": religion and science in the British anti-tobacco movement, 1853–1908', in Stephen Lock, *Ashes to Ashes: The History of Smoking and Health*, Symposium and Witness Seminar Organized by the Wellcome Institute for the History of Medicine and the History of Twentieth Century Medicine Group on 26–27 April 1995 (Amsterdam, 1998) pp. 41–77.
22. P. H. Colomb, *Memoirs of Admiral the Right Honourable Sir Astley Cooper Key* (London, 1898) pp. 92–9, Key to his mother, 23 April 1844.

Chapter 1
1. Isabella Beeton, *Beeton's Book of Household Management* (London, 1861); Perkin, *Women and Marriage*, pp. 247–8; Alexis Soyer, *Soyer's Charitable Cookery: Or the Poor Man's Regenerator* (London, 1848).
2. Arthur Church, *Food: Some Accounts of its Source, Constituents and Uses* (London,

1880, new edition); W. T. Greenup, *Food and its Preparation* (London, 1878); Henry Letheby, *On Food* (London, 1872); F. W. Pavy, *A Treatise on Food and Dietetics, Physiology, and Therapeutically Considered* (London, 1874); Edward Smith, *Practical Dietary for Families, Schools and the Labouring Classes* (London, 1864); W. B. Tegetmeier, *Manual of Domestic Economy* (London, 1875); W. B. Tegetmeier, *The Scholars' Handbook of Household Management and Cookery* (London, 1876). Information is from 'The Sixth Annual Report of the Executive Committee of the National Training School for Cookery for the year ending 31 March 1879', pp. 10–13, Ministry of Education Records, National Archives (NA) London, ED 164/1; The Report of the Northern Union of Schools of Cookery for 1878, F. L. Calder College of Domestic Science Records (Calder Archives) Liverpool John Moores University, Liverpool.

3. For example, Phillis Browne, *The Girls Own Cookery Book* (London, 1882); J. Loveday, *First Course of Cookery Lessons, for Use in Elementary Schools* (London, 1893); Catherine Ryan, *Convalescent Cookery: A Family Handbook* (London, 1881).

4. Mrs Pember Reeves, *Round About a Pound a Week* (London, 1913) pp. 56–9.

5. Anon., *The Report of the Ladies' Sanitary Association to the Seventh International Congress of Hygiene and Demography* (London, 1891) pp. 9–10.

6. Rose Adams, 'The work of the Ladies' Sanitary Association', in *Report of the Congress on Domestic Economy to be taught as a branch of General Education, Birmingham, 1877* (Birmingham, 1877) (hereafter *Domestic Economy Congress Birmingham*) p. 47; Anon., 'Preface', *Birmingham Health Lectures* (Birmingham, 1883); Teachers from the Edinburgh School of Cookery and Domestic Science, 'Sick-room food and cookery', in Edinburgh Health Society, *Health Lectures for the People*, 6th series (Edinburgh, 1886) pp. 121–30.

7. Arthur Gamge, 'Food and body energy', in *Health Lectures for the People*, 4th series (Manchester, 1881) pp. 122–3; John Newton 'Heating, lighting and ventilation', in *Health Lectures for the People*, 8th series (Manchester, 1886) pp. 141–2; Arthur Ransome, 'Soils and sites', in *Health Lectures for the People*, 8th series (Manchester, 1886) pp. 3–6; Arthur Ransome, 'On diet', *Health Lectures for the People*, 9th series (Manchester, 1886) p. 12; Arthur Ransome, 'The money value of health', in *Health Lectures for the People*, 11th series (Manchester, 1887) p. 6; Henry Simpson, 'The dwelling-house in relation to health', in *Health Lectures for the People*, 1st series (Manchester, 1878) p. 115.

8. Arthur Ransome, 'Cleanliness', in *Health Lectures for the People*, 4th series (Manchester, 1881) pp. 8–9.

9. John Taham, 'Special dangers to health in large towns', in *Health Lectures for the People*, 3rd series (Manchester, 1880) pp. 110–11.

10. Henry Ashby, 'Food: quantity – quality – cooking-hours', in *Health Lectures for the People*, 4th series (Manchester, 1881) pp. 23–4.

220   NOTES

11. Philip Birch, 'The food of the household: its bearing on health and disease', in *Health Lectures for the People*, 6th series (Manchester, 1885) pp. 17, 25–6, 33.

12. Revd G. W. Reynolds, 'Thrift: its bearing on health and disease', in *Health Lectures for the People*, 6th series (Manchester, 1885) pp. 117–18; and Henry Simpson, 'Cookery for the household', in *Health Lectures for the People*, 6th series (Manchester, 1885) pp. 137–8, 142.

13. John Priestley, 'The preparation of food', in *Health Lectures for the People*, 9th series (Manchester, 1886) pp. 108–9; John Priestly, 'Diet in relation to disease', in *Health Lectures for the People*, 10th series (Manchester, 1887) p. 137.

14. William M. Maccall, 'The influence of education on health', in *Health Lectures for the People*, 10th series (Manchester, 1887) pp. 97, 102–3.

15. Henry Simpson, 'The care of health in maturity and middle age', in *Health Lectures for the People*, 11th series (Manchester, 1888) p. 121.

16. Alfred H. Carter, 'Facts about food and feeding', in *Birmingham Health Lectures*, 1st series (Birmingham, 1883) pp. 47, 56–7.

17. Elizabeth Bonython and Anthony Burton, *The Great Exhibitor: The Life and Work of Henry Cole* (London, 2003) pp. 6, 269–72.

18. Guthrie Wright, 'The art of preparing food: its place in general education', in *Domestic Economy Congress Birmingham* (Birmingham, 1877) pp. 64–5. At Newcastle 900 people attended classes for artisans and in other places attendance ranged from 500 to 700.

19. Lydia Becker, 'On the teaching of domestic economy in elementary schools', *Report of Second Yearly Congress on Domestic Economy and Elementary Education, Manchester, 1878* (Manchester, 1878) (hereafter *Domestic Economy Congress Manchester*) p. 20.

20. Revd Charles H. Collyns, 'Food and cookery in relation to teaching concerning the same in elementary schools', *Domestic Economy Congress Manchester* (Manchester, 1878) pp. 62–4.

21. Patricia Hollis, *Ladies Elect: Women in English Local Government 1865–1914* (Oxford, 1987) pp. 88–94, 115–25, 144, 151–3, 177, 184, 187–8; Jane Martin, *Women and the Politics of Schooling in Victorian and Edwardian England* (London, 1999) pp. 71–91.

22. For example, Catherine Buckton, *Food and Home Cookery* (Leeds, 1883).

23. 'Miss Margaret Scott interview', *Woman's Herald*, 28 March 1891, Margaret Pillow Papers, Women's Library, London, 7/MEP/2/3; Scott's lecture drafts for Richmond and Petersham Sanitary Association, 7/MEP/1/3; collection of Scott's articles on health and domestic sanitation published in *Women's Help Society* in 1896, 7/MEP/2/5. Margaret Scott, 'Women's work in promoting the cause of hygiene', in *Transactions of the Seventh International Congress of Hygiene and Demography, London, August 10–17th, 1891* (London, 1892) IX, pp. 242–6.

24. Edward Pillow was one of the witnesses as director of the Technical Instruction Committee of the County Council of Norfolk, before the Royal Commission on Secondary Education, PP XLIV (1895) pp. 395, 418–19.

25. Rosemary O'Day and David Englander, *Mr Charles Booth's Inquiry: Life and Labour of the People in London Reconsidered* (London, 1993) pp. 44–5, 58.

26. Sillitoe, *A History of the Teaching of Domestic Subjects*, pp. 111–12.

27. Joyce Goodman, 'Women school board members and women school managers: the structuring of educational authority in Manchester and Liverpool, 1870–1903', in Joyce Goodman and Sylvia Harrop (eds) *Women, Educational Policy-Making and Administration in England: Authoritative Women since 1880* (London, 2000) pp. 59–77; Margaret Simey, *Charitable Effort in Liverpool in the Nineteenth Century* (Liverpool, 1951) pp. 36, 125–6. An Irish woman, Kitty Wilkinson, voluntarily started washhouses in Liverpool and the Rathbones supported her. See Herbert Rathbone, *Memoir of Kitty Wilkinson of Liverpool 1781–1860* (Liverpool, 1927) pp. 31–2, 57–8, 63–6. See also F. L. Calder and E. E. Mann, *A Teachers' Manual of Elementary Laundry Work* (London, 1891).

28. *The Times*, 18 August 1875; Second Report of the Royal Commission appointed to enquire into the working of the Elementary Education Acts, England and Wales, PP XXIX (1887) (hereafter Second Report of the Cross Commission) p. 480.

29. Mrs Fenwick, 'On the practical teaching of domestic economy in elementary schools', in *Domestic Economy Congress Birmingham* (Birmingham, 1877) pp. 65, 67; and Wright, 'The art of preparing food'. In Pycroft, 'Technical classes under county councils in London', in National Union of Women Workers, *Women Workers: The Official Report of the Conference held at Nottingham, on 22, 23, 24 & 25 October 1895* (London, 1895) pp. 13–14, Catherine Buckton referred to instructors by saying that anyone who had experience could teach, although this was not commonly agreed.

30. Christina de Bellaigue, 'The development of teaching as a profession for women before 1870', *Historical Journal*, 44 (2001) pp. 965–71; Frances Widdowson, *Going up into the Next Class: Women and Elementary Teacher Training, 1840–1914* (London, 1983) pp. 14–16.

31. A Somerset Rector, and Assistant Diocesan Inspector of Schools, *Cookery Classes in National Schools. With Practical Directions How to Form Them, Founded on Experience Gained in a Country District* (London, 1880) p. 19; Dina M. Copelman, *London's Women Teachers: Gender, Class and Feminism 1870–1930* (London, 1996) pp. 75–6; Holcombe, *Victorian Ladies at Work*, p. 79; Honnor Morten, 'Nursing as a profession for women', *The Young Woman*, 1 (1892–93) pp. 120–1. At the end of the article she nonetheless stressed the importance of this occupation and gave advice to young readers looking for suitable chances and ways of entering the profession. Technical Education Board, London County Council,

Minutes of Proceedings (hereafter TEB Minutes) 3 July 1893, London Metropolitan Archives (LMA) London.

32. Florence Baddeley, 'Technical work under the county council', in National Union of Women Workers, *Women Workers: The Official Report of the Conference held at Nottingham on 22, 23, 24 & 25 October 1895*, pp. 15–22. For Baddeley, see also *Gloucestershire Chronicle*, 3 November 1923, Gloucestershire Training College of Domestic Science Records, Gloucestershire Record Office (GRO) Gloucester, K/1372; Pycroft, 'Technical classes under county councils in London', pp. 7–14.

33. National Union of Women Workers, *Women Workers: The Official Report of the Conference held at Nottingham on 22, 23, 24 & 25 October 1895* (London, 1895) pp. 37–8.

34. On the sanitary inspector's training, see Roy Acheson 'The British diploma in public health: birth and adolescence', in Elizabeth Fee and Roy Acheson (eds) *A History of Education in Public Health: Health that Mocks the Doctors' Rules* (Oxford, 1991) pp. 44–82; A Lady Inspector, *How to Become a Lady Sanitary Inspector* (London, c.1900); Edith Maynard, *Women in the Public Health Service* (London, 1915); Ministry of Health Records, NA, MH 26/1.

35. Report of the Board of Education for 1909–10 (hereafter Education Report) PP XVI (1911) p. 112. By 1909–10 cookery schools had mostly been renamed 'domestic subjects' schools.

36. Education Report for 1912–13, PP XXV (1914) p. 44.

37. Education Report for 1913–14, PP XVIII (1914–16) pp. 243–4.

38. Margaret Pillow, 'Domestic economy teaching in England', in *Special Reports on Educational Subjects 1896–7*, PP XXV (1897) pp. 162–3; Stone, *The National*, pp. 11–30. In Edinburgh, Christian Guthrie Wright was a leading staff member of the Edinburgh School of Cookery, which, with the support of the local education authorities, was established in 1875 to raise the standard of local women's education. The school contributed to the training of elementary schoolteachers and supplied various public lectures. It also undertook instruction on nursing, more specifically from 1910 onwards. See Tom Begg, *The Excellent Women: The Origins and History of Queen Margaret College* (Edinburgh, 1994) pp. 12, 18–19, 29–30, 57–66, 74–8, 91.

39. On the organization and teachers' training of the Association of Teachers of Domestic Subjects, see Helen Clements, 'The Association of Teachers of Domestic Subjects and the place of domestic science in the school curriculum, 1895–1925' (unpublished M.A. thesis, University of Warwick, 1979); and Yoxall, *A History of the Teaching of Domestic Economy*, pp. 51–6.

40. National Training School for Cookery, Memorandum. Henry Cole to the Executive Committee of the School, 26 November 1873, ED 164/1; Sillitoe, *A History of the Teaching of Domestic Subjects*, pp. 26–31.

41. Rose Owen Cole, *The Official Handbook for the National Training School for Cookery* (London, 1885) pp. 455–6; see also 'The sixth annual report of the National Training School for Cookery for 1879', pp. 10–13, ED 164/1.
42. A Somerset Rector, *Cookery Classes in National Schools*, p. 19 says annual salary would be between £60 and £100 and for three months £25; 'The sixth annual report of the National Training School for Cookery', pp. 18–19, ED 164/1.
43. Regulations for the training of teachers of domestic subjects, PP LXIV (1907) pp. 9–11, 15–16.
44. A. Biggs, 'Domestic economy teaching as a career for women', *Lady's Realm* (1906) pp. 604, 606.
45. Edith Clarke, 'The object and work of the National Training School for Cookery', in *Domestic Economy Congress Birmingham*, p. 63; National Training School for Cookery, Memorandum, ED 164/1.
46. Elizabeth Bird focused on extending the Gloucestershire School of Cookery teaching at the department of Bristol University. See Elizabeth Bird, '"High class cookery": gender, status and domestic subjects, 1890–1930 [1]', *Gender and Education*, 10 (1998) pp. 117–31; Margaret E. Scott, *The History of F. L. Calder College of Domestic Science, 1875–1965* (Liverpool, 1967); Ruth Whitaker, *History of Gloucestershire Training College of Domestic Science* (Gloucester, 1944).
47. Annual reports of the Liverpool Training School of Cookery (hereafter LSC Report) 1880–1915, pp. 3–9. Liverpool Training School of Cookery, Executive Committee Meeting Minutes (hereafter LSC Minutes) 18 December 1879, 8 May 1882, 2 November 1891, 19 February 1894, Calder Archives.
48. LSC Report, 1876–77, p. 9, Calder Archives.
49. LSC Report, 1892, p. 12, Calder Archives.
50. LSC Report, 1893, p. 2, Calder Archives.
51. LSC Report, 1909, p. 7; LSC Minutes, 24 May 1909, Calder Archives.
52. Margaret J. Tuke, *A History of Bedford College for Women 1849–1937* (London, 1939) pp. 232–3, 260–1.
53. LSC Reports for 1881–82, pp. 5–6; for 1893, p. 2; for 1912, p. 7. On emigrants, Report for 1882–83, p. 6 and 1886, p. 3, Calder Archives.
54. LSC Minutes said 2 February 1891, though LSC Report recorded it as 3 February. LSC Minutes, 2 May 1892, 23 May 1892, 14 July 1892, 28 July 1892, 29 August 1892, Calder Archives. Also Scott, *History of Calder College*, pp. 24–5.
55. LSC Minutes, 29 August 1892. Enquiry from London was by Mr Bailey, Seamen's House, London, which conducted the seamen's cookery class. LSC Report for 1892, pp. 8–10. LSC Minutes, 13 March 1893, 10 April 1899, 25 September 1899, 2 October, 1899, Calder Archives; *The Times*, 8 December 1892, 27 January 1893; *The Epicure*, 1 (1894) p. 258.
56. LSC Minutes, 31 October 1892. The training ship *Conway* replied to the school

that it was difficult to carry on the lessons for boys. Minutes, 14 November 1892, 30 January 1893, 6 February 1893, Calder Archives.

57. LSC Minutes, 18 September 1893, Calder Archives.

58. LSC Minutes, 1, 8 and 29 October 1894, Calder Archives.

59. LSC Minutes, 19 May 1895, Calder Archives.

60. LSC Reports for 1893, p. 7; for 1895, pp. 8–9; for 1896, p. 7, Calder Archives.

61. LSC Report for 1897, p. 10, Calder Archives.

62. LSC Report for 1904, pp. 9–10, Calder Archives. On the recognition of cooks on merchant ships, see Sari Mäenpää, 'From pea soup to hors d'oeuvres: the status of the cook on British merchant ships', *The Northern Mariner*, XI (2001) pp. 39–55.

63. LSC Reports for 1911, p. 6; for 1912, p. 7; for 1915, p. 7, Calder Archives. Colonel Alexander conducted a class for 16 men with six weekly lessons during the winter months. Lieutenant-Colonel Stanley's new class comprised eight classes of 20 men in each, held every day for two weeks.

64. Information leaflet, 'The Longfords Eating House (Longfords, 27 January 1885) and Cookery lessons at Longfords House (Tuesday and Wednesday, 20, 21 January 1885, 5.45 p.m.)' K/1372. The Playne family were textile manufacturers in Gloucester. See Barbara Caine, *Destined to be Wives: The Sisters of Beatrice Webb* (Oxford, 1986) pp. 171–6.

65. Extracts from Diaries of Mrs Playne, K/1372.

66. Mary Playne, September 1909, Gloucestershire School of Domestic Science, 'memorandum', K/1372. In 1908, 8172 pupils were taught, of which 5255 were elementary schoolgirls, 2675 adults at evening classes, 81 resident pupils at the Gloucester school, and 161 pupils at Cheltenham.

67. Annual Report of the Gloucestershire School of Cookery and Domestic Economy (hereafter GS Report) for 1914, p. 12; Gloucestershire County Council, Higher Education Subcommittee, Domestic Economy Minor Committee Minutes (hereafter GS Minutes) 21 March 1906, K/1372.

68. GS Reports for 1895, pp. 3–4, 7; for 1896, p. 5; for 1897, pp. 3–4; for 1898, p. 4, K/1372.

69. GS Report, 1899, pp. 3, 6–7, 9, K/1372.

70. GS Reports for 1901–2, p. 4; for 1904–5, p. 9; Gloucestershire School of Domestic Science, Old Girls' Guild Minute, 11 June 1904. Apperley read a paper on domestic science as a preparation for hospital training, K/1372.

71. GS Reports 1899–1913, pp. 3–14, K/1372.

72. GS Reports 1905–11, pp. 10–14, K/1372.

73. GS Report for 1896, pp. 5–6, 8, K/1372.

74. GS Report for 1898, p. 9, K/1372.

75. GS Report for 1901–2, pp. 1, 7, K/1372; Gloucestershire County Council, Annual Report of the late Technical Instruction Committee, 6 July 1903, pp.

93–4, GRO, CE/R2/3/1. Requested by Field-Marshal Sir Evelyn Wood and Colonel Griffin.

76. GS Minutes, 16 December 1914, 17 March 1915, K/1372.
77. Annual Report of the Gloucestershire School of Cookery, Cheltenham Centre, Report, p. 5; GS Report for 1906–07, p. 9, K/1372.
78. Margaret Bryant, *The Unexpected Revolution: A Study in the History of the Education of Women and Girls in the Nineteenth Century* (London, 1979) pp. 114–15; Purvis, 'Domestic subjects since 1870', pp. 156–60 summarizes instruction for middle-class girls.
79. Miss Mitchell, 'The teaching of domestic economy in girls' secondary schools', *Journal of the Society of Arts*, XLV (1897) pp. 952–6; Pillow, 'Domestic economy teaching in England', PP XXV (1897) pp. 181–3, 186.
80. Report of the Consultative Committee of Practical Work in Secondary Schools, PP XX (1913) pp. 304–11.

Chapter 2

1. Anna Davin, *Growing Up Poor: Home, School and Street in London 1870–1914* (London, 1996) pp. 146–53; Carol Dyhouse, *Growing up in Late Victorian and Edwardian England* (London, 1981) pp. 79–114; June Purvis, *A History of Women's Education in England* (Milton Keynes, 1991) pp. 26–9; Annmarie Turnbull, 'Learning her womanly work: the elementary school curriculum, 1870–1914', in Felicity Hunt (ed.) *Lessons for Life: The Schooling of Girls and Women 1850–1950* (Oxford, 1987) pp. 83–99. For discussion on the subject in the twentieth century see Dena Attar, *Wasting Girls' Time: A History and Politics of Home Economics* (London, 1990); and Catherine Manthorpe, 'Science or domestic science? The struggle to define an appropriate science education for girls in early twentieth century England', *History of Education*, 15 (1986) pp. 195–213.
2. For example, Bernard Harris, *The Health of the Schoolchild: A History of the School Medical Service in England and Wales* (Buckingham, 1995) pp. 6–69; J. D. Hirst, 'Public health and public elementary schools', *History of Education*, 20 (1991) pp. 107–18; J. S. Hurt, 'Feeding the hungry schoolchild in the first half of the twentieth century', in Derek J. Oddy and D. Miller (eds) *Diet and Health in Modern Britain* (London, 1985) pp. 178–206.
3. Rosamond Davenport-Hill, 'Cookery teaching under the London School Board', *Macmillan's Magazine*, 1884, reprinted in *Exhibition Cookery Book, Health Exhibition* (London, 1884) pp. 11–12; Mary Davies, 'The teaching of cookery', *Contemporary Review*, 73 (1898) p. 109.
4. Kay-Shuttleworth's career as an educational reformer is most recently examined in R. J. W. Selleck, *James Kay Shuttleworth: Journey of an Outsider*

(London, 1994). See also David McLean, *Education and Empire: Naval Tradition and England's Elite Schooling* (London, 1999); and 'Notes on the introduction and working of the subjects relating to domestic economy in public education, aided by parliamentary votes from 1839 to 1880', Domestic Economy Congress 1881, Royal Society of Arts Archive, PR.GE/121/10/36.

5. Maude Agnes Lawrence, *Special Report on the Teaching of Cookery to Public Elementary School Children in England and Wales* (London, 1907) p. i.

6. Pillow, 'Domestic economy teaching in England', PP XXV (1897) pp. 157–8.

7. William Jolly, *Physical Education and Hygiene in Schools* (London, 1876) p. 20. On HMIs see Nancy Ball, *Her Majesty's Inspectorate, 1839–1849* (London, 1963); and Dennis Lawton and Peter Gordon, *HMI* (London, 1987).

8. Mathias Roth, *On School Hygiene and Scientific Physical Education* (London, 1880) pp. 2, 5, 9; Mathias Roth, *On Scientific Physical Education, and its Practical Introduction into Schools* (London, 1880) pp. 2–4.

9. Report of the Committee of Council on Education, England and Wales for 1884 (hereafter Education Report) PP XXIII (1884–85) p. 135; Report for 1893, PP XXIX (1894) pp. 346–7.

10. H. G. Bowyer, Inspector of Workhouse School, Report for 1876, MH 32/109. Also, Miss Andrews, a Guardian of the Parish of St Pancras, 'The need of domestic economy in bringing up pauper children', *The Schoolmaster*, 25 June 1881, p. 726, Royal Society of Arts Archive, PR.GE/121/10/36.

11. Francis Duke, 'Pauper education', in Derek Fraser (ed.) *The New Poor Law in the Nineteenth Century* (London, 1976) pp. 67–86.

12. Bowyer, Report for 30 August 1862 to Lady Day 1864, on the Parochial Union Schools in the Eastern and Midland Districts, MH 32/108; T. B. Browne, Report on the Parochial Union Schools inspected in the Northern and Western Districts, January 1864, MH 32/108.

13. Edward Tufnell, Report for 1866, MH 32/108; Tufnell, Report for 1868, MH 32/108.

14. A. F. Young and E. T. Ashton, *British Social Work in the Nineteenth Century* (London, 1956) pp. 132–41.

15. Third Annual Report of the Local Government Board, 1873–74, PP XXV (1874) Appendix No. 22, pp. 318–26.

16. Wyndham Holgate, Report for 1875, MH 32/110.

17. Holgate, Report for 1880, MH 32/110.

18. Holgate, Report for 1881, MH 32/110.

19. Miss M. H. Mason, 3 February 1886, 'Boarding Out', MH 32/92.

20. Holgate, Report for 1882, MH 32/112.

21. Holgate, Report for 1886, MH 32/112.

22. Holgate, Report for 1888, MH 32/112.

23. J. R. Mozley, Report for 1887, MH 32/113.

24. Mozley, Report for 1890, MH 32/113.
25. Mozley, Report for 1901, MH 32/113.
26. Tufnell's observations on Senior's report on the education of pauper girls, MH 32/110.
27. Second Report of the Cross Commission, PP XXIX (1887) p. 280; Third Report of the Royal Commission appointed to enquire into the working of the Elementary Education Acts, England and Wales, PP XXX (1887) (hereafter Third Report of the Cross Commission) p. 481.
28. Education Report for 1872–73, PP XXIV (1873) pp. 61–2, 111–12.
29. The Church of Scotland and the counties of Ayr, Bute, Dumfries, Kirkcudbright and Wigtown, in Education Report for 1872–73, PP XXIV (1873) p. 255.
30. Education Report for 1878–79, PP XXIII (1878–79) pp. 632, 764–5.
31. Education Report for 1879–80, PP XXII (1880) pp. 394–5.
32. Joseph Hassell, *Domestic Economy* (London, 1876) p. 3; Joseph Hassell, *Domestic Economy: New Code 1880* (London, n.d.) pp. 1–2; and E. Rice, *Domestic Economy* (London, 1884) pp. 6, 65–6, 121–3, are examples of this.
33. Fanny Calder, 'Practical cookery in elementary schools', *Good Words* (1883) pp. 58–62.
34. Fanny Calder, 'Practical cooking in elementary schools', *The Health Education Literature* (London, 1884) vol. 14, p. 173; Circular 221, Private. Circular to HM Inspectors, Cookery, Education Office, 8 February 1883, F. R. Sandford, ED 142/36.
35. Calder, *Health Education Literature*, pp. 180–1; Edwin Chadwick, 'Sanitation in domestic training', in *Domestic Economy Congress Birmingham*, pp. 49–50.
36. Education Report for 1881–82, PP XXIII (1882) pp. 182, 322–3, 361, 463.
37. Education Report for 1882–83, PP XXV (1883) pp. 257–8, 320–1, 383, 430.
38. Durham District, Education Report for 1883–84, PP XXIV (1884) p. 255.
39. Education Report for 1885–86, PP XXIV (1886) p. 284.
40. Davenport-Hill, 'Cookery teaching under the London School Board', pp. 1–12; Ethel E. Metcalfe, *Memoir of Rosamond Davenport-Hill* (London, 1904) pp. 73, 78; also Second Report of the Cross Commission, PP XXIX (1887) pp. 711,713. Davenport-Hill's work was almost ignored when she joined the cookery committee. There were only 20 centres and in 1882 these were in the experimental stage. Ten years later there were 160. School Board for London, Instruction in Cookery Centres, 1 January 1897, ED 14/37.
41. Education Report for 1885–86, PP XXIV (1886) pp. xx–xxi.
42. Education Report for 1885–86, PP XXIV (1886) pp. 259–60.
43. Ipswich Board, the Eastern Division and Welsh Division, Education Report for 1886–87, PP XXVIII (1887) pp. 309, 359. In Cardiff, for instance, early in 1887, Calder increased girls' attendance at cookery classes from 400 to 600.

44. Third Report of the Cross Commission, PP XXX (1887) pp. 39, 41.
45. Second Report of the Cross Commission, PP XXIX (1887) pp. 479–80, 485; Final Report of the Commissioners appointed to inquire into the Elementary Education Acts, England and Wales, PP XXXV (1888) pp. 142–3.
46. Second Report of the Cross Commission, PP XXIX (1887) p. 749.
47. Third Report of the Cross Commission, PP XXX (1887) p. 227.
48. Second Report of the Cross Commission, PP XXIX (1887) pp. 480, 484.
49. Education Report for 1887–88, PP XXXVIII (1888) pp. 298, 337; Second Report of the Cross Commission, PP XXIX (1887) pp. 710–12.
50. Third Report of the Cross Commission, PP XXX (1887) p. 496; Second Report of the Royal Commissions on Technical Instruction, PP XXXI (1884) pp. 405–6.
51. Issuing grants for cookery classes caused problems of classroom conditions; in one case girls had to stand up for two hours during the demonstration lessons, which caused physical discomfort and made instruction unpopular. Education Report for 1888–89, PP XXIX (1889) pp. 264, 319.
52. Education Report for 1889–90, PP XXVIII (1890) pp. 292, 315–16, 360–1, 371.
53. Fanny Calder, 'Domestic education in elementary schools', *Proceedings of the Literary and Philosophical Society of Liverpool*, XLIII (1888–89) pp. 109–14. Italics are by Calder.

Chapter 3

1. Mary Playne, 'The present position of technical education in domestic science', in *Women in Education, being the transactions of the Education Section of the International Congress of Women* (London, 1900) p. 113.
2. Charles Booth, *Life and Labour of the People in London*, first series, Poverty (1904 edition, first published 1889; this chapter first appeared in the 1891 edition) III, pp. 207, 219–22.
3. Arthur Newsholme, 'The teaching of the laws of health in schools', in *Transactions of the Seventh International Congress of Hygiene and Demography* (London, 1892) IX, pp. 237–41.
4. Arthur Newsholme, 'On the study of hygiene in elementary schools,' *Public Health*, 3 (1890–91) p. 134.
5. John M. Eyler, *Sir Arthur Newsholme and State Medicine, 1885–1935* (Cambridge, 1997) p. 7. Arthur Newsholme's *Hygiene: A manual of Personal and Public Health* (London, 1884) used Edmund Alexander Parkes, *A Manual of Practical Hygiene, Prepared Especially for Use in the Medical Service of the Army* (London, 1864) as a model. He also published a children's handbook, *Lessons for Health* in 1890 (from 1893, *Elementary Hygiene*). *Hygiene*, of which 12,000 copies were printed, was widely circulated.

6. Arthur Newsholme and Margaret Eleanor Scott, *Domestic Economy: Comprising the Laws of Health in their application to Home Life and Work* (London, 1893) pp. v, 102–4, 108–9, 201–2.

7. Lynn McDonald (ed.) *Florence Nightingale on Society and Politics, Philosophy, Science, Education and Literature: Collected Works of Florence Nightingale* (Ontario, 2003) V, pp. 690, 838. Nightingale and Arthur Clough, a poet and a cousin, appointed Burton as first secretary of the Nightingale Fund. Formerly Burton worked at Linton School, Burton-on-Trent, which was twice the size of Lea.

8. Education Report for 1900–01, PP XIX (1901) p. 55.

9. Nightingale to Burton, 7 October 1889. Images provided courtesy of the Clendening History of Medicine Library, Kansas University Medical Center, http://clendening.kume.edu/do/fn/1.burton1.html – 1.burton4.html, 27 October 2005; Nightingale draft [1891], British Library (BL) London, Nightingale Papers, Add.Mss.45811, ff. 17–20.

10. Sir Edward Cook, *The Life of Florence Nightingale* (London, 1913) II, pp. 383–4; Nightingale to Dr William Farr, 13 July 1872, Wellcome Library for the History and Understanding of Medicine, Archives and Manuscripts (Wellcome Library) London, MS 5474/120, MS 5474/121.

11. Nightingale to De'ath, 4 January 1891, 2 January 1892, 20 May 1892, Wellcome Library, MS 5473/1, MS 5473/2, MS 5473/5.

12. Nightingale to Galton, 24 September 1891, Nightingale Papers, Correspondence with Sir Douglas Galton, Add.Mss.45767, ff. 49–50.

13. Nightingale to Frederick Verney, 17 October 1891, in Lynn McDonald (ed.) *Florence Nightingale on Public Health Care: Collected Works of Florence Nightingale* (Ontario, 2004) VI, pp. 587–9.

14. Nightingale to Calder, Nightingale Papers, Add.Mss.45811, f.21 [1891]. LSC Minutes, 9 November 1891; LSC Report for 1892, p. 12, Calder Archives.

15. Nightingale to Calder, 21 November 1892, Calder Archives; Nightingale to Verney, 6 December 1892, in McDonald, *Florence Nightingale on Public Health Care*, VI, p. 596.

16. Fanny Calder, 'Growth and development of domestic science', in Baroness Burdett-Coutts (ed.) *Woman's Mission: A Series of Congress Papers in the Philanthropic Work of Women, by Eminent Writers* (London, 1893) pp. 317–22.

17. Education Report for 1890–91, PP XXVII (1891) p. 348; Report for 1891–92, PP XXVIII (1892) p. 411.

18. Education Report for 1894–95, PP XXVII (1895) pp. 117–18.

19. Education Report for 1891–92, PP XXVIII (1892) pp. 415–29.

20. Education Report for 1892–93, PP XXVI (1893–94) p. 441.

21. Education Report for 1893–94, PP XXIX (1894) pp. 112–13.

22. Education Report for 1896–97, PP XXVI (1897) pp. 184–5.

23. Education Report for 1898–99, PP XX (1899) pp. 295–6.

24. TEB Minutes, 31 July 1893.
25. TEB Minutes, 9 October 1893, 29 June 1896, 6 February 1899, 23 April 1902, 14 January 1903.
26. Ella Pycroft, 'Provision for instruction in domestic economy', February 1894, Technical Education Board Records, LMA, TEB 80/7; Ella Pycroft, 'School of domestic economy for girls', June 1900, TEB 80/8.
27. TEB Minutes, 18 December 1893.
28. Diary of Beatrice Webb, 18 October 1895, typed transcripts, vols 13–16 (1 January 1889–7 March 1898) British Library of Political and Economic Science Archives.
29. Pycroft, 'Technical classes under county councils in London', p. 8.
30. Ibid., pp. 9, 14.
31. Baddeley, 'Technical work under the county council', pp. 15–16; Robert Halstead, 'Some thoughts of a workman concerning the plea for a living wage', *Economic Review*, V (1895) pp. 350–69.
32. National Union of Women Workers, *Women Workers*, pp. 22–8, 35.
33. Pillow, 'Domestic economy teaching in England', PP XXV (1897) pp. 157–86.
34. *British Medical Journal*, 14 February 1914, pp. 262–8.
35. Education Report for 1900–1, PP XIX (1901) pp. 59, 99.
36. General Reports of HM Inspectors of Elementary Schools and Training Colleges for 1901, PP XXV (1902) p. 37.
37. Education Report for 1902–3, PP XXI (1903) pp. 211–12, Report for 1903–4, PP XXV (1905) p. 16.
38. Report of the Inter-Departmental Committee on Physical Deterioration, PP XXXII (1904) (hereafter Report of the Physical Deterioration Committee) pp. 15, 33, 41–3.
39. *British Medical Journal*, 10 December 1904, pp. 1594–5.
40. Report of the Physical Deterioration Committee, PP XXXII (1904) pp. 56, 441–2.
41. Report of the Physical Deterioration Committee, PP XXXII (1904) pp. 42, 251, 255.
42. Report of the Physical Deterioration Committee, PP XXXII (1904) pp. 365, 367.
43. Report of the Physical Deterioration Committee, PP XXXII (1904) pp. 27–8, 35.
44. Report of the Physical Deterioration Committee, PP XXXII (1904) pp. 57, 168, 172, 441.
45. Report of the Physical Deterioration Committee, PP XXXII (1904) pp. 27, 441–2.
46. Report of the Physical Deterioration Committee, PP XXXII (1904) p. 373.
47. Davenport-Hill, 'Cookery teaching under the London School Board', p. 10.
48. Education Report for 1882–83, PP XXV (1883) p. 321; Report for 1885–86, PP XXIV (1886) pp. 284–5.

49. Lord Brabazon, 'Health and physique of our city populations', *Nineteenth Century*, X (1881) pp. 85–6; J. S. Hurt, *Elementary Schooling and the Working Classes 1860–1918* (London, 1979) pp. 101–2.
50. C. S. Loch, 'Cheap dinners for poor school children' (London, ca.1885).
51. School Board for London to Secretary of the Local Government Board, ED 14/24.
52. Education Report for 1890–91, PP XXVII (1891) pp. 369–70.
53. Education Report for 1895–96, PP XXVI (1896) p. 151.
54. Report of Medical Inspection and Feeding Committee, PP XLVII (1906) I, pp. 25–6, 77–8; II, pp. 203–4, 236–8.
55. Report of Medical Inspection and Feeding Committee, PP XLVII (1906) I, pp. 72–3.
56. Report of Medical Inspection and Feeding Committee, PP XLVII (1906) II, pp. 147–50.
57. Robert Blair, 'Preliminary Report', 1905. The five centres selected were: Ackmar Road, Buckingham Street, Columbia Road, Dulwich Hamlet and Old Woolwich Road; Blair to Secretary of the Board of Education, 'School Experiment', 12 January 1906, 27 February 1906, 5 November 1909, ED 14/93.
58. Lawrence, *Special Report on the Teaching of Cookery*, pp. 5–12, 16–17.
59. Report of Medical Inspection and Feeding Committee, PP XLVII (1906) I, p. 7; II, p. 150.
60. Report of Medical Inspection and Feeding Committee, PP XLVII (1906) II, pp. 64, 122–4, 180, 182, 188–9, 227–31.
61. Report on the Working of the Education (Provision of Meals) Act, 1906, PP XXIII (1910) p. 6.
62. Report of Medical Inspection and Feeding Committee, PP XLVII (1906) II, pp. 236–7.
63. Janet Campbell, 'The teaching of physiology and hygiene in the council schools', in *Second International Congress on School Hygiene, London 1907, Transactions* (London, 1908) III, pp. 913–14.
64. Report on the Working of the Education Act, 1906, PP XXIII (1910) pp. 9–12.
65. Annual report for 1908 of the Chief Medical Officer of the Board of Education (hereafter CMO report) PP XXIII (1910) pp. 4, 6–9, 13–15, 42–4, 103–4.
66. CMO report 1910, PP XVII (1911) pp. 236–8; CMO report 1912, PP XXV (1914) p. 17.
67. CMO report 1909, PP XXIII (1910) pp. 28–34; CMO report 1910, PP XVII (1911) pp. 172–3; CMO report 1911, PP XXI (1912–13) p. 155.
68. *British Medical Journal*, 4 September 1907, p. 656.
69. CMO report 1910, PP XVII (1911) pp. 284–5, 289.

70. Anna Davin, 'Imperialism and motherhood', *History Workshop*, V (1978) pp. 9–65.

71. Board of Education, *Some Suggestions for Simple and Nourishing Meals for Home* (London, 1915). This was referred to as Circular 917, and consisted of recipes for enough nourishment even though using less meat, ED 142/44. See also CMO report 1914, PP XVIII (1914–16) pp. 70–5, 211–22.

72. British Medical Association, Report of the Committee on Nutrition, *British Medical Journal Supplement*, 25 November 1933; British Medical Association, *Family Meals and Catering: A Cookery Booklet for Housewives* (London, 1935); Enid Hutchinson, *A History of the British Dietetic Association* (London, 1961) pp. 13–14; E. M. Langley, 'The dietitian in the school meals service', *Nutrition: Dietetics: Catering*, III (1949) pp. 128–30.

73. S. Leff and Vera Leff, *The School Health Service* (London, 1959) pp. 159–61.

74. *British Medical Journal*, 1 October 1904, p. 850.

75. Pycroft to Sir Philip Magnus, 18 February 1903, enclosed in Pillow to Magnus, 20 February 1903, Pillow Family Papers, Norfolk Record Office, Norwich, BR 124/46.

76. *British Medical Journal*, 31 December 1892, p. 1459; 8 October 1904, p. 925; 21 January 1905, p. 162; 28 January 1905, p. 228.

Chapter 4

1. Brian Abel-Smith, *A History of the Nursing Profession* (London, 1960) p. 7; *British Medical Journal*, 28 February 1874, p. 285.

2. Brian Abel-Smith, *The Hospitals, 1800–1948: A Study in Social Administration in England and Wales* (London, 1964) pp. 10, 42–3, 55, 236.

3. F. K. Prochaska, *Philanthropy and the Hospitals of London: The King's Fund, 1897–1990* (Oxford, 1992) pp. 190–1. By 1960, 1600 students had trained there.

4. Abel-Smith, *A History of the Nursing Profession*, p. 7; Anne Summers, 'The costs and benefits of caring: nursing charities, c.1830–c.1860', in Jonathan Barry and Colin Jones (eds) *Medicine and Charity before the Welfare State* (London, 1991) pp. 140–5.

5. Mitchell, 'The teaching of domestic economy in girls' secondary schools', pp. 952–3.

6. *British Medical Journal*, 17 June 1874, p. 847.

7. *The British Journal of Nursing*, 17 January 1903, p. 48.

8. Sheila M. Collins and Edith R. Parker, 'A Victorian matron; no ordinary woman: Eva Charlotte Ellis Lückes (8 July 1854–16 February 1919)', *International History of Nursing Journal*, 7 (2003) pp. 66–74; Margaret McEwan, *Eva C. E. Lückes, Matron, The London Hospital 1880–1919* (The London Hospital League of Nurses, 1958); Susan McGann, 'Eva Charlotte Lückes: pioneer or reactionary? (1854–1919)', *History of Nursing Society Journal*, 3 (1991) pp. 24–9;

Susan McGann, 'Eva Charlotte Lückes: a great maker of matrons (1854–1919)', in Susan McGann, *The Battle of Nurses: A Study of Eight Women who Influenced the Development of Professional Nursing, 1880–1930* (London, 1992), pp. 9–34.

9. McEwan, *Eva C. E. Lückes, Matron*, p. 39.
10. Henry Bonham-Carter, 'Suggestions for improving the management of the nursing department in large hospitals', 1867, pp. 16–17, St Thomas' Hospital Records, Nightingale Collection, LMA, H01/ST/NC/16/6.
11. Anon., *Nursing Guide, Handbook of Nurses' League and Register of Nurses Trained at Guy's Hospital. Edited by the Matron*, 6th edition (London, 1911) p. 7, Guy's Hospital Records, LMA, H9/GY/C/20/001.
12. Nursing Committee, 1893–1904, King's College Hospital Records, Nightingale Institute, King's College London Archives (KCLA) London, 85/1.
13. *British Medical Journal*, 2 February 1878, p. 165; 28 February 1880, p. 338; 14 February 1885, p. 345; 18 January 1890, p. 145; 4 June 1898, p. 1475.
14. Nightingale to Mr and Mrs Bracebridge, Scutari, 7 August 1855, in Sue M. Goldie (ed.) *'I Have Done My Duty': Florence Nightingale and the Crimean War 1854–56* (Manchester, 1987) p. 144. Also, F. B. Smith, *Florence Nightingale: Reputation and Power* (London, 1982) pp. 25–71 for Nightingale's work in the Crimea.
15. Lenna F. Cooper, 'Florence Nightingale's contribution to dietetics', in Adelia M. Beeuwkes, E. Neige Todhunter and Emma Seifrit Weigley (eds) *Essays on History of Nutrition and Dietetics* (Chicago, 1967) pp. 5–11. As Cooper pointed out, Nightingale quoted dietetic research by Dr Robert Christison and examined the diet table of Guy's Hospital in 1857, which consisted of basic sick room diet, not so detailed as those in the late nineteenth century. Florence Nightingale, *Notes on Matters Affecting the Health, Efficiency, and Hospital Administration of the British Army, Founded Chiefly on the Experience of the Late War* (London, 1858) pp. 414–15, Appendix XXIV.
16. Nightingale to Sidney Herbert, 10 December 1854, 8 January 1855, 28 January 1855, in Goldie, *I Have Done My Duty*, pp. 47, 71, 79. Nightingale said she also worked as scavenger, washerwoman, general dealer and storekeeper.
17. S. M. Mitra, *The Life and Letters of Sir John Hall* (London, 1911) pp. 310–17.
18. Nightingale to Hall, 21 May 1856, Correspondence of Sir John Hall, BL, Add.Mss.39867, ff. 156–157.
19. Nightingale to Hall, 27 March 1856, Hall Papers, Add.Mss.39867, f.101.
20. Fitzgerald to Hall, enclosed copies of letters Nightingale to Fitzgerald, 16 April 1856; Fitzgerald to Nightingale, 16 April 1856, Hall Papers, Add.Mss.39867, ff. 113–114.
21. Nightingale to Wear, Barrack Hospital, Scutari, 4 December 1855, Hall Papers, Add. Mss.39867, f.91.
22. 'On the new St Thomas' Hospital', 1878, Nightingale Fund Council Records, LMA, A/NFC84/1.

23. Draft recommendation for training probationers, drawn up by Nightingale, 15 July 1878, A/NFC88/7.

24. Memo: of Instructions to be drawn up for sisters, by Nightingale, 24 August 1878, A/NFC88/8.

25. Memorandum of Instructions by Matron to Ward Sister. On Duties to Probationers. Easter 1879, by S. E. W[ardroper] Nightingale Training School Records, H01/ST/NTS/017.

26. Clarke to Nightingale, 7 August 1879, 12 September 1879, Nightingale Papers, Add. Mss. 45805, ff. 242b, 251.

27. Wardroper to Nightingale, 13 June 1883, Correspondence with Wardroper, Nightingale Papers, Add. Mss.47733, ff. 182–183.

28. Nightingale Training School, Matron's Annual Report for 1883, H01/ST/ NTS/A3/8; Nightingale Fund Council Annual Report for 1883, A/NFC5/23.

29. Wardroper to Nightingale, 28 November 1879, Nightingale Papers, Add.Mss.47733, ff. 56–87, enclosing Probationer Miss Wilson's papers, January 1878–October 1879.

30. Nightingale Fund Council Annual Report for 1910, A/NFC5/50; Report for 1911, A/NFC5/51/1.

31. The Nursing Record, 14 April 1892, p. 295.

32. The house committee of the London Hospital was the administrative body for the whole hospital and was attended by the house governor, house doctors and matron. They mainly discussed problems from the management side of the hospital.

33. The medical council of the London Hospital consisted of house physicians and surgeons.

34. Edith R. Parker and Sheila M. Collins, Learning to Care: A History of Nursing and Midwifery Education at the Royal London Hospital 1740–1993 (The Royal London Hospital Archives and Museum, 1998) pp. 67–8.

35. Eva Lückes, 'How far should our hospitals be training schools for nurses?' [Nightingale Tracts, c.1890]

36. Register of Pupil Probationers, Tredegar House, 1893, Royal London Hospital Records, The Royal London Hospital Archives and Museum (RLHA) London, LH/N/2/1.

37. Lückes to Nightingale, 29 November 1892, Correspondence with Lückes, Nightingale Papers, Add.Mss.47746, ff. 137–138.

38. Lückes to Nightingale, 15 June 1893, Nightingale Papers, Add.Mss.47746, f.166. The classes were started on 12 June.

39. Ibid.

40. Nightingale to Lückes, 19 June 1893. Image provided courtesy of the Clendening History of Medicine Library, Kansas University Medical Center, http://www.clendening.kume.edu/dc/fn/luckes4/html, 2 October 2003.

41. Eva Lückes, *Lecture on General Nursing. Delivered to the Probationers of the London Hospital Training School for Nurses* (London, 1884) pp. 168–9.
42. Ibid., p. 169.
43. Eva Lückes, *General Nursing* (London, 1898) p. 64.
44. Eva Lückes, *Hospital Sisters and their Duties* (London, 1893) 3rd edition, pp. 153–6.
45. Lückes to Nightingale, 15 June 1893; Hospital Nursing Report for 1893, March 1895; Re: Preliminary Training School for Pupil Probationers at Tredegar House, 18 February 1895, enclosed in letter 16 March 1895, Nightingale Papers, Add.Mss.47746, ff. 166, 237, 270. London Hospital, Matron's Annual Letters, No.4, 1897, p. 5, LH/N/7/2/1; London Hospital, Hospital Nursing Report for 1896, 1897, LH/A/17/62; McEwan, *Eva C. E. Lückes, Matron*, p. 18.
46. Hospital Nursing Report for 1896, 1897, 1906, LH/A/17/62; Matron's Annual Letters, No.11, 1904, LH/N/7/2/1.
47. Matron's Annual Letters, No.11, 1904, p. 3, LH/N/7/2/1.
48. Matron's Annual Letters, No.17, 1910 – No. 23, 1916, LH/N/7/2/1. She repeated this advice to private nurses that they were always welcome to attend sick cookery classes to revive their memory along with her opinion on this successful training.
49. Maude Earle, *Sick Room Cookery and Hospital Diet, with Special Recipes for Convalescent and Diabetic Patients* (London, 1897); Florence B. Jack, *The Art of Cooking for Invalids. In the Home and the Hospital* (London, 1896). See also, Mary A. Boland and Mrs Humphry (eds) *The Century Invalid Cookery: For the Use of Nurses in Training Schools, Nurses in Private Practice, Others who tend the Sick* (London, 1898). This is by American authors. Boland worked for the Johns Hopkins Hospital, which was well known for dietetics.
50. Nightingale Training School, Matron's Annual Report for 1883, p. 25, H01/ST/NTS/A/03/008.
51. Timetable of Sick Room Cookery, Papers of Grace Easton, LH/X/85/11.
52. King's College Hospital, Minutes of the Nursing Committee. 14 April 1904, 1 October 1914, KCLA, KH/N/M2; King's College Hospital Lectures to the Nursing Staff, 1891–1938, The Nurses' Training School of King's College Hospital, KCLA, 84/1.
53. *The Nursing Record*, 30 January 1897, pp. 96–7.
54. TEB Minutes, 27 November 1899. The board provided a teacher for the Westminster Hospital free of charge, though another two were charged at the usual rates, 5s for a lesson of two hours.
55. Hon. Sydney Holland, *Two Talks to the Nurses of the London Hospital*, December 1897, p. 6, RLHA; Holland, 'Nursing as a profession: a practical description of the course of training undergone by all professional nurses', reprinted from *The World and His Wife*, no date given, p. 3, LH/X/12/39.

56. Cavell to Lückes, Brussels, 9 September 1908, 17 November 1908, Correspondence of Edith Cavell with Lückes, LH/N/7/7/14, LH/N/7/7/18.
57. Cavell to Lückes, Swardeston Vicarage, Norwich, 13 September 1906, LH/N/7/7/5.
58. Notes of Lecture 3, in Lecture Notebooks of Edith Cavell, 14 August 1896, RLHA; Lecture 3, Diet and Health and Disease, in Medical Lectures Notebook of Grace Easton, c.1907–08, LH/X/85/4.
59. Margaret E. Broadley, *Patients Come First* (London: The London Hospital Special Trustees, 1980) p. 33.
60. Mrs Salmon, 26 October 1923, H01/ST/NTS/Y/23/029.
61. *The British Journal of Nursing*, 18 May 1907, p. 361.
62. *The Times*, 13 April 1907.

Chapter 5

1. Robert Bayliss and Christine Daniels, 'The physical deterioration report of 1904 and education in home economics', *History of Education Society Bulletin*, 41 (1988) pp. 29–39; Davin, 'Imperialism and motherhood'; Ellen Ross, *Love and Toil: Motherhood in Outcast London, 1870–1918* (Oxford, 1993).
2. F. K. Prochaska, *Women and Philanthropy in Nineteenth-Century England* (Oxford, 1980).
3. *The Lancet*, 27 January 1945, p. 124.
4. Celia Davies, 'The health visitor as mother's friend: a woman's place in public health 1900–14', *Social History of Medicine*, 1 (1988) pp. 39–59; Pat Gibb, 'District nursing in the Highlands and islands of Scotland 1890–1940', *History of Nursing Society Journal*, 4 (1992–93) pp. 319–29; Carol Helmstadter, 'From the private to the public sphere: the first generation of lady nurses in England', *Nursing History Review*, 9 (2001) pp. 127–40; Anne Summers, 'Hidden from history? The home care of the sick in the nineteenth century', *History of Nursing Society Journal*, 4 (1992–93) pp. 227–43.
5. Christopher Charlton, 'The National Health Society Almanack, 1883', *Local Population Studies*, 32 (1984) pp. 54–7.
6. A note by Nightingale on Dr Edward Seaton's paper, May 1895. 'Sick Care as for Technical Education', Nightingale Papers, Add.Mss.45813, ff. 68–9; *The Lancet*, 1 June 1895, pp. 1392–3.
7. Anon., 'Rural health missioners', *Public Health*, 5 (1893) p. 133; Florence Nightingale, 'Sick-nursing and health-nursing', in Baroness Burdett-Coutts (ed.) *Woman's Mission: A Series of Congress Papers in the Philanthropic Work of Women, by Eminent Writers* (London, 1893) pp. 191–200; Florence Nightingale, *Rural Hygiene. Health Teaching in Towns and Villages* (London, 1894) pp. 1–26.
8. Select Committee of the House of Lords on Metropolitan Hospitals, etc.

(hereafter Select Committee on Metropolitan Hospitals) PP XVI (1890) First Report, Miss Emily Mansel, Superintendent of Metropolitan and National Nursing Association, p. 538; Mr Arthur William Lacey, Secretary of the East London Nursing Society, pp. 539–40.

9. William Rathbone, *Sketch of the History and Progress of District Nursing from its Commencement in the Year 1859 to the Present Date* (London, 1890) pp. 52–3, 59–60; Mary Stocks, *A Hundred Years of District Nursing* (London, 1960) p. 83.

10. Metropolitan District Nursing Association, Superintendent's Reports, vol. 1 (1876–1880); Annual Reports, vol. 1 (1876) vol. 2 (1877–1884) Guildhall Library, MS.14616, MS.14618.

11. Nightingale to Hughes, 5 June 1894; Nightingale to Hughes, 8 September 1896; Nightingale to Hughes, 20 October 1896; Hughes, n.d., Wellcome Library, MS.5478/4, MS.5478/8/2, MS.5478/11, MS.5478/20/1.

12. Amy Hughes, *Practical Hints on District Nursing* (London, 1897) pp. 2, 39–40, 55–6.

13. Pillow, 'Domestic economy teaching in England', PP XXV (1897) p. 159.

14. Booth, *Life and Labour*, final volume (London, 1902) pp. 154–5; Survey notebooks by G. H. Duckworth, A letter from Lückes, pp. 145–7, A27; Lückes interview, pp. 219–28, B153; Queen Victoria's Jubilee Institute for Nurses, Miss Hadden interview, pp. 1–11, A55, Charles Booth Collection, British Library of Political and Economic Science Archives.

15. *British Medical Journal*, 2 February 1878, p. 165.

16. Anon., 'Queen Victoria's Jubilee Institute for Nurses, Scottish branch, Edinburgh. First annual report, 1889', in William Rathbone, *Sketch of the History and Progress of District Nursing from its Commencement in the Year 1859 to the Present Date* (London, 1890) Appendix B, pp. 105–6.

17. Wright to Leake, 28 September 1904, The Queen's Nursing Institute Collection, Wellcome Library, SA/QNI/S.1/1/7.

18. Guthrie Wright, 'District nursing as a hygiene agency', *Journal of the Royal Sanitary Institute*, XXV (1904) pp. 889–93. Italics by Wright.

19. Amy Hughes, 'The ideal district nurse', reprinted from *The Nursing Times*, 8 May 1909, SA/QNI/P.7/13.

20. Miss Bibby, Miss Colles, Miss Petty and Dr Sykes, *The Pudding Lady: A New Departure in Social Work* (London, 1912) pp. 1, 4, 25, 29; L. N. R. (Ellen Ranyard) *Nurses for the Needy: Or, Bible-women Nurses in the Homes of the London Poor* (London, 1875); National Food Reform Association, *Reason for Food Reform* (London, 1908).

21. Greta Allen, *Practical Hints of Health Visitors* (London, c.1905) pp. 76–9.

22. Nightingale, 'Sick-nursing and health-nursing', p. 192.

23. Select Committee on Metropolitan Hospitals, PP XVI (1890) First Report, pp. 538–9.

24. 'The Metropolitan and National Nursing Association for Providing Trained Nurses for the Sick Poor', 1881. This case was a barrister alone in chambers with rheumatism, only helped by his colleague. A/NFC89/1–2.

25. Select Committee on Metropolitan Hospitals, PP XIII (1892) Third Report, pp. clxx, cvii.

26. Select Committee on Metropolitan Hospitals, PP XVI (1890) First Report, p. 477.

27. Ibid.

28. Private Nursing Report for 1890, February 1892, Lückes to Nightingale, Nightingale Papers, Add.Mss.47746, ff. 87–8.

29. Select Committee on Metropolitan Hospitals, PP XVI (1890) First Report, Miss Mary Louise Sprigg, Deputy Superintendent of the London Association of Nurses, pp. 542–3, and Second Report, PP XIII (1890–91) George Brown, General Practitioner of Threadneedle Street, North London, p. 704.

30. Booth, *Life and Labour*, second series: Industry (London, 1904) V, pp. 322–31; Select Committee on Metropolitan Hospitals, PP XVI (1890) First Report, p. 538.

31. Mrs Dacre Craven, *A Guide to District Nurses and Home Nursing* (London, 1890) pp. 24–5, 38–41; Wilby Hart Diaries, typescript, 'Case 3: 15 December 1907– 22 December 1907, Mr M. – Nervous Breakdown', pp. 1–3; 'Case 6: 10 February 1908–16 March 1908, Mrs B. – Fibroids', pp. 8–9, RLHA, PP/WILBY; Eva C. E. Lückes, *Home Nursing and Sick Room Appliances* (London, 1883) p. 16; National Health Society, *In a Sick Room* (London, 1890) pp. 3, 5; Lionel A. Weatherly, *Lectures on Domestic Hygiene and Home Nursing* (London, 1880) pp. 4–7.

32. Hart Diaries, 'Case 6: Mrs B.', pp. 8–9, PP/WILBY.

33. Lady Acland (née Ovans) 'A few recollections of St Thomas', 1895 to 1903', H01/ST/NTS/Y/23/002/001.

34. Regarding this pneumonia, Hart used the term 'drowning' to explain how patients' lungs filled with water or liquid because of unskilled feeding by nurses.

35. Hart Diaries, pp. 46–7, PP/WILBY.

36. St Thomas' Hospital, House Committee Minutes, 30 May 1900, 27 March 1901, 24 January 1904, 7 February 1906, 9 January 1907, 24 September 1913, H01/ST/A/010/002; Guy's Hospital, Court of Committees Minutes, 18 March 1896, H09/GY/A/003/011/001.

37. Blakestad, 'King's College of Household and Social Science', pp. 75–98; Hutchinson, *A History of the British Dietetic Association*, pp. 5–7; Nyhart, 'Home economists in the hospital', pp. 125–44; Keir Waddington, 'Unsuitable cases: the debate over outpatient admissions, the medical profession and late-Victorian London hospitals', *Medical History*, 42 (1998) p. 29.

38. Select Committee on Metropolitan Hospitals, PP XVI (1890) First Report, William John Nixon, House Governor of the London Hospital, p. 489; Select Committee on Metropolitan Hospitals, PP XIII (1892) Third Report, p. liii.

39. Select Committee on Metropolitan Hospitals, PP XVI (1890) First Report, Sir Edmund Hay Currie, the Management of the London Hospital, p. 121; William Bousfield, Chairman of the Committee of Management, King's College Hospital, p. 94.

40. Select Committee on Metropolitan Hospitals, PP XVI (1890) First Report, pp. 94, 489, 490; Frederick Walker, steward of St Thomas' Hospital, p. 59. Individual hospital records also contain discussions of the quality of food. For example, Guy's Hospital, House Committee Minutes, 18 October 1900, 17 July 1902, 23 October 1902, 19 March 1903, 4 June 1903, H09/GY/A/025/ 003, H09/GY/A/025/004; St Thomas' Hospital, House Committee Minutes, 28 November 1900, H01/ST/A/010/002. St Mary's Hospital, Paddington, Matron Miss Rachel Williams to Bonham-Carter, 22 July 1876, about the matron's duty in that hospital, H01/ST/NC/18/012/ 015/001.

41. Select Committee on Metropolitan Hospitals, PP XVI (1890) First Report, B. E. Broadhurst, private practitioner, fellow of the Royal College of Surgeons, pp. 259–60, 264; Select Committee on Metropolitan Hospitals, PP XIII (1892) Third Report, p. liii.

42. Anonymous memoir of nurse trained at the London Hospital 1906–08, c.1956, LH/X/184/3.

43. King's College Hospital, Minutes of the Committee of Management, 29 July 1885, KII/CM/M12; St Thomas' Hospital, House Committee Minutes, 3 January 1883, 4 April 1883, 6 June 1883, H01/ST/A/010/001.

44. Select Committee on Metropolitan Hospitals, PP XVI (1890) First Report, p. 534.

45. John Ellis, *LHMC 1785–1985: The Story of the London Hospital Medical College, England's First Medical School* (London: London Hospital Medical Club, 1986) p. 59.

46. British Hospital for Diseases of the Skin, *Rules for Diet, and General Instructions of the Guidance of Patients* (London, 1872). General instruction for medicine and ointment was explained, with the method of maintaining personal cleanliness.

47. *British Medical Journal,* 7 December 1889, pp. 1261–2; *The Hospital,* 25 January 1890, pp. 266–7.

48. London Hospital, House Committee Minutes, 13 November 1877, 3 January 1882, 14 March 1882, LH/A/5/38, LH/A/5/40; Draft of Nixon's report, LH/A/17/16; Diet table of the London Hospital, July 1888, LH/Z/2.

49. London Hospital, House Committee Minutes, 26 March 1889, enclosing Nixon, 'Report on Gas and Steam Cooking in the London Hospital Kitchen', 12 March 1889, pp. 3–6, LH/A/5/47. In the new system it only cost one-eighth of a penny per head for each meal.

50. Head and Hutchison, 'Report upon the Diets at the London Hospital', 25 September 1901, LH/A/17/19; London Hospital, House Committee Minutes, 7 October 1901, 2 December 1901, LH/A/5/48; London Hospital, Medical Council Minutes, 27 April 1901, 15 November 1901, 28 November 1901, 21 January 1902, 24 April 1903, 12 March 1905, 8 June 1906, 23 November 1906, RLHA, LM/1/3, LM/1/4, LM/1/5, LM/1/6.

51. Robert Hutchison, *Food and the Principles of Dietetics* (London, 1900) p. 7.

52. Ibid., pp. 69–70, 82–3, 130–4, 377.

53. Hughes, *Practical Hints on District Nursing*, pp. 55–6.

54. Select Committee on Metropolitan Hospitals, PP XVI (1890) First Report, p. 255. At St Georges' Hospital he recommended that the committee establish a soup kitchen and baths to prevent people who did not require medicine crowding into the outpatients' department. Also, support by the Charity Organization Society about outpatient administration is mentioned in Select Committee on Metropolitan Hospitals, PP XIII (1890–91) Second Report, Francis Mead Corner, general practitioner of East London, Poplar, pp. 676–7; Charles Stewart Loch, Secretary of the Charity Organization Society, pp. 759–60; *British Medical Journal*, 11 October 1890, pp. 864–6.

55. Guy's Hospital, Medical Committee Minute Book, 20 October 1892, H09/GY/A/020/001/001–002. Report of subcommittee for instruction to outpatients, including draft of the slip 'How to Feed Children'.

56. *The Times*, 27 November 1884.

57. Invalid Kitchens of London, Annual Report and Balance Sheets 1910, pp. 2–4, LMA, IML/6; 'History of the Invalid Kitchens of London 1905–1929', IML/44; *Daily Express*, 25 January 1915, press cuttings, IML/45; *The British Journal of Nursing*, 56, 22 April 1916, p. 366.

58. Select Committee on Metropolitan Hospitals, PP XIII (1890–91) Second Report, p. 761; Select Committee on Metropolitan Hospitals, PP XIII (1892) Third Report, p. xxxiv.

Chapter 6

1. J. P. Crowdy, 'The science of the soldier's food', *Army Quarterly and Defence Journal*, 110, (1980) pp. 266–79; Sir John Fortescue, *A Short Account of Canteens in the British Army* (Cambridge, 1928); George Armund Furse, *Provisioning Armies in the Field* (London, 1899); Andrew Slade, 'When private contractors fed the army', *Army Quarterly and Defence Journal*, 115 (1985) pp. 160–6.

2. Neil Cantlie, *A History of the Army Medical Department* (London, 1974) II, pp. 376–8.

3. Report of a Committee appointed by the Secretary of State for War to inquire into the Organization of the Army Hospital Corps, Hospital Management and

Nursing in the Field, and the Sea Transport of Sick and Wounded (hereafter Army Hospital Service Inquiry Committee) PP XVI (1883) p. xxviii. For women nurses in military service see Anne Summers, *Angels and Citizens* (London, 1988).

4. John Shepherd, *The Crimean Doctors: A History of the British Medical Services in the Crimean War* (Liverpool, 1991) I, p. 316.

5. George Williams, an ordinary soldier, to his brothers in England. Hospital Ship, *Constantinople*, 13 December 1854, National Army Museum (NAM) Archives 6403–17.

6. Shepherd, *The Crimean Doctors*, II, pp. 591–620 explains Nightingale's work for reform of army sanitation after the war.

7. Margaret Goodman, *Experiences of an English Sister of Mercy* (London, 1862) pp. 110–11, 215–17. Also Shepherd, *The Crimean Doctors*, II, pp. 363–4.

8. Victor Bonham-Carter (ed.) *Surgeon in the Crimea: The Experiences of George Lawson Recorded in Letters to his Family 1854–1855* (London, 1968) pp. 134–5; Shepherd, *The Crimean Doctors*, I, pp. 274–5, II, pp. 500, 502, 505; Jane Williams (ed.) *The Autobiography of Elizabeth Davis* (London, 1857) II, pp. 115–19, 135–6, 151–5, 184–5.

9. Nightingale, *Notes on Matters Affecting the Health, Efficiency, and Hospital Administration of the British Army*, pp. 421, 428.

10. Florence Nightingale, *Notes on Hospitals* (London, 1859) pp. 18–19.

11. Second Report from the Select Committee on the Army before Sebastopol (hereafter Army Before Sebastopol) PP IX (1854–55) pp. 348, 380, 480–1.

12. Cantlie, *History of the Army Medical Department*, II, pp. 217–23; J. B. Neal, 'The history of the Royal Army Medical College', *Journal of the Royal Army Medical Corps*, 13 (1957) pp. 163–72.

13. Parkes to Nightingale, 4 August 1860; Nightingale to Parkes, 9 August 1860, Nightingale Papers, Add.Mss. 45773, ff. 9–10. The Parkes Museum of Hygiene, established after his death, was a special teaching museum for hygiene and used for the practical instruction of sanitary inspectors and district nurses who had to administrate with respect to the sanitation of dwellings; in her book on district nursing Amy Hughes recommended it as the only museum where one could learn about a number of sanitary appliances in detail. Hughes, *Practical Hints on District Nursing*, pp. 41–3. Also, Beverly P. Bergman and Simon A. StJ. Miller, 'Historical perspectives on health: the Parkes Museum of Hygiene and the Sanitary Institute', *Journal of the Royal Society for the Promotion of Health*, 123 (2003) pp. 55–61.

14. Army Medical Department Report for 1873 (hereafter Army Medical Report) PP XLIV (1875) p. 188.

15. *The Nursing Record*, 6 September 1888, p. 307. Their salaries were between £25 and £48 per annum.

16. *British Journal of Nursing*, 5 February 1910, p. 108; National Food Reform Association, *The Feeding of Nurses* (London, 1910) pp. 24–6, 40.

17. Anon., *Standing Orders for the Army Medical Staff in Relation to the Medical Staff Corps* (London, 1894) Appendix 3, pp. 48–9.

18. War Office, *Instructions to Military Hospital Cooks, in the Preparation of Diets for Sick Soldiers* (London, 1860) pp. 3–4, 6–7, recipes pp. 8–34.

19. Alexis Soyer, *A Culinary Campaign* (London, 1857) pp. 101–10. Soyer's work in the Crimea is analysed in Shepherd, *The Crimean Doctors*, II, pp. 367–71. For Soyer's contribution alongside Nightingale, see also Ruth Cowen, *Relish: The Extraordinary Life of Alexis Soyer, Victorian Celebrity Chef* (London, 2006) pp. 256–77.

20. Cantlie, *History of the Army Medical Department*, II, pp. 232–4.

21. Army Hospital Service Inquiry Committee, PP XVI (1883) pp. xxxv–xxxvii.

22. Army Medical Report for 1873, PP XLIV (1875) pp. 39–40.

23. Army Hospital Service Inquiry Committee, PP XVI (1883) pp. 271–4, 278.

24. Army Hospital Service Inquiry Committee, PP XVI (1883) pp. 87–8, 187, 190–1, 600–1.

25. Army Medical Report for 1884, PP XL (1886) p. 39; Report for 1887, PP XLIX (1889) p. 41; Report for 1888, PP XLIII (1890) p. 45; Report for 1890, PP L (1892) p. 47; Cantlie, *History of the Army Medical Department*, II, p. 235.

26. Crawford to Nightingale, 4 September 1882; Nightingale to Crawford, 9 August 1883, Nightingale Papers, Add.Mss.45772, ff. 11–12, 23–24; Cantlie, *History of the Army Medical Department*, II, pp. 277–8.

27. 'Reports of the Executive Committee and the Lady Superintendent, and Balance Sheet for the year ending 31 December 1887', pp. 5–6, ED 164/2.

28. National Training School of Cookery Executive Committee Minute Book (hereafter NTSC Minutes) 28 September 1883, 26 February 1884, 21 March 1884, 14 June 1884, 17 July 1884, 16 February 1885, 6 March 1885, ED 164/2.

29. *Navy and Army Illustrated*, 19 March 1897, p. 218; NTSC Minutes, 3 May 1904, 14 July 1904, ED164/3.

30. Anon., 'Abstract of co-joint report of the advisory and nursing boards, containing a scheme to develop the training of orderlies of the Royal Army Medical Corps as attendants upon the sick and wounded', *Journal of the Royal Army Medical Corps*, V (1905) pp. 292–8.

31. *The British Journal of Nursing*, 8 June 1907, p. 429.

32. Notebook on lectures at the Army School of Cookery, 1905, pp. 116–18, MS of Felix Alexander Hadingue, NAM Archives 7211–62–1.

33. Board of Education, Report of the Special Inspection of London, Westminster, National Training School of Cookery, and other Branches of Domestic Economy, 1910, pp. 5, 13–14, ED 115/57.

34. William Aitken, *On the Growth of the Recruit and Young Soldier, with a View to a*

Judicious Selection of "growing lads" for the Army, and a Regulated System of Teaching for Recruits (London, 1862) pp. vii–ix.

35. Crowdy, 'The science of the soldier's food', pp. 267–8; Slade, 'When private contractors fed the army', p. 161.

36. R. L. V. ffrench Blake, *The Crimean War* (London, 1971) pp. 45, 108.

37. Second Report of the Army Before Sebastopol, PP IX (1854–55) p. 572; Third Report of Army Before Sebastopol, PP IX (1854–55) p. 248.

38. Second Report of the Army Before Sebastopol, PP IX (1854–55) pp. 248–9, 251.

39. First Report of the Army before Sebastopol, PP IX (1854–55) p. 133.

40. Second Report of the Army before Sebastopol, PP IX (1854–55) pp. 204–5.

41. Lysons to his sister, 2 May 1854, 7 September 1855; Lysons to his mother, 19 May 1854, 29 June 1854, 18 August 1854, 25 July 1855, 11 August 1855, in General Sir Daniel Lysons, *The Crimean War: From First to Last* (London, 1895) pp. 19–20, 23–4, 44–5, 64, 203, 206–7, 212–13.

42. John Grant, 'New system of cooking for the army', *Journal of the Royal United Service Institution,* IV (1860) pp. 322, 324–5; Copies of any Reports made to His Royal Highness, the Commander in Chief, or the War Department, respecting the Working of Captain Grant's Kitchens, now in use at the camp at Aldershot and at Woolwich Barracks, PP XXXVII (1857–58) pp. 1, 3, 8.

43. Robert Bell, 'A good plain cook for the army', *Chambers Journal,* 1863, reprinted in *Army Catering Corps Yearbook* (1971–72) pp. 43–5. However, the heavy weight and difficulty of cleaning was discussed in Reports on Captain Grant's Cooking Apparatus, PP XXXII (1863) pp. 1–6.

44. Report of a committee appointed to consider the claims of Captain Grant to Remuneration for the services which he has rendered to the Public by the Introduction of his system of cookery, PP XXXV (1864) pp. 3–4, 8, 19–20.

45. General Report of the Commission appointed for Improving the Sanitary Condition of Barracks and Hospitals, PP XVI (1861) pp. 113–14.

46. Army Medical Report for 1860, PP XXXIII (1862) p. 96; Report for 1863, PP XXXIII (1865) p. 286; Report for 1890, PP L (1892) p. 51; Report for 1898, PP LIII (1899) pp. 63–4; Report for 1897, PP LIV (1898) p. 57. Copies of all correspondence that has taken place this year between the Under Secretary of State for War and Captain Grant, respecting his claims for Remuneration for the Services he has rendered in improving the system of Cooking in the Army, PP XXXII (1862) pp. 3–4; History of the Army Catering Corps, NAM Archives 7004–3; *The Morning Post,* 6 October 1888; *The Times,* 7 September 1867, 23 September 1867, 27 October 1891. The Instructional Kitchen was started under Lieutenant-Colonel Arthur Herbert.

47. War Office, *Instructions to Military Cooks in the preparation of Dinners at the Instructional Kitchen, Aldershot* (London, 1878); War Office, *The Messing of the Soldier. Including Schedules Illustrative of the New System of Military Cooking. Issued by the Direction of Lt.*

Genl. Sir Evelyn Wood, VC, GCB, GCMG, &c. Commanding Aldershot Division, for the Information of the Troops in his Command, and Others whom it may Concern, New edition, revised August 1, 1892 (London, 1892) pp. 3, 8–9, 25–34.

48. War Office, *Manual of Military Cookery, Prepared at the Army School of Cookery* (London, 1910) pp. 1–2, 59–60; War Office, *Manual of Military Cooking and Dietary Mobilization* (London, 1915) p. 39.

49. *The Lancet*, 11 August 1888, pp. 272–3.

50. Committee to inquire into the Question of Soldiers' Dietary, PP XVII (1889) pp. 5–10, 15–16, 19–20.

51. Report of the Commissioner Appointed to Inquire into the Regulations Affecting the Sanitary Condition of the Army, the Organization of Military Hospitals, and the Treatment of the Sick and Wounded, PP XVIII (1857–58) (hereafter Report of the Sanitary Condition of the Army) pp. 86, 93–4.

52. Parkes, *Manual of Practical Hygiene*, pp. 166, 213–16, 274, 591–2.

53. Report of the Sanitary Condition of the Army, PP XVIII (1857–58) pp. 94, 98, 123, 194, 208.

54. Report of the Sanitary Condition of the Army, PP XVIII (1857–58) pp. xxii, xxvii; Report of the Committee on the Conditions under which Canteens and Regimental Institutes are conducted, PP X (1903) pp. xviii, 225.

55. A. M. Davies, *The Food of the Soldier* (Aldershot, 1888) pp. 14, 27–32.

56. James Lane Notter, 'The soldier's food, with reference to health and efficiency for service', *Journal of the Royal United Service Institution*, 33 (1889) p. 556.

57. G. J. H. Evatt, 'The sanitary care of the soldier by his officer, a lecture delivered at the Royal Artillery Institution, Woolwich, 19 January 1894', pp. 24–6, Wellcome Library, RAMC Muniments, RAMC 474.

58. Army Medical Report for 1896, PP LIV (1897) pp. 175–6, 189. Ernest Hanbury Hankin, *Cholera in Indian Cantonments and How to deal with it. Written for the case of Cantonment Magistrates, Medical Officers and others interested in the question* (Allahabad, 1895) pp. 45, 72–6. See also David Arnold, *Science, Technology and Medicine in Colonial India* (Cambridge, 2000) pp. 141–7.

59. Army Medical Report for 1901, PP XXXVIII (1903) pp. 200–3; Report for 1902, PP LI (1904) pp. 209–10; Report for 1903, PP XLVI (1905) p. 223. David Arnold, *Colonizing the Body: State Medicine and Epidemic Disease in Nineteenth-Century India* (Berkeley, 1993) pp. 22–3, 64–7, 87–90.

60. H. E. R. James, *A Manual of Field Cookery* (London, 1912); *Soldier's Small Book*, pp. 22–4, NAM Archives 7211–62–2.

61. Army Medical Report for 1868, PP XLIII (1870) pp. 249–50; Report for 1870, PP XXXVIII (1872) p. 28, 125; Report for 1871, PP XLI (1873) p. 162; Report for 1872, PP XXXVII (1874) p. 162; Report for 1873, PP XLIV (1875) pp. 112, 216–17; Report for 1874, PP XLIV (1876) p. 106; Report for 1875, PP XLIV (1876) p. 73; Report for 1888, PP XLIII (1890) p. 49.

62. Parkes, *Manual of Practical Hygiene*, pp. v–vi; Shepherd, *The Crimean Doctors*, I, pp. 308–9. In Bulgaria, none of the medical officers had training in camp hygiene, which caused the unhealthy condition of the camps. A number of camps had unhygienic cooking sites and soldiers could not wash their clothes to maintain personal cleanliness because the soap was so expensive until the spring of 1855. Army surgeons had, nonetheless, faced earlier problems of widespread sickness among soldiers, such as during the first China War 1841–42, in the West Indies, and during the 1809 Walcheren expedition when a large number of men suffered from a disease known as Walcheren fever. See, for example, Michael Duffy, *Soldiers, Sugar and Seapower: The British Expeditions to the West Indies and the War against Revolutionary France* (Oxford, 1987) pp. 326–7; and David McLean, 'Surgeons of the opium war: the navy on the China coast, 1840–1842', *English Historical Review*, CXXI (2006) pp. 487–504.

63. Report of the Sanitary Condition of the Army, PP XVIII (1857–58) p. 29.

64. Parkes, *Manual of Practical Hygiene*, p. xviii.

65. James Cantlie, 'The relations of the civil and military medical men in Britain' (privately printed, 1897) RAMC 474; and George Evatt, *Army Medical Organisation: A Comparative Examination of the Regimental and Departmental System*, 4th edition (London, 1883) pp. 10, 75–7.

66. Nightingale, *Notes on Matters Affecting the Health, Efficiency, and Hospital Administration of the British Army*, pp. 277–9, 283–6, 448; Report of the Sanitary Condition of the Army, PP XVIII (1857–58) p. 29.

67. Ian Hay, *One Hundred Years of Army Nursing, the Story of the British Army Nursing Services, from the Time of Florence Nightingale to the Present Day* (London, 1953) p. 38.

68. George J. H. Evatt, 'The sanitary care of the soldier by his officer', 1894, pp. 18–19, RAMC 474. He mentioned soldiers' bedding as worse than that for police officers because for the latter sheets were washed once a week, whereas soldiers' sheets were washed only once a month.

69. V. L. Allen, 'The National Union of Police and Prison Officers', *Economic History Review*, XI (1958) p. 133; *The Police Review and Parade Gossip*, 10 April 1893, 30 October 1893, pp. 172, 176, 522.

70. H. K. Allport, Army Form 51, *Health Memoranda for Soldiers* (Gosport, 1906) NAM Archives 8001–1, belonging to Henry Kingston, attached to his *Soldier's Small Book*; Army Health Report for 1907, PP LXIV (1908) p. 48; John S. G. Blair, *'In Arduis Fidelis': Centenary History of the Royal Army Medical Corps* (Edinburgh, 2001) p. 15.

71. Neal to his mother, 27 May 1900, letters of 9007, Private Harry Edward Neal, NAM Archives 8205–41.

72. Rowlandson to his mother, 4 September 1901, 25 September 1901, 9 October 1901, letters of Major Samuel Messiter Rowlandson to his family, NAM Archives 7708–42–159, 7708–42–164A, 7708–42–168.

73. Rowlandson to mother, 8 April 1901, NAM Archives 7708–42–43.
74. Rowlandson to his father, 15 September 1900; Rowlandson to mother, 2 October 1900, 15 October 1900, NAM Archives 7708–42–16, 7708–42–19, 7708–42–20.
75. Hay, *One Hundred Years of Army Nursing*, pp. 49–50.
76. G. Fahey, 'Practical hints on marching and health on active service', *Journal of the Royal Army Medical Corps*, XVIII (1912) p. 415.
77. Porter to his wife, 21 December 1899, 25 January 1900, 19 May 1900; Medical Notes, 13 April 1900 – 12 October 1900, p. 103, National Maritime Museum (NMM) Porter Papers, PTR/6/2.
78. Journal of Chilley Pine, 31 July 1854, NMM, JOD/26.
79. Arthur Ransome, 'Soils and sites', *Health Lectures for the People*, 8th series (Manchester, 1886) pp. 1–21. He quoted on drainage and station sites (pp. 3–7) from Douglas Galton, *Observations on the Construction of Healthy Dwellings, namely Houses, Hospitals, Barracks, Asylums, etc.* (Oxford, 1880). Galton was a member of the commission for improving sanitary conditions in barracks and hospitals in 1861. However, Porter did not find Galton's book that interesting. Porter to wife, 14 December 1897, PTR/5.
80. Nightingale to Galton, 9 August 1896, Nightingale Papers, Add.Mss.45767, ff. 177–178.
81. Journal of Pine, 14 July 1854, JOD/26.
82. Porter to his daughter, 27 October 1899, PTR/6/2.
83. Medical Notes, 3 December 1899–12 April 1900, p. 115, PTR/6/2. Porter to wife, 6 March 1900, 20 April 1900, 2 September 1900, PTR/6/2.
84. Report of the India Plague Commission, PP LXXII (1902) V, pp. 1–9. Its outbreak was officially reported in September 1896 and started to decline in June 1899.
85. Army Medical Report for 1868, PP XLIII (1870) pp. 170–88.
86. Army Medical Report for 1872, PP XXXVII (1874) pp. 160–1. Original information is from Anon., *Seventh Annual Report of the Sanitary Commissioner with the Government of India, 1870* (Calcutta, 1871) p. 42.
87. Sir Garnet Wolseley, *The Soldier's Pocket-Book for Field Service*, 4th edition, revised and enlarged (London, 1882) pp. 258–64.
88. R. C. Eaton, *A Guide to Health: For the Use of Soldiers* (London, 1896) pp. ix, 56–7, 91–2.
89. Hankin, *Cholera in Indian Cantonments*, pp. ii–iii, 30–1, 41. See also Army Medical Report for 1896, PP LIV (1897) pp. 175–6.
90. Army Medical Report for 1898, PP LIII (1899) p. 182; Report for 1899, PP XXXIX (1901) p. 210; Report for 1902, PP LI (1904) p. 209.
91. Army Medical Report for 1903, PP XLVI (1905) pp. 141, 223–5.
92. *The Lancet*, 10 January 1903, pp. 118–19.

93. For example, J. R. Forrest, *The Soldier's Health and How to Preserve It* (Aldershot, 1896); J. Arnallt Jones, *Health Hints for Volunteers* (London, 1900); Sir H. Waite, *How to Keep "FIT," on the Soldier's Guide to Health, in Field, Camp and Quarters* (London, 1901).

94. Allport, *Health Memoranda for Soldiers*, NAM Archives 8001–1.

95. H. K. Allport, 'Training soldiers in personal hygiene', *Journal of the Royal Army Medical Corps*, III (1904) pp. 621–3.

96. Claire Herrick, '"The conquest of the silent foe": British and American military medical reform rhetoric and the Russo–Japanese War', in Roger Cooter, Mark Harrison and Steve Sturdy (eds) *Medicine and Modern Warfare* (Amsterdam, 1999) pp. 99–129.

97. W. G. MacPherson, 'The sanitary instructions issued to the Japanese Army on mobilization', p. 387 and 'Japanese field service health memoranda', pp. 403–12. 'Japanese rules for the prevention of cholera and plague amongst soldiers', p. 413, all in War Office, *The Russo-Japanese War: Medical and Sanitary Reports from Officers Attached to the Japanese and Russian Forces in the Field* (London, 1908). Japanese Army, Man-Dainikki (Japanese Army Minute Books on Manchuria) in Rikugunsyo Dainikki (Japanese Army Minute Books) 18 January 1904, 23 June 1904, 14 September 1904, 11 January 1905, 5 June 1905, 7 June 1905, the National Institute for Defense Studies, Tokyo, Archives, RikuManFu/M37–5, M37–15, M37–20, M38–13, M40–2.

98. Army Medical Report for 1904, PP LXVIII (1906) pp. 124–6, 224–47.

99. G. J. Stoney Archer, 'A lecture on hygiene', *Journal of the Royal Army Medical Corps*, V (1905) pp. 743–6.

100. Army Medical Report for 1906, PP LXIV (1908) p. 216; Report for 1907, PP LXIV (1908) pp. 47–9, 80, 109–10; Anon., 'The school of army sanitation, Aldershot', *Journal of the Royal Army Medical Corps*, XI (1908) pp. 482–5.

101. Army Medical Report for 1906, PP LXIV (1908) pp. 54–6.

102. C. H. Melville, 'Course of lectures on army sanitation', *Journal of the Royal Sanitary Institute*, XXXII (1911) pp. 170–1.

103. Army Medical Report for 1908, PP LII (1909) p. 3; Report for 1909, PP XLVII (1911) p. 4; Report for 1910, PP XLVII (1911) p. 4.

Chapter 7

1. Report of the Sanitary Condition of the Army, PP XVIII (1857–58) p. 379; Nightingale, *Notes on Matters Affecting Health, Efficiency and Hospital Administration of the British Army*, p. 448.

2. David Stewart, 'Hospital ships in the Second Dutch War', *Journal of the Royal Naval Medical Service*, 34 (1948) pp. 29–35.

3. J. C. Goddard, 'An insight into the life of Royal Naval surgeons during the

Napoleonic War, Part I', *Journal of the Royal Naval Medical Service*, 77 (1991) pp. 206–19; J. C. Goddard, 'Part II', *Journal of the Royal Naval Medical Service*, 78 (1991) pp. 27–34.

4. T. P. Gillespie, 'The diet and health of seamen in the West Indies at the end of the eighteenth century: some remarks on the work of Leonard Gillespie, MD', *Journal of the Royal Naval Medical Service*, 37 (1951) pp. 187–92.

5. Janet Macdonald, *Feeding Nelson's Navy: The True Story of Food at Sea in the Georgian Era* (London, 2004) pp. 15–44, 104–16, 166–8, Appendix 6.

6. Anon., 'Abstract from "Captain James Cook," by Kitson (1907) pp. 331–341', *Journal of the Royal Naval Medical Service*, 26 (1940) pp. 329–35; for explanation of the edibility of fish with caution of poison, see James Duncan Gatewood, *Naval Hygiene* (London, 1910) pp. 538–69. Gatewood was a medical inspector of the United States Navy. See also Journal of Robert Guthrie, 31 December 1829, HMS *Seringapatam*, NMM, JOD/16; R. T. Williamson, 'Captain James Cook, RN, FRS, and his contribution to medical science', *Journal of the Royal Naval Medical Service*, 14 (1928) pp. 19–22.

7. Richard J. Cyriax, *Sir John Franklin's Last Arctic Expedition: The Franklin Expedition, a Chapter in the History of the Royal Navy* (London, 1939) pp. 42, 137–41; Drs James Donnet and Thomas R. Fraser, 'Paper on scurvy', in Report of the Committee appointed by the Lords Commissioners of the Admiralty to enquire into the causes of the Outbreak of Scurvy in the recent Arctic Expedition, PP LVI (1877) pp. xiii–xxiii: the sledge parties' diet (pemmican, dry preserved potatoes and no lime juice) on the Arctic expedition of Captain Sir S. Nares in 1875–76 showed further consideration of the nutritive value of food. Preserved vegetables lost anti-scorbutic and nutritional value during the preservation process. See also Sir Francis L. McClintock, *The Voyage of the "Fox" in the Arctic Seas: A Narrative of the Discovery of the Fate of Sir John Franklin and his Companions* (London, 1859) pp. 7–10; R. M'Cormick, *Voyages of Discovery in the Arctic and Antarctic Seas* (London, 1884) II, pp. 172–5; Len Stephens, *History of the Naval Victualling Department and its Association with Plymouth* (Plymouth, 1996) Chapter 8.

8. Journal of Henry Piers, 15 March 1851, 23 October 1851, 3 November 1851, 16 February 1852, NMM, JOD/102. Also, Ann Savours, 'The diary of Assistant Surgeon Henry Piers, HMS *Investigator*, 1850–54', *Journal of the Royal Naval Medical Service*, 76 (1990) pp. 33–8. Piers served under Surgeon Alexander Armstrong.

9. William Edward Parry, *Journal of A Voyage for the Discovery of a North West Passage from the Atlantic to the Pacific; Performed in the Years 1819–20, in His Majesty's Ships Hecla and Griper under the Orders of William Edward Parry*, second edition (London, 1821) 2 January 1820, pp. 132–3. Crops were pale in colour though had the same taste. See Revd Edward Parry, *Memoirs of Rear-Admiral Sir Edward*

Parry (London, 1857) pp. 101–2 for his exercise instruction in 1819 at Winter Harbour for eight to nine months.

10. McClintock, *The Voyage of the "Fox" in the Arctic Seas*, pp. 6–7; Robert F. Scott, *The Voyage of the 'Discovery'* (London, 1905) I, pp. 61–2, 299–300, 337, 442–8, 541–3. Tins were limited to 50–60 lbs each for easy handling. There is a photograph of cress and mustard in the polar regions on p. 546.

11. E. L. Atkinson, 'A method of growing yeast for making bread', *Journal of the Royal Naval Medical Service*, 1 (1915) pp. 202–3.

12. Anon., 'Regulations and instructions, for the medical officers of the Her Majesty's Fleet, 1825', *Journal of the Royal Naval Medical Service*, 87 (2001) pp. 17–18.

13. Statistical Report on the Health of the Navy for years 1830, 1831, 1832, 1833, 1834, 1835 and 1836 (hereafter Navy Health Report) PP XXX (1840) p. xviii. Wilson's remarks on healthcare for body and mind were recognized as progress in social medicine. See G. H. G. Southwell-Sander, 'The development of naval preventive medicine', *Journal of the Royal Naval Medical Service*, 43 (1956) p. 66.

14. A. G. Bath, 'The victualling of the navy', *Journal of the Royal United Service Institution*, 84 (1939) pp. 744–68; Anthony Carew, *The Lower Deck of the Royal Navy 1900–39* (Manchester, 1981) pp. 1–37; W. E. Clayton, 'Victualling the navy: as it was and as it is', *Brassey's Naval Annual* (1936) pp. 95–6; Peter Kemp, *The British Sailor: A Social History of the Lower Deck* (London, 1970); Christopher Lloyd and Jack L. S. Coulter, *Medicine and the Navy 1200–1900* (London, 1963) IV, 1815–1900; Eugene L. Rasor, *Reform in the Royal Navy: A Social History of the Lower Deck 1850 to 1880* (Connecticut, 1976) pp. 100–3; James Watt, 'The influence of nutrition upon achievement in maritime history', in Catherine Gessler and Derek J. Oddy (eds) *Food, Diet and Economic Change: Past and Present* (Leicester, 1993) pp. 62–82; Lionel Yexley (James Woods) *The Inner Life of the Navy* (London, 1908).

15. Clayton, 'Victualling the navy', pp. 92–3, said that 'presumably they were considered to be saving on their rations by leaving them, and hence the term "Savings".'

16. R. A. Rombough, 'Medical services of the Royal Navy in the nineteenth century, "nursing afloat"', *History of Nursing Bulletin*, 2 (1987) pp. 33, 38.

17. Booth, *Life and Labour*, second series: Industry (London, 1903) III, pp. 362–3. Booth mentioned that their wages were varied; 70–80s a month for steamships, 55s a month for sailing vessels and 28–30s for weekly boats. For example, *The Times*, 27 January 1893.

18. Navy Health Report for 1830–36, PP XXX (1840) pp. x–xiii.

19. Kenneth J. Carpenter, *The History of Scurvy and Vitamin C* (Cambridge, 1986) pp. 233–8; Christopher C. Lloyd, 'Victualling of the fleets in the eighteenth and nineteenth century', in J. Watt, E. J. Freeman and W. F. Bynum (eds) *Starving Sailors: The Influence of Nutrition upon Naval and Maritime History* (National

Maritime Museum, 1981) p. 11; G. J. Milton-Thompson, 'Two hundred years of the sailor's diet', in J. Watt, E. J. Freeman and W. F. Bynum (eds) *Starving Sailors: The Influence of Nutrition upon Naval and Maritime History* (National Maritime Museum, 1981) p. 31; Ivan M. Sharman, 'Vitamin requirements of the human body', in J. Watt, E. J. Freeman and W. F. Bynum (eds) *Starving Sailors: The Influence of Nutrition upon Naval and Maritime History* (National Maritime Museum, 1981) pp. 17–26.

20. West to Director-General Sir William Burnett, 5 July 1844, HMS *Bittern*, East Coast of Africa, Journal of Maurice West, NMM, JOD/167; Porter to wife, 28 October 1911, PTR/7/3.

21. Richard Barrie Behenna (ed.) *A Victorian Sailor's Diary: Richard Behenna of Vergan, 1833–1898* (Cornwall: Institute of Cornish Studies, 1981) pp. 14–16, 20.

22. Alexander Armstrong, *Observations of Naval Hygiene and Scurvy, More Particularly as the Latter Appeared During a Polar Voyage* (London, 1858) pp. 20–1; Gavin Milroy, *The Health of the Royal Navy Considered, in a Letter Addressed to the Rt Hon. Sir John S. Pakington* (London, 1862) pp. 60–4; William M'Kenzie Saunders, *Hygienic, Medical and Surgical Hints for Young Officers of the Royal and of the Merchant Navy* (London, 1856) pp. 5–7.

23. Anon., *The Seaman's Medical Guide in Preserving Health of a Ship's Crew*, new edition (London, 1873) pp. 14–18; Harry Leach, *The Ship Captain's Medical Guide* (London, 1868) p. 4. Revised by William Spooner, 9th edition (London, 1885) pp. 4–12.

24. Thomas J. Turner, 'Hygiene of the naval and merchant marine', in Albert H. Buck (ed.) *A Treatise on Hygiene and Public Health* (London, 1879) II, p. 177. Thomas Turner was medical director of the United States Navy.

25. G. C. Cook, 'Disease in the nineteenth century merchant navy: the Seamen's Hospital Society's experience', *The Mariner's Mirror*, 87 (2001) pp. 460–1; R. W. Coppinger, 'Tropical naval hygiene', in Andrew Davidson (ed.) *Hygiene and Diseases in Warm Climates* (London, 1893) pp. 98–111.

26. Thomas Francis Adkins, 'Cooking on board ship', in William Johnston Smith (ed.) *A Medical and Surgical Help for Ship-Masters and Officers in the Merchant Navy; Including First Aid to the Injured* (London, 1900) p. 293.

27. Sir Henry Keppel, *A Sailor's Life under Four Sovereigns* (London, 1899) I, p. 32; John Laffin, *Jack Tar: The Story of the British Sailor* (London, 1969) pp. 78–87.

28. A copy of the medical statistical returns of Baltic and Black Sea fleets during the years 1854 and 1855 (hereafter Baltic and Black Sea Fleets) PP IX (1857) pp. 75–7. Death from disease ratio was 43.6 per 1000; Lloyd and Coulter, *Medicine and the Navy*, IV, p. 147; Shepherd, *The Crimean Doctors*, I, pp. 330–5.

29. Burnett to Secretary of Admiralty, 28 December 1854, 'Report to the Board of Admiralty on the state of Health of the Seamen and Marines serving in the Black Sea and Crimea', Admiralty Records, NA, ADM 97/216.

30. Baltic and Black Sea Fleets, PP IX (1857) p. 37.

31. Milroy, *Health of the Royal Navy Considered*, pp. 4–5, 24, 37–43, 58–9.

32. Ibid., pp. 61–3.

33. John D. Macdonald, *Outline of Naval Hygiene* (London, 1881) pp. 162–3; Milroy, *Health of the Royal Navy Considered*, p. 57.

34. Queen's Regulations, 497, 498, 499, 501(Captain's Roles) extracts in appendix of Macdonald, *Outline of Naval Hygiene*, pp. 301–3.

35. *The Times*, 25 April 1865; Frederick Warren, *A Letter to the Secretary of State for War: On the Subject of Remuneration for a Newly Invented Cooking Apparatus* (London, 1868) p. 3.

36. Hutchison, *Food and the Principles of Dietetics*, pp. 387–9; Letheby, *On Food*, pp. 177–9; Sir Henry Thompson, *Food and Feeding* (London, 1899) 10th edition, pp. 99–102.

37. Warren to Secretary of Admiralty, 11 September 1870, ADM 1/6245.

38. Warren to Secretary of Admiralty, 6 July 1868; Warren to Secretary of Admiralty, 8 July 1868, enclosing 'Second Report on Captain Warren's Cooking Apparatus from HMS *Pembroke*', by Senior Lieutenant John Moyer, Staff Surgeon Thomas Seccombe, Paymaster Arthur Speed, ADM 1/6075.

39. Bryson and Champ to Secretary of Admiralty, 13 July 1868, ADM 1/6075.

40. Report of the Committee, appointed to enquire into the System of Savings of Provisions, and Victualling in the Royal Navy, with appendices (London, 1870) (hereafter Report of the Savings Committee) pp. 7, 23, ADM 1/6156.

41. Report of the Savings Committee, ADM 1/6156, pp. 4 5, 8 10.

42. Ibid., p. 14.

43. Ibid., pp. 26, 33–6, 38.

44. Ibid., p. 6.

45. 'New School of Cookery and Trained Cooks for the Navy', 28 June 1872, enclosed copy of a letter from Secretary of Admiralty Vernon Lushington to Warren, 23 August 1870; Warren to Stewart, 3 December 1871, ADM 1/6245.

46. Warren to Secretary of Admiralty, 11 September 1870, enclosing copy of a letter from War Office, Douglas Galton, to the Quartermaster General, 21 August 1867. Successful trials of Warren's apparatus were expected to be published for guidance in the army circular. Memoranda and Minute, 21 November 1870, 26 May 1871, 31 May 1871, 14 June 1871, ADM 1/6245.

47. Molyneux to Stewart, 4 January 1872, ADM 1/6245.

48. Glyn to Mundy, 1 September 1873; Lushington to Mundy, 17 September 1873 which mentioned that Warren's service would cease on 31 October of that year. ADM 1/6245.

49. Circular, No. 64 N. Admiralty, 27 September 1873, Ship's Cooks (trained cooks and cooks' mates) Robert Hall, to all Commanders-in-Chief, Flag

Officers, Captains, Commanders, and Commanding Officers of HM ships and vessels. *Navy List*, 1874, p. 441.

50. Alexander Rattray, Journal of HM Frigate *Bristol*, Particular Service Station between 29 January–20 November 1871, ADM 101/263.

51. Alexander Quinlan and N. E. Mann, *Cookery for Seamen* (Liverpool, 1894); ADM 12/1273.

52. *The Lancet*, 5 May 1894, p. 1113.

53. Secretary of Admiralty to Admiral Sir Charles Ogle, Commander-in-Chief, Portsmouth, 14 November 1846, f. 109, NMM, LBK/32; Navy Health Report for 1867, PP XLI (1868–69) Appendix III, pp. 133–4, Appendix IV, p. 157; Report for 1868, PP XLVII (1870) pp. 48–51.

54. Navy Health Report for 1869, PP XLV (1871) Appendix, p. 256; Report for 1871, PP XLVI (1873) pp. 3–4.

55. A. F. Grimbly, 'On real economy in recruiting', *Journal of the Royal Naval Medical Service*, 7 (1921) pp. 135–8; Navy Health Report for 1900, PP XLII (1901) pp. 4–5.

56. Report of the Committee appointed by the Lords Commissioners of the Admiralty to inquire into the State of Greenwich Hospital Schools, 1859, in Report of the Commissioners appointed to Inquire into Greenwich Hospital (hereafter Greenwich Hospital School Committee 1860) PP XXX (1860) p. lxxxix.

57. Greenwich Hospital School Committee 1860, PP XXX (1860) pp. 74, 81.

58. Thomas Brassey, *British Seamen as Described in Recent Parliamentary and Official Documents* (London, 1877) p. 72; J. McA. Holmes, 'The training service as seen in HMS *Impregnable*', *Journal of the Royal Naval Medical Service*, 13 (1927) pp. 130–5. The timetable of daily routine is on pp. 133–4.

59. Thomas Holman, *Life in the Royal Navy*, third edition (London, 1892) pp. 11–12.

60. C. K. Bushe, 'HMS *Ganges*, naval training establishment for boys, and the sick quarters, Shotley', *Journal of the Royal Naval Medical Service*, 15 (1929) pp. 14–23; H. W. Nicholls, 'Notes from a training establishment', *Journal of the Royal Naval Medical Service*, 14 (1928) pp. 170–7; D. L. Summers, *HMS Ganges 1866–1966: One Hundred Years of Training Boys for the Royal Navy* (Shotley Gate, 1966) p. 54.

61. R. C. Munday, 'Comparisons of the naval military, RAF, and civil medical services with private practice, part ix', *Journal of the Royal Naval Medical Service*, 38 (1951) pp. 150–1.

62. Report of the Committee on the Details of Naval Commissariat Duties, on System of Victualling Boys in the Training Ships, and of Providing for the Miscellaneous Expenditure in connexion therewith, with appendix (London, 1872) (hereafter Report of Victualling Boys) pp. 3–8, ADM 116/153.

63. Report of Victualling Boys, pp. 22–3, 25, 28, 32; Kennedy to Captain J. Wilson of *Impregnable*, 21 January 1873, ADM 116/153.

64. Greenwich Hospital School Committee 1860, PP XXX (1860) pp. xlv, lxxix.
65. Burney to Secretary of Admiralty, 9 November 1870, ADM 169/19; Burney to Secretary of Admiralty, 10 July 1874, ADM 169/65. On medical examination in 1881 the fleet surgeon complained about this reduced diet in that it caused weakness among Greenwich boys. See H. D. Turner, *The Cradle of the Navy: The Story of the Royal Hospital School at Greenwich and at Holbrook, 1694–1980* (York, 1990) pp. 87–9.
66. Report of the Committee appointed by the Lords Commissioners of the Admiralty to enquire into Greenwich Hospital School, PP XVI (1882) pp. xvi–xviii; Robert Christison, 'The dietary of the boys in the Greenwich Hospital School and of the pensioners in Greenwich Hospital', in Greenwich Hospital School Committee 1860, PP XXX (1860) pp. lxxvi–lxxvii. He commented that the current diet for the boys was too scanty, though the pensioners' was sufficient.
67. Armstrong to Burney, 29 May 1882, ADM 169/118.
68. Burney to Secretary of Admiralty, 17 June 1882; Hadlow to Secretary of Admiralty, 2 November 1882, ADM 169/118.
69. Hadlow to Secretary of Admiralty, 2 November 1882, Lloyd to Reid, 21 March 1883; Fleet Surgeon Alexander Turnbull to Reid, 16 July 1883, ADM 169/118.
70. Alston Kennerley, 'Ratings for the Mercantile Marine: the roles of charity, the state and industry in the pre-service education and training of ratings for the British Merchant Navy, 1879–1939', *History of Education*, 28 (1999) pp. 36–7; Metropolitan Asylums Board, Annual Report of the Committee of Management of the Metropolitan Training Ship *Exmouth*, lying off Grays, Essex (hereafter Annual Report of *Exmouth*) 1883, p. 6, LMA, MAB/2527, 'Epitome of subjects taught on board the *Exmouth*', in Annual Report of *Exmouth* for 1885, p. 8, MAB/2529; Summers, *HMS Ganges 1866–1966*, pp. 24–5.
71. Sir Allan Powell, *The Metropolitan Asylums Board and its Work, 1867–1930* (London: Metropolitan Asylums Board, 1930) pp. 47–8. The guardians for the poor in Whitechapel and Poplar managed the first training ship *Goliath*. It was destroyed by fire in 1875 and then replaced by *Exmouth*, which the Admiralty lent and the Metropolitan Asylums Board ran. In 1905 it was inaugurated and the new ship was built at the same time. Poor Law School, Return of *Exmouth* Training Ship, 25 March 1908, ED 132/5. Return of All Vessels of the Royal Navy used for training Boys and where stationed in the years 1868, 1869 and 1870, PP XL (1870) pp. 2–3. There were on average 654 boys trained on *St Vincent* in 1868 and 609 in 1870, and 674 boys trained in *Impregnable* in 1868 and 561 in 1870. 'Boys admitted and discharged 1876 to 1914', in Annual Report of *Exmouth* for 1914, Appendix II, p. 15, MAB/2558. Archibald Cowie, 'The supply of British seamen', *Contemporary Review*, 73 (1898) pp. 861–2.

72. Annual Report of *Exmouth* for 1882, pp. 6–8, MAB/2526; Report for 1892, p. 2, MAB/2536. The commander of *Impregnable* said that *Exmouth* boys were better than those of any other mercantile training ship in 1882. In 1892 the Metropolitan Board of Guardians commented that boys became healthier through training and as a result many of them were of service to the country. Some of the Japanese visitors were Professor N. Kanai of the Imperial University of Tokyo on 6 August 1909, Admiral Count Togo, chief of the Imperial Japanese Navy (accompanied by Rear-Admiral, Sir Charles Ottley, secretary of the Imperial Defence) Commander S. Saito on 5 July 1911, and Captain Kiyokazu Abo, naval attaché to the Japanese embassy (with Admiral W. Henderson) on 16 May 1914. Report for 1909, p. 7, MAB/2553; Report for 1911, p. 6, MAB/2555; Report for 1914, p. 7, MAB/2558.

73. Annual Report of *Exmouth* for 1878, p. 24, MAB/2522; Report for 1880, p. 21, MAB/2524; Report for 1883, pp. 27, 42, MAB/2527; Report for 1884, pp. 23, 28, MAB/2528; Report for 1885, pp. 22, 32–3, MAB/2529; Report for 1892, pp. 23–4, MAB/2536; Report for 1893, p. 25, MAB/2537.

74. Annual Report of *Exmouth* for 1903, p. 19, MAB/2547; Minutes of the Proceedings of the Training Ship *Exmouth* Committee (hereafter *Exmouth* Minutes) 16 November 1903, MAB/1302; Report for 1905, p. 13, MAB/2549; *Exmouth* Minutes, 6 March 1905, MAB/1304.

75. *Exmouth* Minutes, 20 January 1908, 20 July 1908, 28 September 1908, 23 November 1908, MAB/1308. First Colmore purchased 20 books and after visits by Mr Butler, a school examiner, and Nicholson for cookery he decided to purchase 100 copies.

76. *Exmouth* Minutes, 21 June 1909, 10 October 1910, 6 May 1912, MAB/1309, MAB/1310, MAB/1312; Nicholson, 'Report as to instruction in Cookery', 19 April 1909, ED 132/5.

Chapter 8

1. Surgeon E. A. Shaw's analysis of Mediterranean fever was an example of such research. He revealed from experiments that it was transmitted from goats' milk. H. V. Wyatt, 'Royal Navy surgeons and the transmission of brucellosis by goats' milk', *Journal of the Royal Naval Medical Service*, 85 (1999) pp. 112–17.

2. Clayton, 'Victualling the navy', pp. 97–8. Clayton pointed out that the general messing system was still deemed ideal and practical even in the 1930s; in some cases he could find no progress since the canteen committees of the early 1900s. There was still a problem of varied food bills among ships because young men who were in charge of messing had not enough knowledge to purchase suitable foods, so they were inclined to obtain tinned food from the canteen, which did not support good health. See also Charles Dawe, 'Diet and

disease in the Royal Navy', *Journal of the Royal Naval Medical Service*, 13 (1927) pp. 273–6, 283–5.

3. Navy Health Report for 1911, PP LIII (1912–13) p. 16.

4. Navy Health Report for 1874, PP XLVIII (1875) pp. 6–7; Report for 1875, PP XLVIII (1876) pp. 47–8, 261–2; Report for 1883, PP XLIX (1884–85) p. 23; Report for 1885, PP XLII (1886) pp. xv, 94–5; Report for 1893, PP LIV (1894) pp. 83–4; Report for 1894, PP LXV (1895) pp. 30–2, 78–80; Report for 1911, PP LIII (1912–13) p. 67.

5. Navy Health Report for 1865, PP XLVI (1867–68) pp. 107–8; Report for 1867, PP XLI (1868–69) pp. 86–7; Report for 1868, PP XLVII (1870) p. 240.

6. Navy Health Report for 1873, PP XLI (1874) Appendix, pp. 8–9.

7. Thomas B. Shaw, 'Water-boats and the supply of drinking water from the shore to HM ships', *Journal of the Royal Naval Medical Service*, 4 (1918) pp. 41–7; Thomas B. Shaw, 'The ship's water supply', *Journal of the Royal Naval Medical Service*, 5 (1919) pp. 48–71; T. J. Underhill, 'Points of interest respecting preserved food, more particularly that supplied to the fleet', *Journal of the Royal Naval Medical Service*, 8 (1922) pp. 241–6.

8. Kenneth Chivers, 'Henry Jones versus the Admiralty', *History Today*, 10 (1960) pp. 247–54; Navy Health Report for 1867, PP XLI (1868–69) Appendix III, pp. 132–40, 152–3; Talbot to Secretary of Admiralty, 25 May 1854, enclosing reports by Surgeon John Adams, HMS *Mænder*, Surgeon William Loney, HMS *Hydra*, Surgeon Andrew Moffit, HMS *Penguin*, and Assistant Surgeon in charge, Fred Le Roux, HMS *Dart*, ADM 97/211; Edward Moore (supplier of Moore's Milk) to Burnett, 26 October 1854, ADM 97/215; Medical Inspector Alexander M'Kecknie to Burnett, 25 September 1854, HM Hospital ship *Belleisle*, ADM 97/214.

9. Navy Health Report for 1871, PP XLVI (1873) Appendix, pp. 208–9; *British Medical Journal*, 8 November 1873, pp. 548–9.

10. Lloyd and Coulter, *Medicine and the Navy*, IV, p. 214.

11. Anon., 'Royal Naval Hospital at Haslar near Gosport', *Journal of the Royal Naval Medical Service*, 34 (1948) pp. 76–8.

12. Navy Health Reports for years 1830–36, PP XXX (1840) pp. xiv–xvi.

13. Burnett to Secretary of Admiralty, 18 May 1854, ADM 97/211.

14. Donald R. McNeil, 'Medical care aboard Australia-bound convict ships, 1786–1840', *Bulletin of the History of Medicine*, 26 (1952) pp. 117–40.

15. Journal of West, 6 August 1843, HMS *Bittern*, Coast of West Africa, JOD/167.

16. Deas to Burnett, 27 December 1854, HMS *Sanspareil*, Balaclava, ADM 97/216; Assistant Surgeon Herbert MacKarsie to Burnett, 9 February 1855, ADM 97/218.

17. Allan to Burnett, 30 September 1842, ADM 97/156.

18. Cowan to his mother, 30 January 1856, Royal Naval Hospital, Malta, PTR/1.

19. Wilson to Burnett, 'Report on the Lunatic Department of the Royal Naval Hospital, Haslar for the year ending 31 March 1854', pp. 11, 22–5, ADM 97/210.

20. Greenwich Hospital School Committee 1860, PP XXX (1860) pp. xiii, 89–90.

21. William Tait, *A History of Haslar Hospital* (Portsmouth, 1906) pp. 149–51.

22. Journal of Guthrie, 16 April 1830, 2 June 1830, HMS *Seringapatam*, at Tahiti, JOD/16; James McIlroy to Thomas McIlroy, 24 February 1843, HMS *Persian*, at sea off West Africa, NMM, LBK/41; and Rombough, 'Medical services of the Royal Navy', p. 35.

23. Davidson to Burnett, 4 February 1854, Therapia, ADM 97/217; J. Stewart to H. Stewart, 11 April 1854, enclosed in J. Stewart to Burnett, 18 April 1854, ADM 97/210.

24. Pat Gould, 'The story of the Royal Naval Nursing Service up to 1914', *History of Nursing Bulletin*, 2 (1987) pp. 20–5; Kathleen M. Harland, 'A short history of Queen Alexandra's Royal Naval Nursing Service', *Journal of the Royal Naval Medical Service*, 70 (1984) pp. 59–61; Richard Huntsman, Mary Bruin and Deborah Holttum, 'Light before dawn: naval nursing and medical care during the Crimean War', *Journal of the Royal Naval Medical Service*, 88 (2002) pp. 9–17; Marjorie E. Penney, 'Letters from Therapia, 1855', *Blackwoods Magazine*, 275 (1954) pp. 413–21; Shepherd, *The Crimean Doctors*, I, pp. 50, 107, II, pp. 549–50.

25. Gregory Clark, *'Doc': 100 Year History of the Sick Berth Branch* (London, 1984) pp. 11–23; G. O. M. Dickenson, 'The origin of the sick berth staff, Royal Navy', *Journal of the Royal Naval Medical Service*, 3 (1927) pp. 161, 164–5, 168–9; S. Jenkinson, 'Extract from a naval scrap book', *Journal of the Royal Naval Medical Service*, 42 (1956) p. 121.

26. Report to the Lords Commissioners of the Admiralty of the Committee approved to inquire into the Organisation and Training of the Sick-Berth Staff of the Navy, and Nursing Staff of the Royal Naval Hospitals (hereafter Report of Sick Berth Staff) PP XVII (1884) pp. v, vii, xii–xiii; Lloyd and Coulter, *Medicine and the Navy*, IV, p. 64.

27. Inspector-General James Dick to Storekeeper and Cashier, W. Mitchell, 9 October 1886; Dick to Mitchell, 13 October 1886; Assistant Storekeeper and Cashier John Charlton to Dick, 1 November 1886, ADM 305/62; *Navy and Army Illustrated*, 19 February 1897, p. 112; C. T. Parsons, 'The modernisation of Haslar', *Journal of the Royal Naval Medical Service*, 72 (1986) p. 107; Tait, *A History of Haslar Hospital*, p. 5.

28. Morgan to Medical Director-General, Sir John Watt Reid, 28 April 1883, ADM 305/55; Dick to Reid, 4 February 1885, ADM 305/59. The superintendent of the hospital recommended the hospital's current cook as lecturer for the sick-berth staff.

29. Report of Sick Berth Staff, PP XVII (1884) pp. 12, 23. Parkhurst said generally cookery instruction at hospitals was too basic, such as peeling potatoes.

30. Clark to Rear Admiral Sir Anthony Hoskyns, 6 November 1883, ADM 116/220. Clarke to Clark, 1 May 1895; Clarke to Dick, 26 September 1895, regarding commencement of a course from 8 October for three weeks, ADM 1/7278.

31. Dick to Reid, 8 July 1885, ADM 305/60; Gerald Sickel, *Historical Notes on Haslar and the Naval Medical Profession* (London, 1903) reprinted from *The Guy's Hospital Gazette*, p. 28.

32. Clarke to Clark, 1 May 1895; Clarke to Dick, 26 September and 8 November 1895. Memorandum of 'Ships' Cook's Certificate (£5 5s for four weeks)' using 'Cookery for the sick and convalescent (£4 for three weeks)' in *The Terms and Rules for the Local Classes of the National Training School of Cookery, January 1895*, p. 15. Clarke to Clark, 3 October 1895. Inspector-General, Duncan Hilston to Dick, 12 October 1895 includes the plan that the sick-room cookery course was to be prepared the same as for the London Hospital nurses. It was divided into two groups at Haslar Hospital, 12 probationers for the practical course from 10 a.m. to noon, another 12 had training from 2 p.m. to 4 p.m.; Hilston to Dick, 1 November 1895, ADM 1/7278. NTSC Minutes, 3 April 1894, 6 May 1894, 29 May 1894, 19 June 1894, 3 November 1894, 17 December 1895, ED 164/3. *The Lancet*, 7 February 1903, p. 393.

33. Treasury, Francis Browntt to Secretary of Admiralty, 1 August 1895, ADM 1/7278; NTSC Minutes, 26 February 1903, ED 164/3.

34. Porter to wife, 10 May 1891, 28 November 1891, HMS *Scout*, at Malta, PTR/2.

35. Report to the Lords Commissioners of the Admiralty of the Committee on the Rank, Pay and Position of Naval Medical Officers, PP XXII (1881) pp. xiii–xiv; Report to the Lords Commissioners of the Admiralty of the Committee on the Training of Naval Medical Officers, PP LV (1899) pp. 4–5, 9.

36. Case E. 302 vol. 1, Training of: Medical Officers, Sick Berth Staff, Nursing Sisters, Dispensers. Report of the Committee etc. (1898)–1899, minute, 21 March 1899, ADM 116/516; Report of the Training of Naval Medical Officers, PP LV (1899) p. 4; Cook, 'Disease in the nineteenth century merchant navy'; Coppinger, 'Tropical naval hygiene'. The London School of Tropical Medicine was established in 1899 at the Royal Albert Dock Hospital before moving to St Pancras.

37. Grant to Norbury, 15 June 1898; Louisa Hogg to Hilston, 20 June 1899, ADM 116/516.

38. Second Report of the Committee on the Training of Medical Officers, & c., (London, 1899) pp. 1–3, ADM 116/516.

39. Captain William Hamilton to Commander-in-Chief, Plymouth, Lord Charles Scott, 12 December 1900; Hamilton, HMS *Duke of Wellington*, to Commander-in-Chief, Portsmouth, Admiral Sir Charles Hotham, 12 February 1901, with comments from Admiral Charles Holland, ADM 1/7447.

40. William Spooner, 'Dietary scales in connection with the health of seamen',

Public Health, official organ of the Congress of Hygiene and Demography, 1891 special daily numbers, pp. 149–50.

41. Henry E. Armstrong, 'The hygiene of merchant ships, with special regards to seamen, a paper read at the International Congress of Hygiene and Demography, Section IX at Budapest', *Public Health*, 7 (1894) pp. 62, 65–6; *The Lancet*, 5 May 1894, p. 1113.

42. Report of the Committee appointed by the Board of Trade, to inquire into certain questions affecting the Mercantile Marine, PP LLXII (1903) pp. 464–5.

43. Report of the Committee appointed to Inquire into the question of Navy Rations, Meal Hours, the Prices Paid for "Savings," and the management of Canteens, PP XLII (1901) p. 7.

44. Ibid., pp. 6, 9.

45. Report of the Committee Appointed to Inquire into the Question of Naval Cookery, the Organisation of the Cookery Schools at the Home Ports, Bread-making in HM Ships, and kindred matters (London, 1905) (hereafter Report of Naval Cookery) pp. 1–4, 9, ADM 1/7953.

46. *Euryalus* further report on cooking trials, from Commander-in-Chief, North America and West Indies, Admiral Sir Day Bosanquet to Secretary of Admiralty, 1 October 1906, ADM 1/7953.

47. Report of Naval Cookery, ADM 1/7953, p. 5.

48. Report of Naval Cookery, p. 6, Appendix II, p. 21, ADM 1/7953. The training of cooks was planned for six months, from laying a fire to cleaning and baking.

49. Report of Naval Cookery, pp. 9, 17, Appendix III, pp. 22–34, ADM 1/7953; Anon., *Handbook of Naval Cookery* (1914) pp. 99–106, 134–5.

50. Greene to Secretary of Treasury, 9 September 1907; Captain Mark Kerr, HMS *Drake*, 15 June 1906, reported untrained cooks and monotonous diet were largely changed by skilled cooks under clean and more hygienic conditions of cooking. He reported again on 5 December 1906. *Carnarvon* and *Venerable* also reported improvement and claimed better fitted galleys for cooks, 30 June 1906; boys and youths on *Euryalus* gained weight, Bosanquet reported on 1 October 1906; *King Edward VII* also reported hygienic cooking, 14 June 1906; Greene to Treasury, 18 September 1907, ADM 1/7953. A circular letter issued 16 January 1908 on ships' cooks by C. I. Thomas stated that they were important to maintain 'health and comfort of the crews', in Carew, *Lower Deck of the Royal Navy*, appendix iv, pp. 382–5.

51. Pillow to Clarke, 11 March 1905, ADM 1/7953.

52. Pillow to Clarke, 30 March 1905, Pillow Papers, BR 124/48.

53. Pillow to Clarke, 'Special Report upon the Preserved Vegetables provided in the Kitchen', 30 March 1905, Pillow Papers, BR 124/48.

54. Kathleen Harland, *A History of the Queen Alexandra's Royal Naval Nursing Service* (Portsmouth, 1990) pp. 14–23. At least three years' experience at civilian

hospitals was required for nurses, Mildred L. Hughes, 'The naval nursing service', *Journal of the Royal Naval Medical Service*, 8 (1922) pp. 182–90; Lloyd and Coulter, *Medicine and the Navy*, pp. 269–70; R. W. Mussen, 'The Royal Naval Medical School', *Journal of the Royal Naval Medical Service*, 33 (1947) pp. 61–7.

55. *Aberdeen Daily Journal*, 15 May 1915, PTR/7/5.

56. Hoskyn to Porter, 22 April 1908. When Hoskyn wrote to Porter there were only 17 patients, PTR/7/3; 'A Scale of Diet for Patients in the Royal Naval Hospitals and Marine Infirmaries, revised, April 1908', PTR/7/5.

57. Cowan to Porter, 7 April 1886, PTR/3; Porter to wife, HMS *Scout* at Malta, 26 March 1890; Porter to wife, HMS *Scout* at Piraeus, Athens, 19 April 1890, PTR/2; Porter to wife, 30 March 1900, PTR/6/2.

58. Report of the Committee on the Naval Medical Service, 1909, II, Sick Berth and Nursing Staff, pp. 3–4, Appendix A, pp. 20–1, ADM 116/1244.

59. NTSC Minutes, 31 March 1909, 14 March 1911, ED 164/4; Report of the National Training School of Cookery in 1910 shows that 18 navy accountant officers and four army officers joined the course, p. 5, ED 115/57. In 1911 seven army non-commissioned officers from the Royal Army Medical Corps also spent four weeks at the school.

60. 'Notes on what Miss Lückes has done for Her Majesty's Queen Alexandra's Royal Nursing Service', enclosed in Porter to First Sea Lord, Admiral Prince Louis of Battenberg, 26 April 1913, headed 'Submission with Reference to the Decoration of the Royal Red Cross', PTR/9.

61. Porter to wife, 4 August 1909, 8 August 1909, 26 October 1911, 27 October 1911, PTR/7/3.

62. Porter to wife, 31 July 1912, PTR/7/4.

63. The Committee on the System of Ordering, Receiving, Issuing and Accounting for Food Supplies on Other Stores in Connection therewith at the Royal Naval Hospitals at Haslar, Plymouth and Chatham (London, 1910) pp. 6–8, 30–1, Appendix B, pp. 46–7, ADM 1/8317.

64. Report on visit to Glasgow Royal Infirmary, Glasgow Western Infirmary, Royal Infirmary Edinburgh, the General Infirmary Leeds, and the General Hospital Birmingham, January 1905, by Secretary E. W. Morris, Steward G. Hills and Matron's Assistant A. McIntosh, LH/A/17/21.

65. NTSC Minutes, 21 May 1912, 18 June 1912, 15 October 1912. £102 for teaching paymasters, ED 164/4.

66. Anon., *Manual of Instruction for the Royal Naval Sick Berth Staff* (London, 1914) Chapter XXI, Cooking for the Sick, pp. 388–404.

67. Lückes to Lady Porter, 15 August 1918; Porter to First Sea Lord, 26 April 1913, PTR/9.

68. *Regulations for Queen Alexandra's Royal Naval Nursing Service* (London, 1911).

69. Wilsmore to Porter, 25 April 1913, PTR/9.

70. Report of the Committee on the Naval Medical Service, I, Officers on the Active List, 1909, pp. 16–23; Appendix III of Admiralty to Treasury, 28 March 1911, mentioned that the payment of navy medical officers should be slightly higher than those of the army. Enclosure of Treasury letter dated 19 January 1911. ADM 116/243.

71. Anon., *Manual of Instruction for the Royal Naval Sick Berth Staff*, pp. 451–4.

72. Clark, *'Doc': 100 Year History*, pp. 123–4.

73. C. E. Hamilton, 'A suggested improved diet on the East Indies station', *Journal of the Royal Naval Medical Service*, 5 (1919) pp. 284–5.

74. *British Medical Journal*, 31 August 1907, p. 503.

75. Ibid., p. 523.

Conclusion

1. Heath to Selby-Bigge, 21 June 1913, ED 24/1789.

2. Board of Education, Statistics of Public Education in England and Wales, 1907–8 (hereafter Educational Statistics) PP LXVIII (1909) p. lxxvii; Statistics for 1912–13, PP L (1914–16) p. 253.

3. Memorandum on an inquiry into the Demand for and the Supply of Domestic Subjects Teachers for Public Elementary Schools and into the need for an increased Grant to Training Schools, ED 24/1789. This was despite fewer training schools for teachers of domestic subjects. In 1896–97 there were 27 schools in Britain. In 1907–8 there were 18 (England and Wales); in 1913–14, 14 were recorded. Pillow, 'Domestic economy teaching in England', pp. 162–3; Educational Statistics for 1907–8, PP LXVIII (1909) pp. 269, 425; Statistics for 1913–14, PP LI (1914–16) p. 177.

4. Maude Agnes Lawrence, *General Report on the Teaching of Domestic Subjects to Public Elementary School Children in England and Wales* (London, 1912) pp. 11, 32.

5. Second Report of the Cross Commission, PP XXIX (1887) p. 482.

6. For example, Hospital Nursing Report, 1896, LH/A/17/62; Matron's Annual Letters, No.11, 1904, LH/N/7/2/1; Morten, 'Nursing as a profession for women', pp. 120–1.

7. ADM 12/922, ADM 12/945, ADM 12/967, ADM 12/1286.

8. Director of Victualling, O. Murray to the Secretary of N. Branch, 28 September 1906 and C. E. Gifford, 'Increase of cooks' mates required', memoranda and minute, 16 April 1907, ADM 1/7953.

9. Statement of the First Lord of the Admiralty, Explanatory of the Navy Estimates, 1910–11, PP LXI (1910) pp. 5, 11–12.

10. Army Estimates of the Effective and Non-Effective Services, for 1871–72, PP XXXVIII (1871) p. 23; for 1880–81, PP XLI (1880) p. 23; for 1887–88, PP XLVIII (1889) p. 27; for 1894–95, PP LII (1894) p. 28.

11. *The Times*, 10 March, 1915.
12. Education Report for 1890–91, PP XXVII (1891) p. 348; Report for 1891–92, PP XXVIII (1892) p. 411.
13. Report on the Working of the Education Act, 1906, PP XXIII (1910) pp. 9–12.
14. Hughes, *Practical Hints on District Nursing*, pp. 55–6.
15. Anon., *Report of the Ladies' Sanitary Association*, p. 10.
16. Ella Pycroft, 'History of training schools for teachers of domestic economy in England', *Journal of the Society of Arts*, XLV (1897) pp. 966–71.
17. Report of Medical Inspection and Feeding Committee, PP XLVII (1906) II, pp. 188–9.
18. Booth, *Life and Labour*, second series: Industry (London, 1904) V, pp. 319–21.
19. For example, Imperial Japanese Navy, *The Surgical and Medical History of the Naval War Between and Japan and China During 1894–95* (Tokyo, 1901) pp. 492–511, 515–18, 523–5; The Royal Navy asked advice from the Japanese navy for beriberi, as the latter had more experience of this disease. Charles Dundas, captain and naval attaché of British embassy to Captain Kenji Ide, the Imperial Japanese Navy, 16 April 1910, Tokyo. It enclosed a draft copy from the medical department of the Japanese navy for this enquiry, 20 April 1910. Taishikantsuki Bukan tono Oufuku Bunsyo (correspondence, between military attaché and the foreign embassies) 1910, The National Institute of Defense Studies, BuOuBun/M–19. For the United States Army, Department of War, *Manual for Army Cooks* (Washington, 1883) pp. 3–4, 7.
20. Journal of Pine, 14 July 1854, JOD/26; Porter to his daughter, 27 October 1899, PTR/6/2.
21. Bosanquet to Secretary of Admiralty, 1 October 1906; Greene to Secretary of Treasury, 9 September 1907, 18 September 1907; Report of Naval Cookery, p. 5, ADM 1/7953.
22. *British Medical Journal*, 20 September 1924, pp. 510–11; Dorothy E. Linsay and D. Noël Paton, *Report upon a Study of the Diet of the Labouring Classes in the City of Glasgow Carried out During 1911–1912, Under the Auspices of the Corporation of the City* (Glasgow, 1913) pp. 9, 34.
23. Hardy, *Health and Medicine in Britain*, pp. 97–100; John Boyd Orr, *Food, Health and Income: Report on a Survey of Adequacy of Diet in Relation to Income* (London, 1936) pp. 5, 9–10, 36–8, 45–50.
24. Rose M. Simmonds, *Handbook of Diets* (London, 1937) second edition, pp. 17–18.
25. Ruth Pybus, 'The protective diet', *Edinburgh Post-Graduate Lectures in Medicine*, III (1942–43) pp. 69–71.

Bibliography

Unpublished Material
Archival Sources

1. Official Papers
(a) In the National Archives (NA), London; Admiralty Records; Series: ADM 1/;
   ADM 12/; ADM 97/; ADM 101/; ADM 116/; ADM 169/; Haslar Hospital
   Records: ADM 305/; Ministry of Education Records Series: ED 14/; ED 24/;
   ED 115/; ED 132/; ED 142/; ED 164/; Ministry of Health Records Series:
   MH 26/; MH 32/

2. Private Collections
(a) In the British Library (BL), London; Hall Papers; Nightingale Papers;
   Nightingale Tracts

(b) At the British Library of Political and Economic Science Archives, London;
   Charles Booth Collection, Survey notebooks; Diary of Beatrice Webb

(c) At the Guildhall Library, London; Metropolitan District Nursing Association
   Records

(d) At the King's College London Archives (KCLA), London; King's College
   Hospital, Minutes of the Committee of Management KH/CM; King's College
   Hospital, Nursing Committee KH/N; The Nurses' Training School of King's
   College Hospital 84/1; Nightingale Institute 85/1

(e) At the London Metropolitan Archives (LMA), London; Guy's Hospital
   Records, Administrative Records H09/GY/A; Guy's Hospital Records, Staff
   Records H09/GY/C; Invalid Kitchens of London Records IML/; Metropolitan
   Asylums Board Records MAB/; Nightingale Fund Council A/NFC; St Thomas'
   Hospital Records, Administrative Records H01/ST/A; St Thomas' Hospital
   Records, Nightingale Collection H01/ST/NC; St Thomas' Hospital Records,
   Nightingale Training School H01/ST/NTS; Technical Education Board
   Records, London County Council TEB/

(f) At the National Army Museum (NAM), London

Archives 6403-17, a letter of George Williams; Archives 7004-3, History of the Army Catering Corps; Archives 7211-62, MS of Felix Alexander Hadingue; Archives 7708-42, letters of Major Samuel Messiter Rowlandson; Archives 8001–1, belonging to Henry Kingston, attached to his *Soldier's Small Book*; H. K. Allport, Army Form 51, *Health Memoranda for Soldiers* (Gosport, 1906); Archives 8205-41, letters of 9007, Private Harry Edward Neal

(g) At the National Maritime Museum (NMM), London
Journal of Robert Guthrie JOD/16; Journal of Chilley Pine JOD/26; Journal of Henry Piers JOD/102; Journal of Maurice West JOD/167; Letterbook of Admiral Sir Charles Ogle LBK/32; Letterbook of James McIlroy LBK/41; Sir James Porter Papers PTR/

(h) At the Royal London Hospital Archives and Museum (RLHA), London; Royal London Hospital Records; London Hospital, Administrative Records LH/A; London Hospital, Nursing Records LH/N; London Hospital, Records from unofficial sources LH/X; Subject files LH/Z; London Hospital, Medical Council Records LM/1; Wilby Hart Diaries, typescript and manuscript PP/WILBY; Lecture Notebooks of Edith Cavell

(i) At the Royal Society of Arts Archive, London; Domestic Economy Congresses 1877–1881 PR.GE/121/10/36

(j) In the Wellcome Library for the History and Understanding of Medicine, Archives and Manuscripts (Wellcome Library), London; Correspondence of Florence Nightingale; Royal Army Medical Corps, Muniments Collection RAMC/; The Queen's Nursing Institute Collection SA/QNI/

(k) In the Women's Library, London; Margaret Pillow Papers 7/MEP/

(l) At the F. L. Calder College Archives (Calder Archives), Liverpool John Moores University, Liverpool; F. L. Calder College of Domestic Science Records; Liverpool Training School of Cookery, Annual Reports 1876–1915; Executive Committee Meeting Minutes, 1891–1909; The Report of the Northern Union of Schools of Cookery for 1878; Letter from Nightingale to Calder

(m) At the Gloucestershire Record Office (GRO), Gloucester; Gloucestershire Training College of Domestic Science Records K/1372; Gloucestershire School of Cookery and Domestic Economy, Annual Reports 1895–1914; Gloucestershire County Council, Higher Education Sub-Committee, Domestic Economy Minor Committee Minutes 1906–1915; Old Girl's Guild Minutes 1904; Gloucestershire County Council, Annual Report of the late Technical Instruction Committee CE/R2/3/1

(n) At the Norfolk Record Office, Norwich; Pillow Family Papers; Letterbooks of Margaret Pillow BR 124/

(o) In the Clendening History of Medicine Library, Kansas University Medical Center; Nightingale Collection, http://clendening.kume.edu/dc/fn; Letter from Nightingale to Lückes; Correspondence with Burton

(p) At the National Institute for Defense Studies, Tokyo, Japan; Man-Dainikki (Japanese Army Minute Books on Manchuria), in Rikugunsyo Dainikki; (Japanese Army Minute Books); RikuManFu/M37; M38; M40; Japanese Navy Records; Taishikantsuki Bukan tono Oufuku Bunsyo (Correspondence, between military attaché and the foreign embassies) for 1910; BuOuBun/M-19

Newspapers and Journals

British Journal of Nursing   British Medical Journal
Contemporary Review   Economic Review
Journal of Royal Army Medical Corps   Journal of the Royal Naval Medical Service
Journal of the Royal Sanitary Institute   Journal of the Royal United Service Institution
Lady's Realm   Navy and Army Illustrated
Navy List   Nineteenth Century
Parliamentary Accounts and Papers   Public Health
The Epicure   The Hospital
The Lancet   The Morning Post
The Nursing Record   The Police Review and Parade Gossip
The Times

Secondary Sources

Abel-Smith, Brian (1960) *A History of the Nursing Profession* (London)
    (1964) *The Hospitals, 1800–1948: A Study in Social Administration in England and Wales* (London)
Acheson, Roy (1991) 'The British diploma in public health: birth and adolescence', in Elizabeth Fee and Roy Acheson (eds) *A History of Education in Public Health: Health that Mocks the Doctors' Rules* (Oxford) pp. 44–82
Acland, Lady (née Ovans) 'A few recollections of St Thomas', 1895 to 1903', H01/ST/NTS/Y/23/002/001
Adams, Rose (1877) 'The work of the Ladies' Sanitary Association', in *Report of the Congress on Domestic Economy to be Taught as a Branch of General Education, Birmingham, 1877* (Birmingham) pp. 47–9
Adkins, Thomas Francis (1900) 'Cooking on board ship', in William Johnston Smith (ed.) *A Medical and Surgical Help for Ship-Masters and Officers in the Merchant Navy; Including First Aid to the Injured* (London) pp. 293–300

Aitken, William (1862) *On the Growth of the Recruit and Young Soldier, with a View to a Judicious Selection of "Growing Lads" for the Army, and a Regulated System of Teaching for Recruits* (London)

A Lady Inspector (*c*.1900) *How to Become a Lady Sanitary Inspector* (London)

Allen, Greta (*c*.1905) *Practical Hints of Health Visitors* (London)

Allen, V. L. (1958) 'The National Union of Police and Prison Officers', *Economic History Review*, XI, pp. 133–43

Allport, H. K. (1904) 'Training soldiers in personal hygiene', *Journal of the Royal Army Medical Corps*, III, pp. 621–3

(1906) *Health Memoranda for Soldiers* (Gosport) Army Form 51, NAM Archives 8001–1, belonging to Henry Kingston, attached to his *Soldier's Small Book*

Andrews, Miss, a Guardian of the Parish of St Pancras (1881) 'The need of domestic economy in bringing up pauper children', *The Schoolmaster*, 25 June, p. 726, Royal Society of Arts Archive, PR.GE/121/10/36

Anon. (1871) *Seventh Annual Report of the Sanitary Commissioner with the Government of India, 1870* (Calcutta)

Anon. (1873) *The Seaman's Medical Guide in Preserving Health of a Ship's Crew*, new edition (London)

Anon. (1883) *Birmingham Health Lectures* (Birmingham)

Anon. (1890) 'Queen Victoria's Jubilee Institute for Nurses, Scottish branch, Edinburgh. First annual report, 1889', in William Rathbone, *Sketch of the History and Progress of District Nursing from its Commencement in the Year 1859 to the Present Date* (London) Appendix B, pp. 105–7

Anon. (1891) *The Report of the Ladies' Sanitary Association to the Seventh International Congress of Hygiene and Demography* (London)

Anon. (1893) 'Rural health missioners', *Public Health*, 5, pp. 131–3

Anon. (1894) *Standing Orders for the Army Medical Staff in Relation to the Medical Staff Corps* (London)

Anon. (1900) *Longman's 'Ship' Series, Domestic Economy Readers*, Book 2 (London)

Anon. (1905) 'Abstract of co-joint report of the advisory and nursing boards, containing a scheme to develop the training of orderlies of the Royal Army Medical Corps as attendants upon the sick and wounded', *Journal of the Royal Army Medical Corps*, V, pp. 292–303

Anon. (1908) 'The school of army sanitation, Aldershot', *Journal of the Royal Army Medical Corps*, XI, pp. 482–5

Anon. (1911) *Nursing Guide, Handbook of Nurses' League and Register of Nurses Trained at Guy's Hospital. Edited by the Matron*, 6th edition (London) Guy's Hospital Records, LMA, H9/GY/C/20/001

Anon. (1914) *Handbook of Naval Cookery*

Anon. (1914) *Manual of Instruction for the Royal Naval Sick Berth Staff* (London)

Anon. (1940) 'Abstract from "Captain James Cook," by Kitson (1907) pp. 331–341', *Journal of the Royal Naval Medical Service*, 26, pp. 329–35

Anon. (1948) 'Royal Naval Hospital at Haslar near Gosport', *Journal of the Royal Naval Medical Service*, 34, pp. 76–8

Anon. (2001) 'Regulations and instructions, for the medical officers of the Her Majesty's Fleet, 1825', *Journal of the Royal Naval Medical Service*, 87, pp. 6–81

Archer, G. J. Stoney (1905) 'A lecture on hygiene', *Journal of the Royal Army Medical Corps*, V, pp. 712–46

Armstrong, Alexander (1858) *Observations of Naval Hygiene and Scurvy, More Particularly as the Latter Appeared During a Polar Voyage* (London)

Armstrong, Henry E. (1894) 'The hygiene of merchant ships, with special regards to seamen, a paper read at the International Congress of Hygiene and Demography, Section IX at Budapest', *Public Health*, 7, pp. 62–6

Arnold, David (1993) *Colonizing the Body: State Medicine and Epidemic Disease in Nineteenth-Century India* (Berkeley)
    (2000)*Science, Technology and Medicine in Colonial India* (Cambridge)

Ashby, Henry (1881) 'Food: quantity – quality – cooking-hours', in *Health Lectures for the People*, 4th series (Manchester) pp. 15–26

A Somerset Rector, and Assistant Diocesan Inspector of Schools (1880) *Cookery Classes in National Schools. With Practical Directions How to Form Them, Founded on Experience Gained in a Country District* (London)

Atkins, P. J. (1991) 'Sophistication detected: or, the adulteration of the milk supply, 1850–1914', *Social History*, 16, pp. 317–39

Atkinson, E. L. (1915) 'A method of growing yeast for making bread', *Journal of the Royal Naval Medical Service*, 1, pp. 202–3

Attar, Dena (1990) *Wasting Girls' Time: A History and Politics of Home Economics* (London)

Baddeley, Florence (1895) 'Technical work under the county council', in National Union of Women Workers, *Women Workers: The Official Report of the Conference held at Nottingham on 22, 23, 24 & 25 October 1895* (London) pp. 15–22

Ball, Nancy (1963) *Her Majesty's Inspectorate, 1839–1849* (London)

Barnsby, George (1971) 'The standard of living in the Black Country during the nineteenth century', *Economic History Review*, 2nd series, 24, pp. 220–39

Bath, A. G. (1939) 'The victualling of the navy', *Journal of the Royal United Service Institution*, 84, pp. 744–68

Bayliss, Robert and Christine Daniels (1988) 'The physical deterioration report of 1904 and education in home economics', *History of Education Society Bulletin*, 41, pp. 29–39

Becker, Lydia (1878) 'On the teaching of domestic economy in elementary schools', *Report of Second Yearly Congress on Domestic Economy and Elementary Education, Manchester, 1878* (Manchester) pp. 19–22

Beeton, Isabella (1861) *Beeton's Book of Household Management* (London)

Begg, Tom (1994) *The Excellent Women: The Origins and History of Queen Margaret College* (Edinburgh)

Behenna, Richard Barrie (ed.) (1981) *A Victorian Sailor's Diary: Richard Behenna of Vergan, 1833–1898* (Cornwall)

Bell, Frances and Robert Millward (1998) 'Public health expenditures and mortality in England and Wales, 1870–1914', *Continuity and Change*, 13, pp. 221–49

Bell, Robert (1971–72) 'A good plain cook for the army', *Chambers Journal*, 1863, reprinted in *Army Catering Corps Yearbook*, pp. 43–5

Bergman, Beverly P. and Simon A. StJ. Miller (2003) 'Historical perspectives on health: the Parkes Museum of Hygiene and the Sanitary Institute', *Journal of the Royal Society for the Promotion of Health*, 123, pp. 55–61

Bibby, Miss, Miss Colles, Miss Petty and Dr Sykes (1912) *The Pudding Lady: A New Departure in Social Work* (London)

Biggs, A. (1906) 'Domestic economy teaching as a career for women', *Lady's Realm*, pp. 601–6

Birch, Philip (1885) 'The food of the household: its bearing on health and disease', in *Health Lectures for the People*, 6th series (Manchester) pp. 17–36

Bird, Elizabeth (1998) '"High Class Cookery": gender, status and domestic subjects, 1890–1930 [1]', *Gender and Education*, 10, pp. 117–31

Blair, John S. G. (2001) *'In Arduis Fidelis': Centenary History of the Royal Army Medical Corps* (Edinburgh)

Blakestad, Nancy L. (1997) 'King's College of Household and Social Science and the origins of dietetics education', in David F. Smith (ed.) *Nutrition in Britain: Science, Scientists and Politics in the Twentieth Century* (London) pp. 75–98

Board of Education (1915) *Some Suggestions for Simple and Nourishing Meals for Home* (London)

Boland, Mary A. and Mrs Humphry (eds) (1898) *The Century Invalid Cookery: For the Use of Nurses in Training Schools, Nurses in Private Practice, Others who tend the Sick* (London)

Bonham-Carter, Henry (1867) 'Suggestions for improving the management of the nursing department in large hospitals', St Thomas' Hospital Records, Nightingale Collection, LMA, H01/ST/NC/16/6

Bonham-Carter, Victor (ed.) (1968) *Surgeon in the Crimea: The Experiences of George Lawson Recorded in Letters to his Family 1854–1855* (London)

Bonython, Elizabeth and Anthony Burton (2003) *The Great Exhibitor: The Life and Work of Henry Cole* (London)

Booth, Charles (1904) *Life and Labour of the People in London*, first series, Poverty (London) III

(1902–4) *Life and Labour of the People in London*, second series, Industry (London) III, V and final volume

Brabazon, Lord (1881) 'Health and physique of our city populations', *Nineteenth Century*, X, pp. 80–9

Brassey, Thomas (1877) *British Seamen as Described in Recent Parliamentary and Official Documents* (London)

Briggs, Emily (1900) 'Cookery', in Thomas Alfred Spalding, *The Work of the London School Board* (London) pp. 226–7

British Hospital for Diseases of the Skin (1872) *Rules for Diet, and General Instructions of the Guidance of Patients* (London)

British Medical Association, Report of the Committee on Nutrition (1933) *British Medical Journal Supplement*, 25 November

(1935) *Family Meals and Catering: A Cookery Booklet for Housewives* (London)

Broadley, Margaret E. (1980) *Patients Come First* (London: The London Hospital Special Trustees)

Browne, Phillis (1882) *The Girls Own Cookery Book* (London)

Bryant, Margaret (1979) *The Unexpected Revolution: A Study in the History of the Education of Women and Girls in the Nineteenth Century* (London)

Burnett, John (1966) *Plenty and Want: A Social History of Food in England from 1815 to the Present* (London)

(1966) 'Trends in bread consumption', in T. Barker, J. McKenzie and J. Yudkin (eds) *Our Changing Fare* (London) pp. 61–75

Buckton, Catherine (1883) *Food and Home Cookery* (Leeds)

Bushe, C. K. (1929) 'HMS *Ganges*, naval training establishment for boys, and the sick quarters, Shotley', *Journal of the Royal Naval Medical Service*, 15, pp. 14–23

Caine, Barbara (1986) *Destined to be Wives: The Sisters of Beatrice Webb* (Oxford)

Calder, Fanny (1883) 'Practical cookery in elementary schools', *Good Words*, pp. 58–62

(1884) 'Practical cooking in elementary schools', *The Health Education Literature* (London) vol. 14, pp. 171–84

(1888–89) 'Domestic education in elementary schools', *Proceedings of the Literary and Philosophical Society of Liverpool*, XLIII, pp. 109–20

(1893) 'Growth and development of domestic science', in Baroness Burdett-Coutts (ed.) *Woman's Mission: A Series of Congress Papers in the Philanthropic Work of Women, by Eminent Writers* (London) pp. 317–22

Calder, F. L. and E. E. Mann (1891) *A Teachers' Manual of Elementary Laundry Work* (London)

Campbell, Janet (1908) 'The teaching of physiology and hygiene in the council schools', in *Second International Congress on School Hygiene, London 1907, Transactions* (London) III, pp. 913–14

Cantlie, James (1897) 'The relations of the civil and military medical men in Britain' (privately printed) RAMC 474

Cantlie, Neil (1974) *A History of the Army Medical Department* (London)

Carew, Anthony (1981) *The Lower Deck of the Royal Navy 1900–39* (Manchester)

Carpenter, Kenneth J. (1986) *The History of Scurvy and Vitamin C* (Cambridge)

(1994) *Protein and Energy: A Study of Changing Ideas in Nutrition* (Cambridge)

Carter, Alfred H. (1883) 'Facts about food and feeding', in *Birmingham Health Lectures*, 1st series (Birmingham) pp. 47–67

Chadwick, Edwin (1877) 'Sanitation in domestic training', *Domestic Economy Congress Birmingham*, pp. 49–50

Charlton, Christopher (1984) 'The National Health Society Almanack, 1883', *Local Population Studies*, 32, pp. 54–7

Chivers, Kenneth (1960) 'Henry Jones versus the Admiralty', *History Today*, 10, pp. 247–54

Christison, Robert (1860) 'The dietary of the boys in the Greenwich Hospital School and of the pensioners in Greenwich Hospital', in Greenwich Hospital School Committee 1860, PP XXX, pp. lxxvi–lxxviii

Church, Arthur (1880) *Food: Some Accounts of its Source, Constituents and Uses* (London, new edition)

Clark, Gregory (1984) *'Doc': 100 Year History of the Sick Berth Branch* (London)

Clarke, Edith (1877) 'The object and work of the National Training School for Cookery', *Domestic Economy Congress Birmingham* (Birmingham) pp. 62–5

Clayton, W. E. (1936) 'Victualling the navy: as it was and as it is', *Brassey's Naval Annual*, pp. 92–101

Clements, Helen (1979) 'The Association of Teachers of Domestic Subjects and the place of domestic science in the school curriculum, 1895–1925' (unpublished M.A. thesis, University of Warwick)

Cole, Rose Owen (1885) *The Official Handbook for the National Training School for Cookery* (London)

Collins, Sheila M. and Edith R. Parker (2003) 'A Victorian matron; no ordinary woman: Eva Charlotte Ellis Lückes (8 July 1854–16 February 1919)', *International History of Nursing Journal*, 7, pp 66–74

Collyns, Revd Charles H. (1878) 'Food and cookery in relation to teaching concerning the same in elementary schools', *Domestic Economy Congress Manchester* (Manchester) pp. 62–4

Colomb, P. H. (1898) *Memoirs of Admiral the Right Honourable Sir Astley Cooper Key* (London)

Cook, Edward (1913) *The Life of Florence Nightingale* (London) II

Cook, G. C. (2001) 'Disease in the nineteenth century merchant navy: the Seamen's Hospital Society's experience', *The Mariner's Mirror*, 87, pp. 460–71

Cooper, Lenna F. (1967) 'Florence Nightingale's contribution to dietetics', in Adelia M. Beeuwkes, E. Neige Todhunter and Emma Seifrit Weigley (eds) *Essays on History of Nutrition and Dietetics* (Chicago) pp. 5–11

Copelman, Dina M. (1996) *London's Women Teachers: Gender, Class and Feminism 1870–1930* (London)

Coppinger, R. W. (1893) 'Tropical naval hygiene', in Andrew Davidson (ed.) *Hygiene and Diseases in Warm Climates* (London) pp. 81–112

Cowen, Ruth (2006) *Relish: The Extraordinary Life of Alexis Soyer, Victorian Celebrity Chef* (London)

Cowie, Archibald (1898) 'The supply of British seamen', *Contemporary Review*, 73, pp. 855–65

Craven, Mrs Dacre (1890) *A Guide to District Nurses and Home Nursing* (London)

Crowdy, J. P. (1980) 'The science of the soldier's food', *Army Quarterly and Defence Journal*, 110, pp. 266–79

Cyriax, Richard J. (1939) *Sir John Franklin's Last Arctic Expedition: The Franklin Expedition, a Chapter in the History of the Royal Navy* (London)

Davenport-Hill, Rosamond (1884) 'Cookery teaching under the London School Board', *Macmillan's Magazine*, 1884, reprinted in *Exhibition Cookery Book, Health Exhibition* (London) pp. 1–12

Davies, A. M. (1888) *The Food of the Soldier* (Aldershot)

Davies, Celia (1988) 'The health visitor as mother's friend: a woman's place in public health 1900–14', *Social History of Medicine*, 1, pp. 106–14

Davies, Mary (1898) 'The teaching of cookery', *Contemporary Review*, 73, pp. 106–14

Davin, Anna (1978) 'Imperialism and motherhood', *History Workshop*, V, pp. 9–65
(1996) *Growing Up Poor: Home, School and Street in London 1870–1914* (London)

Dawe, Charles (1927) 'Diet and disease in the Royal Navy', *Journal of the Royal Naval Medical Service*, 13, pp. 273–285

de Bellaigue, Christina (2001) 'The development of teaching as a profession for women before 1870', *Historical Journal*, 44, pp. 963–88

Dickenson, G. O. M. (1927) 'The origin of the sick berth staff, Royal Navy', *Journal of the Royal Naval Medical Service*, 3, pp. 161–73

Donnet, Drs James and Thomas R. Fraser (1877) 'Paper on scurvy', in Report of the Committee appointed by the Lords Commissioners of the Admiralty to enquire into the causes of the Outbreak of Scurvy in the recent Arctic Expedition, PP LVI, pp. v–xxix

Duffy, Michael (1987) *Soldiers, Sugar and Seapower: The British Expeditions to the West Indies and the War against Revolutionary France* (Oxford)

Duke, Francis, 'Pauper education', in Derek Fraser (ed.) (1976) *The New Poor Law in the Nineteenth Century* (London) pp. 67–86

Dyhouse, Carol (1981) *Growing up in Late Victorian and Edwardian England* (London)

Earle, Maude (1897) *Sick Room Cookery and Hospital Diet, with Special Recipes for Convalescent and Diabetic Patients* (London)

Eaton, R. C. (1896) *A Guide to Health: For the Use of Soldiers* (London)

Edinburgh Health Society (1886) *Health Lectures for the People*, 6th series (Edinburgh)

Ellis, John (1986) *LHMC 1785–1985: The Story of the London Hospital Medical College, England's First Medical School* (London: London Hospital Medical Club)

Evatt, George (1883) *Army Medical Organisation: A Comparative Examination of the Regimental and Departmental System*, 4th edition (London)
(1894) 'The sanitary care of the soldier by his officer', RAMC 474

Eyler, John M. (1997) *Sir Arthur Newsholme and State Medicine, 1885–1935* (Cambridge)

Fahey, G. (1912) 'Practical hints on marching and health on active service', *Journal of the Royal Army Medical Corps*, XVIII, p. 415

Fenwick, Mrs (1877) 'On the practical teaching of domestic economy in elementary schools', in *Domestic Economy Congress Birmingham* (Birmingham) pp. 65–7

ffrench Blake, R. L. V. (1971) *The Crimean War* (London)

Floud, Roderick, Kenneth Wachter and Annabel Gregory (1990) *Height, Health and History: Nutritional Status in the United Kingdom, 1750–1930* (Cambridge)

Forrest, J. R. (1896) *The Soldier's Health and How to Preserve It* (Aldershot)

Fortescue, John (1928) *A Short Account of Canteens in the British Army* (Cambridge)

French, Michael and Jim Phillips (2000) *Cheated not Poisoned? Food Regulation in the United Kingdom, 1875–1938* (Manchester)

Furse, George Armund (1899) *Provisioning Armies in the Field* (London)

Galton, Douglas (1880) *Observations on the Construction of Healthy Dwellings, namely Houses, Hospitals, Barracks, Asylums, etc.* (Oxford)

Gamge, Arthur (1881) 'Food and body energy', in *Health Lectures for the People*, 4th series (Manchester) pp. 111–26

Gatewood, James Duncan (1910) *Naval Hygiene* (London)

Gibb, Pat (1992–93) 'District nursing in the Highlands and islands of Scotland 1890–1940', *History of Nursing Society Journal*, 4, pp. 319–29

Gibson, E. H. (1954) 'Baths and washhouses in the English public health agitation 1839–48', *Journal of the History of Medicine and Allied Sciences*, IX, pp. 391–406

Gillespie, T. P. (1951) 'The diet and health of seamen in the West Indies at the end of the eighteenth century: some remarks on the work of Leonard Gillespie, MD', *Journal of the Royal Naval Medical Service*, 37, pp. 187–92

Goddard, J. C. (1991) 'An insight into the life of Royal Naval surgeons during the Napoleonic War, Part I', *Journal of the Royal Naval Medical Service*, 77, pp. 206–22
 (1991) 'An insight into the life of Royal Naval surgeons during the Napoleonic War, Part II', *Journal of the Royal Naval Medical Service*, 78, pp. 27–36

Goldie, S. M. (ed.) (1987) *'I Have Done My Duty': Florence Nightingale and the Crimean War 1854–56* (Manchester)

Goodman, Joyce (2000) 'Women school board members and women school managers: the structuring of educational authority in Manchester and Liverpool, 1870–1903', in Joyce Goodman and Sylvia Harrop (eds) *Women, Educational Policy-Making and Administration in England: Authoritative Women since 1880* (London) pp. 59–77

Goodman, Margaret (1862) *Experiences of an English Sister of Mercy* (London)

Gould, Pat (1987) 'The story of the Royal Naval Nursing Service up to 1914', *History of Nursing Bulletin*, 2, pp. 20–5

Grant, John (1860) 'New system of cooking for the army', *Journal of the Royal United Service Institution*, IV, pp. 322–5

Greenup, W. T. (1878) *Food and its Preparation* (London)

Grimbly, A. F. (1921) 'On real economy in recruiting', *Journal of the Royal Naval Medical Service*, 7, pp. 135–8

Halstead, Robert (1895) 'Some thoughts of a workman concerning the plea for a living wage', *Economic Review*, V, pp. 350–69

Hamilton, C. E. (1919) 'A suggested improved diet on the East Indies station', *Journal of the Royal Naval Medical Service*, 5, pp. 280–6

Hamlin, Christopher (1990) *A Science of Impurity: Water Analysis in Nineteenth Century Britain* (Bristol)

Hankin, Ernest Hanbury (1895) *Cholera in Indian Cantonments and How to Deal with it: Written for the Case of Cantonment Magistrates, Medical Officers and others Interested in the Question* (Allahabad)

Hardy, Anne (1999) 'Food, hygiene, and the laboratory: a short history of food poisoning in Britain, *circa* 1850–1950', *Social History of Medicine*, 12, pp. 293–311

(2001) *Health and Medicine in Britain since 1860* (Basingstoke)

(2003) 'Exorcizing Molly Malone: typhoid and shellfish consumption in urban Britain 1860–1960', *History Workshop Journal*, 55, pp. 73–90

Harland, Kathleen M. (1984) 'A short history of Queen Alexandra's Royal Naval Nursing Service', *Journal of the Royal Naval Medical Service*, 70, pp. 59–65

(1990) *A History of the Queen Alexandra's Royal Naval Nursing Service* (Portsmouth)

Harris, Bernard (1995) *The Health of the Schoolchild: A History of the School Medical Service in England and Wales* (Buckingham)

Hassell, Joseph (1876) *Domestic Economy* (London)

(n.d.) *Domestic Economy: New Code 1880* (London)

Hay, Ian (1953) *One Hundred Years of Army Nursing, the Story of the British Army Nursing Services, from the Time of Florence Nightingale to the Present Day* (London)

Helmstadter, Carol (2001) 'From the private to the public sphere: the first generation of lady nurses in England', *Nursing History Review*, 9, pp. 127–40

Herrick, Claire (1999) '"The conquest of the silent foe": British and American military medical reform rhetoric and the Russo–Japanese War', in Roger Cooter, Mark Harrison and Steve Sturdy (eds) *Medicine and Modern Warfare* (Amsterdam) pp. 99–129

Hilton, Matthew (1995) '"Tabs", "fags" and the "boy labour problem" in late Victorian and Edwardian Britain', *Journal of Social History*, 28, pp. 587–607

(1998) 'Retailing history as economic and cultural history: strategies of survival by specialist tobacconists in the mass market', *Business History*, 40, pp. 115–37

Hilton, Matthew and Simon Nightingale (1998) '"A microbe of the devil's own make": religion and science in the British anti-tobacco movement, 1853–1908', in Stephen Lock, *Ashes to Ashes: The History of Smoking and Health*, Symposium and Witness Seminar Organized by the Wellcome Institute for the History of Medicine and the History of Twentieth Century Medicine Group on 26–27 April 1995 (Amsterdam) pp. 41–77

Hirst, J. D. (1991) 'Public health and public elementary schools', *History of Education*, 20, pp. 107–18

Holcombe, Lee (1973) *Victorian Ladies at Work: Middle-Class Working Women in England and Wales 1850–1914* (London)

Hollis, Patricia (1987) *Ladies Elect: Women in English Local Government 1865–1914* (Oxford)

Holman, Thomas (1892) *Life in the Royal Navy*, third edition (London)

Holmes, J. McA. (1927) 'The training service as seen in HMS *Impregnable*', *Journal of the Royal Naval Medical Service*, 13, pp. 130–5

Hughes, Amy (1897) *Practical Hints on District Nursing* (London)
(1909) 'The ideal district nurse', reprinted from *The Nursing Times*, 8 May, SA/QNI/P.7/13

Hughes Mildred L. (1922) 'The naval nursing service', *Journal of the Royal Naval Medical Service*, 8, pp. 182–90

Huntsman, Richard, Mary Bruin and Deborah Holttum (2002) 'Light before dawn: naval nursing and medical care during the Crimean War', *Journal of the Royal Naval Medical Service*, 88, pp. 9–27

Hurt, J. S. (1979) *Elementary Schooling and the Working Classes 1860–1918* (London)
(1985) 'Feeding the hungry schoolchild in the first half of the twentieth century', in Derek J. Oddy and D. Miller (eds) *Diet and Health in Modern Britain* (London) pp. 178–206

Hutchinson, Enid (1961) *A History of the British Dietetic Association* (London)

Hutchison, Robert (1900) *Food and the Principles of Dietetics* (London)

Imperial Japanese Navy (1901) *The Surgical and Medical History of the Naval War Between and Japan and China During 1894–95* (Tokyo)

Jack, Florence B. (1896) *The Art of Cooking for Invalids: In the Home and the Hospital* (London)

James, H. E. R. (1912) *A Manual of Field Cookery* (London)

Jenkinson, S. (1956) 'Extract from a naval scrap book', *Journal of the Royal Naval Medical Service*, 42, pp. 120–2

Jolly, William (1876) *Physical Education and Hygiene in Schools* (London)

Jones, J. Arnallt (1900) *Health Hints for Volunteers* (London)

Kemp, Peter (1970) *The British Sailor: A Social History of the Lower Deck* (London)

Kennerley, Alston (1999) 'Ratings for the Mercantile Marine: the roles of charity, the state and industry in the pre-service education and training of ratings for the British Merchant Navy, 1879–1939', *History of Education*, 28, pp. 31–51

Keppel, Henry (1899) *A Sailor's Life under Four Sovereigns* (London)

Laffin, John (1969) *Jack Tar: The Story of the British Sailor* (London)

Langley, E. M. (1949) 'The dietitian in the school meals service', *Nutrition: Dietetics: Catering*, III, pp. 128–30

Lawrence, Maude Agnes (1907) *Special Report on the Teaching of Cookery to Public Elementary School Children in England and Wales* (London)

(1912) *General Report on the Teaching of Domestic Subjects to Public Elementary School Children in England and Wales* (London)

Lawton, Dennis and Peter Gordon (1987) *HMI* (London)

Leach, Harry (1868) *The Ship Captain's Medical Guide* (London)

(1885) *The Ship Captain's Medical Guide*, revised by William Spooner, 9th edition (London)

Leff, S. and Vera Leff (1959) *The School Health Service* (London)

Letheby, Henry (1872) *On Food: Its Varieties, Chemical Composition, Nutritive Value, Comparative Digestibility, Physiological Functions and Uses, Preparation, Ancillary Treatment, Preservation, Adulteration, etc., Being the Substance of Four Canter Lectures, delivered before the Society of the Encouragement of Arts* (London)

Linsay, Dorothy E. and D. Noël Paton (1913) *Report upon a Study of the Diet of the Labouring Classes in the City of Glasgow Carried out During 1911–1912, Under the Auspices of the Corporation of the City* (Glasgow)

Lloyd, Christopher C. (1981) 'Victualling of the fleets in the eighteenth and nineteenth century', in J. Watt, E. J. Freeman and W. F. Bynum (eds) *Starving Sailors: The Influence of Nutrition upon Naval and Maritime History* (National Maritime Museum) pp. 9–15

Lloyd, Christopher C. and Jack L. S. Coulter (1963) *Medicine and the Navy 1200–1900* (London) IV, 1815–1900

L. N. R. (Ellen Ranyard) (1875) *Nurses for the Needy: Or, Bible-women Nurses in the Homes of the London Poor* (London)

Loch, C. S. (*c.*1885) 'Cheap dinners for poor school children' (London)

Loveday, J. (1893) *First Course of Cookery Lessons, for Use in Elementary Schools* (London)

Lubbock, John (1879) *Addresses, Political and Educational* (London)

Lückes, Eva C. E. (1883) *Home Nursing and Sick Room Appliances* (London)

(1884) *Lecture on General Nursing. Delivered to the Probationers of the London Hospital Training School for Nurses* (London)

(1893) *Hospital Sisters and their Duties* (London) 3rd edition

(1898) *General Nursing* (London)

Lysons, Daniel (1895) *The Crimean War: From First to Last* (London)

Maccall, William M. (1887) 'The influence of education on health', in *Health Lectures for the People*, 10th series (Manchester) pp. 97–112

McClintock, Francis L. (1859) *The Voyage of the "Fox" in the Arctic Seas: A Narrative of the Discovery of the Fate of Sir John Franklin and his Companions* (London)

M'Cormick, R. (1884) *Voyages of Discovery in the Arctic and Antarctic Seas* (London) 2 vols

Macdonald, Janet (2004) *Feeding Nelson's Navy: The True Story of Food at Sea in the Georgian Era* (London)

Macdonald, John D. (1881) *Outline of Naval Hygiene* (London)

McDonald, Lynn (ed.) (2003) *Florence Nightingale on Society and Politics, Philosophy, Science, Education and Literature: Collected Works of Florence Nightingale* (Ontario) V (ed.) (2004) *Florence Nightingale on Public Health Care: Collected Works of Florence Nightingale* (Ontario) VI

McEwan, Margaret (1958) *Eva C. E. Lückes, Matron, The London Hospital 1880–1919* (The London Hospital League of Nurses)

McGann, Susan (1991) 'Eva Charlotte Lückes: pioneer or reactionary? (1854–1919)', *History of Nursing Society Journal*, 3, pp. 24–9

(1992) 'Eva Charlotte Lückes: a great maker of matrons (1854–1919)', in Susan McGann, *The Battle of Nurses: A Study of Eight Women who Influenced the Development of Professional Nursing, 1880–1930* (London) pp. 9–34

McKeown, Thomas (1976) *The Modern Rise of Population* (London)

McLean, David (1999) *Education and Empire: Naval Tradition and England's Elite Schooling* (London)

(2006) *Public Health and Politics in the Age of Reform: Cholera, the State and the Royal Navy in Victorian Britain* (London)

(2006) 'Surgeons of the opium war: the navy on the China coast, 1840–1842', *English Historical Review*, CXXI, pp. 487–504

McNamee, Betty (1966) 'Trends in meat consumption', in T. Barker, J. McKenzie and J. Yudkin (eds) *Our Changing Fare* (London) pp. 76–93

McNeil, Donald R. (1952) 'Medical care aboard Australia-bound convict ships, 1786–1840', *Bulletin of the History of Medicine*, 26, pp. 117–40

Mäenpää, Sari (2001) 'From pea soup to hors d'oeuvres: the status of the cook on British merchant ships', *The Northern Mariner*, XI, pp. 39–55

Manthorpe, Catherine (1986) 'Science or domestic science? The struggle to define an appropriate science education for girls in early twentieth century England', *History of Education*, 15, pp. 195–213

Martin, Jane (1999) *Women and the Politics of Schooling in Victorian and Edwardian England* (London)

Matthews, Derek (1986) 'Laissez-faire and the London gas industry in the nineteenth century: another look', *Economic History Review*, 2nd series, 39, pp. 244–63

Maynard, Edith (1915) *Women in the Public Health Service* (London)

Melville, C. H. (1911) 'Course of lectures on army sanitation', *Journal of the Royal Sanitary Institute*, XXXII, pp. 169–247

Metcalfe, Ethel E. (1904) *Memoir of Rosamond Davenport-Hill* (London)

Millward, Robert and Sally Sheard (1995) 'The urban fiscal problem, 1870–1914: government expenditure and finance in England and Wales', *Economic History Review*, 2nd series, 48, pp. 501–35

Milroy, Gavin (1862) *The Health of the Royal Navy Considered, in a Letter Addressed to the Rt Hon. Sir John S. Pakington* (London)

Milton-Thompson, G. J. (1981) 'Two hundred years of the sailor's diet', in J. Watt, E. J. Freeman and W. F. Bynum (eds) *Starving Sailors: The Influence of Nutrition upon Naval and Maritime History* (National Maritime Museum) pp. 27–34

Mitchell, Miss (1897) 'The teaching of domestic economy in girls' secondary schools', *Journal of the Society of Arts*, XLV, pp. 952–6

Mitra, S. M. (1911) *The Life and Letters of Sir John Hall* (London)

Morten, Honnor (1892–93) 'Nursing as a profession for women', *The Young Woman*, 1, pp. 120–1

Munday, R. C. (1951) 'Comparisons of the naval military, RAF, and civil medical services with private practice, part ix', *Journal of the Royal Naval Medical Service*, 38, pp. 148–55

Mussen, R. W. (1947) 'The Royal Naval Medical School', *Journal of the Royal Naval Medical Service*, 33, pp. 61–7

National Food Reform Association (1908) *Reason for Food Reform* (London)
(1910) *The Feeding of Nurses* (London)

National Health Society (1890) *In a Sick Room* (London)

National Union of Women Workers (1895) *Women Workers: The Official Report of the Conference held at Nottingham on 22, 23, 24 & 25 October 1895* (London)

Neal, J. B. (1957) 'The history of the Royal Army Medical College', *Journal of the Royal Army Medical Corps*, 13, pp. 163–72

Newsholme, Arthur (1884) *Hygiene: A Manual of Personal and Public Health* (London)
(1890–91) 'On the study of hygiene in elementary schools,' *Public Health*, 3, pp. 134–6
(1892) 'The teaching of the laws of health in schools', in *Transactions of the Seventh International Congress of Hygiene and Demography, London, August 10–17th, 1891* (London) IX, pp. 237–41

Newsholme, Arthur and Margaret Eleanor Scott (1893) *Domestic Economy: Comprising the Laws of Health in their application to Home Life and Work* (London)

Newton, John (1886) 'Heating, lighting and ventilation', in *Health Lectures for the People*, 8th series (Manchester) pp. 133–56

Nicholls, H. W. (1928) 'Notes from a training establishment', *Journal of the Royal Naval Medical Service*, 14, pp. 170–7

Nightingale, Florence (1858) *Notes on Matters Affecting the Health, Efficiency, and Hospital Administration of the British Army, Founded Chiefly on the Experience of the Late War* (London)
(1859) *Notes on Hospitals* (London)
(1893) 'Sick-nursing and health-nursing', in Baroness Burdett-Coutts (ed.) *Woman's Mission: A Series of Congress Papers in the Philanthropic Work of Women, by Eminent Writers* (London) pp. 191–200
(1894) *Rural Hygiene. Health Teaching in Towns and Villages* (London)

Notter, James Lane (1889) 'The soldier's food, with reference to health and efficiency for service', *Journal of the Royal United Service Institution*, 33, pp. 537–65

Nyhart, Lynn K. (1997) 'Home economists in the hospital 1900–1930', in Sarah Stage and Virginia B. Vincenti (eds) *Rethinking Home Economics: Women and the History of a Profession* (Ithaca) pp. 125–44

O'Day, Rosemary and David Englander (1993) *Mr Charles Booth's Inquiry: Life and Labour of the People in London Reconsidered* (London)

Oddy, Derek J. (1970) 'Working-class diets in late nineteenth-century Britain', *Economic History Review*, 2nd series, 23, pp. 314–23

— (1990) 'Food, drink and nutrition', in F. M. L. Thompson (ed.) *The Cambridge Social History of Britain 1750–1950* (Cambridge) II, pp. 251–78

— (2003) *From Plain Fare to Fusion Food: British Diet from the 1890s to the 1990s* (Woodbridge, Suffolk)

Orr, John Boyd (1936) *Food, Health and Income: Report on a Survey of Adequacy of Diet in Relation to Income* (London)

Parker, Edith R. and Sheila M. Collins (1998) *Learning to Care: A History of Nursing and Midwifery Education at the Royal London Hospital 1740–1993* (The Royal London Hospital Archives and Museum)

Parkes, Edmund Alexander (1864) *A Manual of Practical Hygiene, Prepared Especially for Use in the Medical Service of the Army* (London)

Parry, Edward (1857) *Memoirs of Rear-Admiral Sir Edward Parry* (London)

Parry, William Edward (1821) *Journal of A Voyage for the Discovery of a North West Passage from the Atlantic to the Pacific; Performed in the Years 1819–20, in His Majesty's Ships Hecla and Griper under the Orders of William Edward Parry*, second edition (London)

Parsons, C. T. (1986) 'The modernisation of Haslar', *Journal of the Royal Naval Medical Service*, 72, pp. 107–10

Pavy, F. W. (1874) *A Treatise on Food and Dietetics, Physiology, and Therapeutically Considered* (London)

Pember Reeves, Mrs (1913) *Round About a Pound a Week* (London)

Penney, Marjorie E. (1954) 'Letters from Therapia, 1855', *Blackwoods Magazine*, 275, pp. 413–21

Perkin, Joan (1989) *Women and Marriage in Nineteenth-Century England* (London)

Phillips, Jim and Michael French (1998) 'Adulteration and food law, 1899–1939', *Twentieth Century British History*, 9, pp. 350–69

Pillow, Margaret (1897) 'Domestic economy teaching in England', *Special Reports on Educational Subjects 1896–7*, PP XXV, pp. 157–86

Playne, Mary (1900) 'The present position of technical education in domestic science', in *Women in Education, Being the Transactions of the Education Section of the International Congress of Women* (London) pp.113–16

Powell, Allan (1930) *The Metropolitan Asylums Board and its Work, 1867–1930* (London: Metropolitan Asylums Board)

Priestley, John (1886) 'The preparation of food', in *Health Lectures for the People*, 9th series (Manchester) pp. 107–24

— (1887) 'Diet in relation to disease', in *Health Lectures for the People*, 10th series (Manchester) pp. 137–53

Prochaska, F. K. (1980) *Women and Philanthropy in Nineteenth-Century England* (Oxford)

(1992) *Philanthropy and the Hospitals of London: The King's Fund, 1897–1990* (Oxford)

Purvis, June (1985) 'Domestic subjects since 1870', in Ivor F. Goodson (ed.) *Social Histories of the Secondary Curriculum: Subjects for Study* (London) pp. 145–76

—— (1991) *A History of Women's Education in England* (Milton Keynes)

Pybus, Ruth (1942–43) 'The protective diet', *Edinburgh Post-Graduate Lectures in Medicine*, III, pp. 69–88

Pycroft, Ella (1895) 'Technical classes under county councils in London', in National Union of Women Workers, *Women Workers: The Official Report of the Conference Held at Nottingham, on 22, 23, 24 & 25 October 1895* (London) pp. 7–14

—— (1897) 'History of training schools for teachers of domestic economy in England', *Journal of the Society of Arts*, XLV, pp. 966–71

Quinlan, Alexander and N. E. Mann (1894) *Cookery for Seamen* (Liverpool)

Ransome, Arthur (1881) 'Cleanliness', in *Health Lectures for the People*, 4th series (Manchester) pp. 1–14

—— (1886) 'Soils and sites', *Health Lectures for the People*, 8th series (Manchester) pp. 1–21

—— (1886) 'On diet', *Health Lectures for the People*, 9th series (Manchester) pp. 1–16

—— (1887) 'The money value of health', *Health Lectures for the People*, 11th series (Manchester) pp. 1–16

Rasor, Eugene L. (1976) *Reform in the Royal Navy: A Social History of the Lower Deck 1850 to 1880* (Connecticut)

Rathbone, Herbert (1927) *Memoir of Kitty Wilkinson of Liverpool 1781–1860* (Liverpool)

Rathbone, William (1890) *Sketch of the History and Progress of District Nursing from its Commencement in the Year 1859 to the Present Date* (London)

Reynolds, Revd G. W. (1885) 'Thrift: its bearing on health and disease', in *Health Lectures for the People*, 6th series (Manchester) pp. 115–31

Rice, E. (1884) *Domestic Economy* (London)

Rombough, R. A. (1987) 'Medical services of the Royal Navy in the nineteenth century, "nursing afloat"', *History of Nursing Bulletin*, 2, pp. 33–9

Ross, Ellen (1993) *Love and Toil: Motherhood in Outcast London, 1870–1918* (Oxford)

Roth, Mathias (1880) *On School Hygiene and Scientific Physical Education* (London)

—— (1880) *On Scientific Physical Education, and its Practical Introduction into Schools* (London)

Ryan, Catherine (1881) *Convalescent Cookery: A Family Handbook* (London)

Saunders, William M'Kenzie (1856) *Hygienic, Medical and Surgical Hints for Young Officers of the Royal and of the Merchant Navy* (London)

Savours, Ann (1990) 'The diary of Assistant Surgeon Henry Piers, HMS *Investigator*, 1850–54', *Journal of the Royal Naval Medical Service*, 76, pp. 33–8

Scott, Margaret (1892) 'Women's work in promoting the cause of hygiene', *Transactions of the Seventh International Congress of Hygiene and Demography, London, August 10–17th, 1891* (London) IX, pp. 242–6

Scott, Margaret E. (1967) *The History of F. L. Calder College of Domestic Science, 1875–1965* (Liverpool)

Scott, Robert F. (1905) *The Voyage of the 'Discovery'* (London)

Selleck, R. J. W. (1994) *James Kay Shuttleworth: Journey of an Outsider* (London)

Sharman, Ivan M. (1981) 'Vitamin requirements of the human body', in J. Watt, E. J. Freeman and W. F. Bynum (eds) *Starving Sailors: The Influence of Nutrition upon Naval and Maritime History* (National Maritime Museum) pp. 17–26

Shaw, Thomas B. (1918) 'Water-boats and the supply of drinking water from the shore to HM ships', *Journal of the Royal Naval Medical Service*, 4, pp. 41–7

(1919) 'The ship's water supply', *Journal of the Royal Naval Medical Service*, 5, pp. 48–71

Sheard, Sally (2000) 'Profit is a dirty word: the development of public baths and wash-houses in Britain 1847–1915', *Social History of Medicine*, 13, pp. 63–85

Shepherd, John (1991) *The Crimean Doctors: A History of the British Medical Services in the Crimean War* (Liverpool) 2 vols

Sickel, Gerald (1903) *Historical Notes on Haslar and the Naval Medical Profession* (London) reprinted from *The Guy's Hospital Gazette*

Sillitoe, Helen (1933) *A History of the Teaching of Domestic Subjects* (London, reprint 1966)

Simey, Margaret (1951) *Charitable Effort in Liverpool in the Nineteenth Century* (Liverpool)

Simmonds, Rose M. (1937) *Handbook of Diets* (London) second edition

Simpson, Henry (1878) 'The dwelling-house in relation to health', *Health Lectures for the People*, 1st series (Manchester) pp. 111–32

(1885) 'Cookery for the household', *Health Lectures for the People*, 6th series (Manchester) pp. 137–42

(1888) 'The care of health in maturity and middle age', *Health Lectures for the People*, 11th series (Manchester) pp. 119–35

Slade, Andrew (1985) 'When private contractors fed the army', *Army Quarterly and Defence Journal*, 115, pp. 160–6

Smith, Edward (1864) *Practical Dietary for Families, Schools and the Labouring Classes* (London)

Smith, F. B. (1979) *The People's Health 1830–1910* (London)

(1982) *Florence Nightingale: Reputation and Power* (London)

Southwell-Sander, G. H. G. (1956) 'The development of naval preventive medicine', *Journal of the Royal Naval Medical Service*, 43, pp. 54–71

Soyer, Alexis (1848) *Soyer's Charitable Cookery: Or the Poor Man's Regenerator* (London)

(1857) *A Culinary Campaign* (London)

Spooner, William (1891) 'Dietary scales in connection with the health of seamen', *Public Health*, official organ of the Congress of Hygiene and Demography, special daily numbers, pp. 149–53

Stephens, Len (1996) *History of the Naval Victualling Department and its Association with Plymouth* (Plymouth)

Stewart, David (1948) 'Hospital ships in the Second Dutch War', *Journal of the Royal Naval Medical Service*, 34, pp. 29–35

Stocks, Mary (1960) *A Hundred Years of District Nursing* (London)

Stone, Dorothy (1966) *The National: The Story of the Pioneer College, the National Training College of Domestic Subjects* (London)

Summers, Anne (1988) *Angels and Citizens* (London)

———— (1991) 'The costs and benefits of caring: nursing charities, *c.*1830–*c.*1860', in Jonathan Barry and Colin Jones (eds) *Medicine and Charity before the Welfare State* (London) pp. 133–48

———— (1992–93) 'Hidden from history? The home care of the sick in the nineteenth century', *History of Nursing Society Journal*, 4, pp. 227–43

Summers, D. L. (1966) *HMS Ganges 1866–1966: One Hundred Years of Training Boys for the Royal Navy* (Shotley Gate)

Szreter, Simon (1988) 'The importance of social intervention in Britain's mortality decline *c.*1850–1914: a re-interpretation of the role of public health', *Social History of Medicine*, 1, pp. 1–37

Taham, John (1880) 'Special dangers to health in large towns', in *Health Lectures for the People*, 3rd series (Manchester) pp. 110–11

Tait, William (1906) *A History of Haslar Hospital* (Portsmouth)

Tegetmeier, W. B. (1875) *Manual of Domestic Economy* (London)

———— (1876) *The Scholars' Handbook of Household Management and Cookery* (London)

Thompson, Henry (1899) *Food and Feeding* (London)

Tuke, Margaret J. (1939) *A History of Bedford College for Women 1849–1937* (London)

Turnbull, Annmarie (1987) 'Learning her womanly work: the elementary school curriculum, 1870–1914', in Felicity Hunt (ed.) *Lessons for Life: The Schooling of Girls and Women 1850–1950* (Oxford) pp. 83–99

———— (1994) 'An isolated missionary: the domestic subjects teacher in England, 1870–1914', *Women's History Review*, 3, pp. 81–100

Turner, H. D. (1990) *The Cradle of the Navy: The Story of the Royal Hospital School at Greenwich and at Holbrook, 1694–1980* (York)

Turner, Thomas J. (1879) 'Hygiene of the naval and merchant marine', in A. H. Buck (ed.) *A Treatise on Hygiene and Public Health* (London) II, pp. 177–228

Underhill, T. J. (1922) 'Points of interest respecting preserved food, more particularly that supplied to the fleet', *Journal of the Royal Naval Medical Service*, 8, pp. 241–57

United States Army, Department of War (1883) *Manual for Army Cooks* (Washington)

Vicinus, Martha (1985) *Independent Women: Work and Community for Single Women 1850–1920* (London)

Waddington, Keir (1998) 'Unsuitable cases: the debate over outpatient admissions, the medical profession and late-Victorian London hospitals', *Medical History*, 42, pp. 26–46

(2003) '"Unfit for human consumption": tuberculosis and the problem of infected meat in late Victorian Britain', *Bulletin of the History of Medicine*, 77, pp. 636–61

Waite, H. (1901) *How to Keep "FIT," on the Soldier's Guide to Health, in Field, Camp and Quarters* (London)

War Office (1860) *Instructions to Military Hospital Cooks, in the Preparation of Diets for Sick Soldiers* (London)

(1878) *Instructions to Military Cooks in the preparation of Dinners at the Instructional Kitchen, Aldershot* (London)

(1892) *The Messing of the Soldier. Including Schedules Illustrative of the New System of Military Cooking. Issued by the Direction of Lt. Genl. Sir Evelyn Wood, VC, GCB, GCMG, &c. Commanding Aldershot Division, for the Information of the Troops in his Command, and Others whom it may Concern, New edition, revised August 1, 1892* (London)

(1908) *The Russo-Japanese War: Medical and Sanitary Reports from Officers Attached to the Japanese and Russian Forces in the Field* (London)

(1910) *Manual of Military Cookery, Prepared at the Army School of Cookery* (London)

(1915) *Manual of Military Cooking and Dietary Mobilization* (London)

Warren, Frederick (1868) *A Letter to the Secretary of State for War: On the Subject of Remuneration for a Newly Invented Cooking Apparatus* (London)

Watt, James (1993) 'The influence of nutrition upon achievement in maritime history', in Catherine Gessler and Derek J. Oddy (eds) *Food, Diet and Economic Change: Past and Present* (Leicester) pp. 62–82

Weatherly, Lionel A. (1880) *Lectures on Domestic Hygiene and Home Nursing* (London)

Whitaker, Ruth (1944) *History of Gloucestershire Training College of Domestic Science* (Gloucester)

Widdowson, Frances (1983) *Going up into the Next Class: Women and Elementary Teacher Training, 1840–1914* (London)

Williams, Jane (ed.) (1857) *The Autobiography of Elizabeth Davis* (London) 2 vols

Williamson, R. T. (1928) 'Captain James Cook, RN, FRS, and his contribution to medical science', *Journal of the Royal Naval Medical Service*, 14, pp. 19–22

Wohl, Anthony S. (1983) *Endangered Lives: Public Health in Victorian Britain* (Cambridge)

Wolseley, Garnet (1882) *The Soldier's Pocket-Book for Field Service*, 4th edition, revised and enlarged (London)

Wright, Christian Guthrie (1877) 'The art of preparing food: its place in general education', in *Domestic Economy Congress Birmingham* (Birmingham) pp. 64–5

(1904) 'District nursing as a hygiene agency', *Journal of the Royal Sanitary Institute*, XXV, pp. 889–93

Wyatt, H. V. (1999) 'Royal Navy surgeons and the transmission of brucellosis by goats' milk', *Journal of the Royal Naval Medical Service*, 85, pp. 112–17

Yelling, J. A. (1986) *Slums and Slum Clearance in Victorian London* (London)

Yexley, Lionel (James Woods) (1908) *The Inner Life of the Navy* (London)

Young, A. F. and E. T. Ashton (1956) *British Social Work in the Nineteenth Century* (London)

Yoxall, Ailsa (1913) *A History of the Teaching of Domestic Economy: Written for the Association of Teachers of Domestic Subjects in Great Britain* (London, reprint 1965)

Index

119, 207, 213; analysis of food
values, 12, 70; and medical doctors,
13, 72, 91, 95, 99, 101, 105, 111,
208–9; and nurses, 90–2, 105, 109,
113, 209; dietitians, 22, 69, 72, 106,
205, 213; in Britain, 7, 14, 23, 43,
105–6; in the United States, 8;
research and study, 10, 14, 44, 70,
92, 105–6, 109–10, 113, 115, 121,
142, 153, 206, 211, 213
district nursing, 3, 20, 30–1, 67, 73,
79, 93–7, 99–101, 104, 119, 210;
organizations, 93, 95, 102, 112
domestic economy education, 11, 18,
42, 49, 64, 113; centres, 29, 31,
45–6, 48, 50, 55, 57, 63–5, 67–8;
cookery, 2–3, 5, 16, 19, 33, 35, 41,
43, 45, 59, 67, 203, 209; domestic
economy congresses, 5, 16, 24;
domestic economy schools, 5, 56,
209; domestic subjects, 5, 6, 18,
22–5, 30, 33, 91, 99, 204;
housewifery, 5, 24, 30, 34, 42, 46,
55, 60–1; infant care, 5, 38, 41, 55,
60–1, 67–8, 111; laundry work, 5,
19, 24, 37–8, 40, 46, 50;
mothercraft, 58, 61, 65, 67–9;
syllabus, 23, 27, 34, 42, 48, 53, 65,
80, 86; textbooks, 34, 42, 86, 94,
120
du Sautoy, Cathelin, 85
Duckworth, George, 97
dysentery, 136, 155

Earle, Maud, 84
East London Nursing Society, 95,
100
Easton, Grace, 86
Eaton, Robert, 139
Ecole Belge d'Infirmières Diplômées,
88
Edinburgh, 13, 20

education: Acts, 34, 36, 40, 115;
Board of Education, 3, 24, 36, 63,
66, 68, 204, 208; codes, 35, 47, 58;
Cross Commission, 40, 47–8, 205,
207; Education Department, 3, 42,
43, 51, 54, 63, 97; educationists,
3–4, 16–17, 19–20, 27, 33, 45, 47,
59, 61, 70, 88; elementary, 5, 45, 57,
97, 115, 168, 207; grant system, 43,
54, 58; higher, 20, 106; secondary,
20, 50
Egypt, 115
Egyptian campaign, 122–3, 126
Eichholz, Alfred, 61
enteric fever, 131, 137, 139–41, 211
epidemic diseases: beriberi, 8, 151;
cholera, 6, 19, 127, 136, 139, 181;
plague, 137–40, 152; smallpox, 31,
175; tuberculosis, 10, 66–7, 165,
213
Evatt, George, 130, 134, 135

Fenwick, Mrs, 20
First World War, 88, 143, 165, 174,
213
Fitzgerald, David, 77
food: adulteration, 10; handling, 2, 10,
69, 140–1, 152, 155, 198, 211;
preserved, 108, 132, 146–7, 151,
157–8, 162, 166, 175–6, 190,
192–3; protein, 8, 110, 151, 174;
safety, 10, 11; Sale of Food and
Drugs Act, 10; supply, 3, 106, 131,
137, 146, 154, 196, 198
Fortescue, Sir John, 115
France, 134
Franklin, Sir John, 146
French army, 130
French navy, 161
Furse, George Armund, 115

Galton, Sir Douglas, 14, 137

75, 80, 81, 82, 85, 86, 87, 88, 89, 91,
92, 100–3, 105–6, 108, 110–11,
157, 180, 183, 196–8, 205, 214; diet
reform, 107–9, 197; management
of, 197; nursing, 185; preliminary
training school, 73, 82, 84; private
nursing institution, 81, 85, 101, 102;
sickroom cookery training, 184, 205
London School Board, 46, 63, 97
Longmore, Thomas, 119
Lückes, Eva, 82–5, 88–9, 91, 97, 198;
and Royal Navy, 198; private
nursing, 101, 103, 104; sickroom
cookery, 4, 30, 71, 81, 82, 83, 85,
86, 87, 101, 183; training for nurses,
75, 80–1, 88, 90, 196, 201, 209
Lysons, Daniel, 127

Macdonald, John, 155
Mackay, Alexander, 158
Mackenzie, Eliza, 180, 181
Mackenzie, John, 181
Mackenzie, Stephen, 108
McKeown, Thomas, 8, 9
Mackinnon, William, 123
Maclean, Alexander, 119
MacPherson, William, 140
Maidstone, 45
malaria, 137, 182
Mallan, Robert, 170
malnutrition, 59, 66–9, 214
Manchester, 17, 26, 44, 60, 62
Manchuria, 141
Mann, Miss, 27, 28, 163, 171
Manson, Patrick, 186
Marine Society, 168
Markham, Alfred, 161
Martin, Alfred, 166
Martin, George, 159
Martin, William, 48
medical inspection and feeding
committee, 63, 209

Medical Research Council, 213
Mediterranean, 132, 175
Mercantile Marine, 167–70, 184, 189
merchant seamen, 150; Merchant
Shipping Act, 29; nautical cookery
schools, 55, 56, 153, 163, 171, 189.
Metropolitan and National
Association of Providing Trained
Nurses (Bloomsbury nurses), 95,
96, 100, 102
Metropolitan Association for
Befriending Young Servants, 36, 37
Metropolitan Asylums Board, 169,
171
Metropolitan Police Force, 135
Middlesex Hospital, 75, 181
military medicine, 119, 211
Milroy, Gavin, 152, 155
Minnesota State University, 76
Molyneux, Robert, 161
Moore, Edward, 177
Morgan, David, 183
Munday, Richard, 165
Mundy, Sir Rodney, 161
Musson, E. M., 120

National Food Reform Association,
99
National Health Society, 13, 18, 22, 93
National Insurance Act, 72
National Training School of Cookery,
2, 12, 23–5, 29, 86, 108, 123–5, 173,
180, 182–5, 187, 189–90, 192–3,
195, 197, 201; teacher training, 46,
55, 79, 83, 84, 196
National Union of Women Workers,
21, 57
naval brigade, 137, 138, 154, 159, 166,
175, 191, 211
Neal, Harry, 136, 137
needlework, 5, 13, 16, 22, 30, 34,
36–8, 50, 54–6, 208